Jo Ippolito Christensen, author of the best-selling, award-winning *The Needlepoint Book: 303 Stitches with Patterns and Projects,* has taught many courses in needlepoint and has taught Creative Stitchery at the University of Alaska and William Carey College, Mississippi. She is the author of *Trapunto,* and is also the coauthor of *Bargello Stitchery, Cross Stitchery, Needlepoint Simplified,* and *Appliqué and Reverse Appliqué.*

This world is but canvas to our imaginations.

HENRY DAVID THOREAU
A Week on the Concord and Merrimac Rivers
(1849). Wednesday

Teach Yourself Needlepoint

Jo Ippolito Christensen

Drawings by Lynn Lucas Jones
Designs by Cynthia Murrell Pendleton
Photographs by
Richard D. Moats, James T. Long, and Paul Hagerty

A SPECTRUM BOOK

Prentice-Hall, Inc., Englewood Cliffs, New Jersey 07632

Library of Congress Cataloging in Publication Data

CHRISTENSEN, JO IPPOLITO.
    Teach yourself needlepoint.

    (The Creative handcrafts series)   (A Spectrum Book)
    Includes indexes.
    1. Canvas embroidery. I. Title.
TT778.C3C483   746.4'4   78–838
ISBN 0-13-888024-7
ISBN 0-13-888016-6 pbk.

In the interest of a good design for the cover of this book, the usual canvas painting procedure was replaced by special methods which are normally not used in needlepoint. Please see page 68 for proper canvas painting procedure. Cover: Long Stitch Landscape, page 109.

A SPECTRUM BOOK

Printed in the United States of America

10 9 8 7 6 5 4 3

PRENTICE-HALL INTERNATIONAL, INC., *London*
PRENTICE-HALL OF AUSTRALIA PTY., LIMITED, *Sydney*
PRENTICE-HALL OF CANADA, LTD., *Toronto*
PRENTICE-HALL OF INDIA PRIVATE, LIMITED, *New Delhi*
PRENTICE-HALL OF JAPAN, INC., *Tokyo*
PRENTICE-HALL OF SOUTHEAST ASIA PTE., LTD., *Singapore*
WHITEHALL BOOKS, LIMITED, *Wellington, New Zealand*

This book is dedicated to Sonie Ashner
of The Morningside Knit Shop, Kansas City, Missouri,
who kindled the fires of my imagination.

Foreword

Living in different parts of the United States has given me the opportunity to come to know and love many wonderful people. Some I have known very briefly; others have been friendships of a longer tenure. Getting to know all about a person and what makes that particular person interesting is indeed fascinating.

I have felt so blessed to marry a man who served his country in the military because this provided me with the opportunity to live in new communities, to meet new people, and observe their customs, habits, exchange recipes, and watch their children grow and develop. I first met the Christensen family of Geneva, New York when I was a newlywed. Betty Christensen (Jo's mother-in-law) was the most talented, efficient and domesticated homemaker I had ever met. Her house always had the aroma of a holiday—her family was the best fed in the community. Being the mother of six daughters provided her with plenty of reasons to become an excellent seamstress. Needless to say, the daughters were always well-dressed. When an only son grows up in such a household it is quite natural that he would marry a girl with equal talents. This John did when he married Jo.

Jo has combined the ingredients that so many modern women are reaching for—she is the wife of an outstanding military officer, the mother of a growing son, and she continues to pursue and attain her goals in her chosen field.

For those who are familiar with her past books, I am certain this new book, *Teach Yourself Needlepoint*, will prove to be of equal interest. *Teach Yourself Needlepoint* does exactly as it says. The book begins with a thorough discussion of supplies and basic methods used in stitching needlepoint. The color and design chapter is written in easy-to-understand language. It offers unique checklists on color and design so that the reader can test his or her original designs against it.

Several unique features of the book: a chart is included that tells the reader the amount of yarn needed to stitch one square inch of about 175 stitches. There are instructions for making the "Easy Project Planner," which is useful in several ways. It helps you to figure out how many square inches there are of each color in your design. It can also be used to enlarge and reduce designs and even in drawing from real life.

Complete instructions for blocking and framing are given. Nothing is left for you to guess at. Other finishing techniques discussed are a man's tie, a box top, a purse, and a bell pull, to mention a few.

There is a preview of things to come in the field of needle-point in the way of interesting three-dimensional needlepoint.

Explicit how-to drawings and photographs of the almost 175 stitches are included in the book. There is a chapter of supplemental designs for you to stitch with your own colors and stitches. Let your imagination go to work!

Fifty-nine projects are described in detail. A black and white photograph of each, a color photograph of many, a drawing showing which stitches are used and where they are used, and some closeup photographs illustrate each project. The text accompanying each stitch warns the reader of possible pitfalls and gives hints for a more successful project, as well as teaching the basics. A large variety of techniques and styles is included in this well-illustrated book.

For those who are familiar with Jo's previous work, I am certain this edition will prove to be equally exciting in new ideas and methods. *Teach Yourself Needlepoint* will give the beginner confidence and the skilled professional a new outlook.

CONNIE HANSEN
Wife of The Honorable George Hansen,
Congressman from Idaho

Preface

Teach *Yourself Needlepoint* really does as it says. It takes you back to school. You'll learn the basics about supplies and equipment in Part One. It will also give you instructions for the procedures of doing needlepoint, as well as hints to help you over some of the errors you might make, or have made.

The "Easy Project Planner" helps you enlarge and reduce designs, draw from real life, and best of all, figure out how much yarn you'll need to buy for your project. Instructions to make the Easy Project Planner are included in the book. The chart beginning on page 9 tells how much yarn is needed to stitch one square inch of 174 stitches.

Part Two gives lessons on color and design. It pares art terms down to lay language. Excellent photographs and drawings illustrate the various points about hue, value, intensity, form, texture, line, and many others. Unique checklists on color and on design allow you to check your own design against a list to see if it is artistically sound. Instructions are given for making the miraculous black glass. It is an invaluable aid in selecting colors for your needlepoint. It can be made in less than an hour, and for a small amount of money.

If you are not interested in designing your own projects, complete instructions for fifty-nine projects are given in Part Three. The projects are arranged in order of increasing difficulty and are divided into five levels. Projects for Beginners starts out at rock bottom. The projects and the instructions are easy enough so that even an adult—or a child—who has never threaded a needle can work a stitch. Advanced Beginners offers projects that are just a little harder, but no new techniques are introduced. Intermediate gives you an opportunity to learn more new stitches and how to use them. Advanced gives you an opportunity to study how color choices affect a design. The Expert projects deal with combining techniques you already know with more advanced procedures, such as three-dimensional needlepoint.

Complete information to make each project is given through graphs, drawings, charts, and black and white photos, as well as color photos. The text picks up where these graphics leave off.

Part Four gives *clear* diagrams of the 174 stitches used in the making of the projects. Numbers tell you what to stitch and when. Each is also illustrated with a black and white photo. Handy charts tell the characteristics of each stitch.

Flawless finishing is a must, for without it, even the most expert stitching is overlooked. Learn to block and frame a picture with the no-guess photo series and the many drawings.

Other finishing techniques are also described with text, drawings, and photos.

Although Part Six is the end of this book, it is just the beginning of your needlepoint career. Use the extra designs presented here and add your own colors and stitches. From there it is just one small step to your own designs!

Do not hesitate to try new things and experiment beyond what you think you can do. You will never learn by refusing to try new techniques! I hope you will come to love needlepoint as I do!

JO IPPOLITO CHRISTENSEN
Ocean Springs, Mississippi

A word
of thanks

Many, many people have helped put this book together. I could not have done it all alone.

Lynn Lucas Jones has produced, again, fantastically clear diagrams to tell you how to do the stitches and how to put projects together. Many were reprinted from *The Needlepoint Book* by Jo Christensen, published by Prentice-Hall.

Cindy Pendleton's inimitable style is evident in the many imaginative designs that she has created for you to stitch. Most of them appear in Part Six, Supplemental Designs, although some are stitched and appear in Part Three, The Projects.

Many of Jim Long's black and white photographs were also reprinted from *The Needlepoint Book*. Richard Moats and Paul Hagerty took the rest of the hundreds of photographs, both color and black and white. Without their good work, stitching from this book would be guesswork on your part. A stamina award goes to Dick Moats, who helped me decorate a Christmas tree in July in the Mississippi heat and humidity!

My heartfelt thanks go to the many people who allowed me to use their lovely needlepoint pieces. They are: Jackie Beaty, Pat Biesiot, Betty Christensen, Nyla Christensen, Ruth Ippolito, Kay Kendall, Carole Key, Mickey McKitrick, Joan McMahon, Marlene Meek, Lois Ann Necaise, Needleworks Ltd. of New Orleans, Louisiana, Betty Powers, Kathy Smith, Wayne Stephens, and Linda Wilson.

Thanks, also, to Luciano Ippolito, who allowed me to re-produce one of his paintings in needlepoint; he also designed the Mississippi River-boat Gambler vest.

My husband, Major John J. Christensen, USAF, even made two projects. He did many odd jobs for the book, including proofreading. He scrubbed pots and pans to save my fingernails! He cooked and cleaned and did laundry and . . .

Others who proofread include: Ruth Frantz, Betty Herman, Cea Linton, Bonnie Long, Mickey McKitrick, Marlene Meek, Mary Savage, Kathy Smith, Wayne Stephens, and Denise Wokutch.

Katherine Wright took hour after hour of dictation, typed many letters, and typed what seemed like a never-ending manuscript. Thank you, Katherine.

A very special thanks goes to Wayne Stephens, who cheerfully took on (and even performed with animation) those dull jobs that no one else wanted: checking and double-checking.

My editor, Lynne Lumsden, made everything seem like it was my idea! All the work was easier with her brilliant guidance! A very special thank you goes to Maria Carella, the production editor, who nearly worked herself to death trying to make the book error-free in the face of ever-pressing deadlines. I especially appreciate the "extra mile" that assistant art director Jeannette Jacobs ran to make this book easy to work from. We certainly can't forget Dave Hetherington, for an excellent job in coordinating the manufacturing details. And I would also like to acknowledge my appreciation to the staff of Intergraphic Technology, Inc., for their professionalism in meeting a very tight schedule—and doing it beautifully.

The following have graciously allowed me to reprint their work: Chottie Alderson—Chottie's Plaid and Rainbow Plaid stitches from *Stitchin' with Chottie*; Dover Publications, Inc., New York—designs from their *Stained Glass Pattern Book*, by Ed Sibbett, Jr. (Plate 28, Fig. 3–45, and various designs in Part Six); Doris Drake—excerpt from page 45 and alphabet on pages 54 and 55 of *Doris Drake's Needlepoint Designs*, dragon fly, page 17, and adaptation of J, O, & Y, pages 40-42, and alphabet, pages 47-48 of *Needlepoint Designs II* by Doris Drake; Orest S. Poliszczuk—reproduction of an original wedding invitation cover design by Orest S. Poliszczuk, June 1975, titled "Hutzul Wedding;" Famous Artist School, Westport, Connecticut, value scale in Figure 2–1 and in Plate 48.

The following companies have kindly consented to my using their products in photographs: Leatherpoint Creations, Inc.—pre-finished belt (Plate 43), wallet and credit card case (Plate 2); the Wooden Purse in Chapter 5 and in Plate 40 is courtesy of the Jacmore Company, 36 West 25th Street, New York, N.Y. This purse is no longer available, but there are other styles of handbags and handles from Jacmore which will work with this needlepoint project; and the pre-finished evening purse in Chapter 5 is courtesy of the Markann Company, New Rochelle, N.Y.

Contents

SUPPLIES AND BASIC PROCEDURES

COLOR
AND DESIGN

THE
PROJECTS

SUPPLIES AND BASIC PROCEDURES

In order to "teach yourself needlepoint," you will need to know the range of materials available to create needlepoint pieces and how to choose the right ones for your projects. Part One, Supplies and Basic Procedures, introduces the vocabulary of needlepoint. The two chapters describe in detail the supplies and basic procedures you must become acquainted with. What is needlepoint canvas? How do you choose the right type? What yarns are used with which type of canvas? How much yarn do you need? What needles are used for these projects?

In the first chapter, a chart shows you how to judge the amount of yarn that each kind of stitch will require for a given area. To help you design your own pieces, as well as work up the designs in this book, you also learn to make an Easy Project Planner. With it, you can estimate the amount of each color of yarn needed for an original design. The Planner will also help you draw original designs from real life.

The second chapter deals with how to label, store, and use the materials you have selected. It tells you how to stitch, how to begin and end a color, and how *not* to knot. Especially useful for the serious student is the discussion of how to prepare your yarn for perfect coverage. You will learn how to smooth, roll, strip, and thicken or thin your yarn. You will also learn when to use these techniques for specific canvases and stitches.

Supplies

Needlepoint is available in various forms: (1) pre-worked (the design is worked for you—you fill in the background), (2) painted canvases (a design painted by you or someone else on needlepoint canvas), (3) charted designs (a design drawn on graph paper and transferred to canvas by you as you stitch), (4) pre-finished articles (blank canvas or painted canvas for you to stitch as part of an already finished article—pillow, purse, etc.), and (5) blank canvas. This book will teach you how to work with all of these. Part One gives you the basic information about the yarn, canvas, needles, and basic procedures that you need to make the projects in this book.

Canvas

Needlepoint is worked on a canvas made especially for it. The threads are so loosely woven that holes are created at regular intervals. The threads are called mesh.

Penelope canvas

When these threads are woven in pairs as in Figure 1–1, the canvas is called Penelope. Each *pair* of threads is considered one mesh. The pairs of threads running one way on the canvas are woven more closely together than the pairs running across them. These tightly woven pairs should always run vertically on your design.

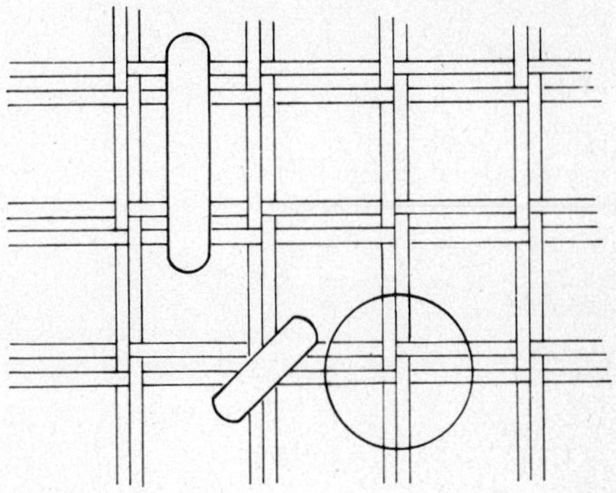

Fig. 1–1. Penelope canvas (junction of mesh circled).

Mono canvas

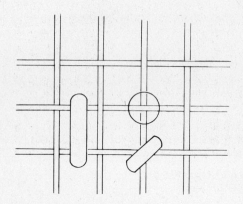

Fig. 1–2. Regular Mono canvas (junction of mesh circled).

When one canvas thread equals one mesh (Figure 1–2), the canvas is called Mono canvas. There are two kinds of Mono canvas: regular Mono and Interlock Mono. The threads of regular Mono canvas are woven over, under, over, under, and so on. This alternation makes the junctions of the mesh unstable. Many people feel, as I do, that it is difficult to work on.

The Basketweave Stitch (page 192) is well suited to regular Mono canvas. Note that there are special instructions for working it on regular Mono canvas.

Interlocking Mono canvas stabilizes the junctions of mesh by intertwining a small thread around each junction of the mesh (Figure 1–3).

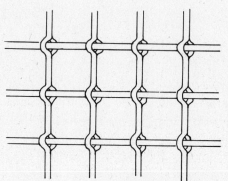

Fig. 1–3. Interlock Mono canvas.

After the words Penelope and Mono there usually appears a number. This number refers to the number of mesh per linear inch. In this book we will be working with Penelope 3½, 5, 7, and 10 and with Mono 10, 12, 14, 16, and 18 (Figure 1–4 a–g).

Fig. 1–4a. Penelope 4 canvas worked with rug yarn.

Fig. 1–4b. Penelope 7 canvas worked with rug yarn.

2

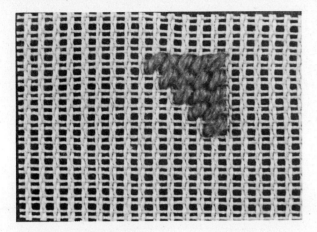

Fig. 1–4c. Penelope 10 canvas worked with Persian yarn.

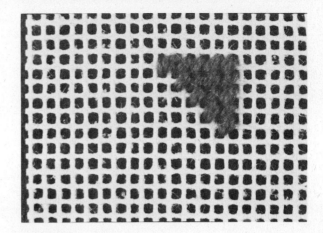

Fig. 1–4d. Interlock Mono 10 canvas worked with Persian yarn.

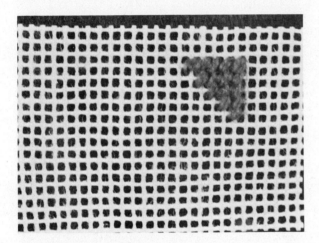

Fig. 1–4e. Interlock Mono 14 canvas worked with Persian yarn.

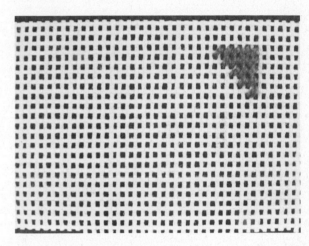

Fig. 1–4f. Regular Mono 18 canvas worked with Persian yarn.

Fig. 1–4g. Silk gauze 40 worked with embroidery floss.

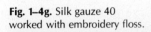

Fig. 1–4h. Nylon canvas, 10 mesh per inch.

Plastic canvas

We will also be using plastic canvas, which usually comes seven mesh per inch. The plastic canvas is nice because it has no raw edges and holds its shape (Figure 1–5). It is somewhat awkward to work on because it does not bend easily (see page 84).

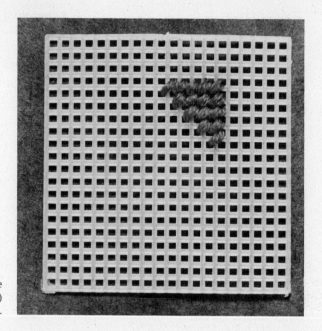

Fig. 1–5. 3″ plastic square (7 mesh per inch) worked with Persian yarn.

Breakaway (waste) canvas

Beware of Breakaway (or waste) canvas (Figure 1–6). It is very light in weight and does not hold up well for needlepoint. It is tempting to buy it, for the price is much lower than that of good quality needlepoint canvas. Breakaway canvas is designed for even stitching on fabric. It *dissolves* when wet. Needlepoint is dampened when it is blocked (see page 293). It would not do to have the canvas dissolve under your hard-worked needlepoint stitches.

Fig. 1–6. Breakaway canvas: Penelope 13 worked with Persian yarn.

A blunt-end tapestry needle is used for needlepoint. The needle must drop easily through the hole in the canvas, yet the proper thickness of yarn needed to cover the canvas must be able to pass through the eye of the needle.

Use the following chart as a guide in choosing a needle of the proper size.

Canvas Size	Needle Size
3-5	13
7-8	16
10	18-20
12-14	20
16-20	22
22-24	24

(See Figure 1–7.)

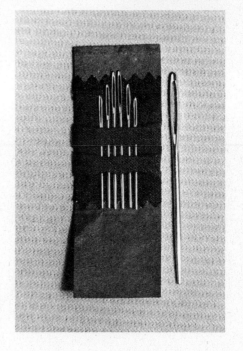

Fig. 1–7. Blunt-end tapestry needles: sizes 22, 20, 18, 20, 22, and 13 (from left to right).

Threading the needle

Many of my students think threading the needle is the hardest part of needlepoint. One group even came to class with several needles already threaded!

For those who can keep track of a tiny piece of paper, Figure 1–8 shows an infallible method for threading the needle. However, I always lose the paper!

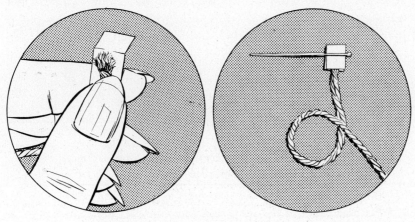

Fig. 1–8a & b. Threading the needle—the paper way.

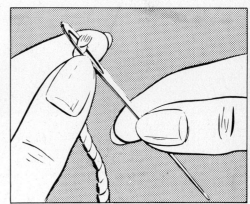

Fig. 1–9. Threading the needle—my way.

I usually give the yarn an extra twist and put it between the end of my left thumbnail and my index finger. Then I slip the needle between my fingers (Figure 1–9). It *usually* works!

When that doesn't work, I try folding the yarn over the tip of the needle and passing it through the eye of the needle as in Figure 1–10.

You may find a metal needle-threader made especially for yarn helpful. Attach it to the margin of your canvas with a piece of yarn to keep track of it.

I heartily recommend that you practice needle threading. It's a *very* important part of needlepoint.

Fig. 1–10a, b, c. Threading the needle—the loop method.

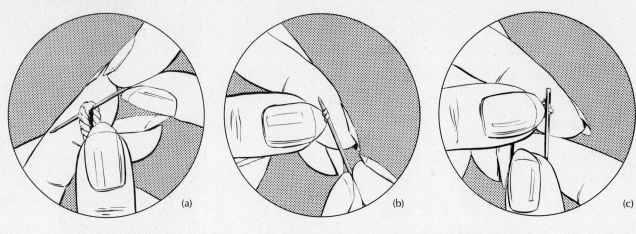

(a) (b) (c)

Yarn

Many kinds of yarn can be used with needlepoint. However, for the most part, wool needlepoint yarn is used, because it is woven with long, strong fibers that help it stand up to the rough needlepoint canvas. It is also moth-proofed.

Needlepoint yarn is sold in dye-lots. That means the color can change slightly from one vat of dye to the next, so the lots are numbered. Yarn purchased from different dye-lots will probably not match perfectly. Be sure you buy enough yarn in the same dye-lot to complete your project. (See the chart on pages 9-19.) If you do miscalculate, work the new dye-lot in by using the same procedure as for shading (page 152).

Tapestry yarn

There are two kinds of needlepoint yarn: tapestry and Persian. Tapestry (Figure 1–11a) is a tightly twisted 4-ply yarn that looks like knitting worsted. It is sold in 40-yard, 12½-yard, 10-yard, and 8.8-yard skeins. Its tight twist makes a nice, smooth stitch. It is my favorite for this reason. This same tight twist makes it difficult to separate the plies for shading or for thickening or thinning the yarn (page 31). When you do separate tapestry yarn, its smooth look is lost. Except for a few brands, tapestry yarn does not have much variety in colors.

6

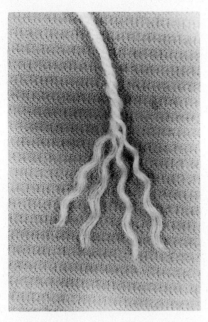

Fig. 1–11a. Four-ply tapestry yarn.

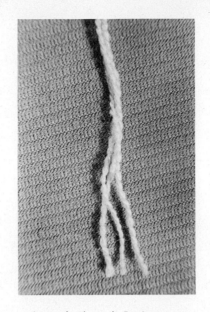

Fig. 1–11b. Three-ply Persian yarn.

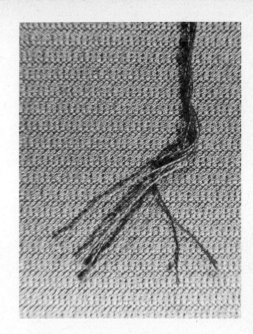

Fig. 1–11c. Six-ply embroidery floss.

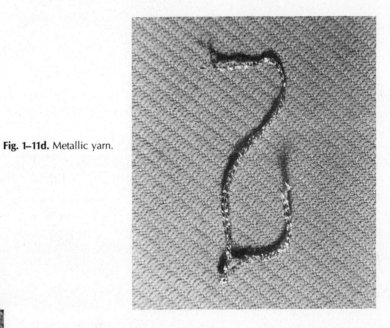

Fig. 1–11d. Metallic yarn.

Fig. 1–11e. Angora.

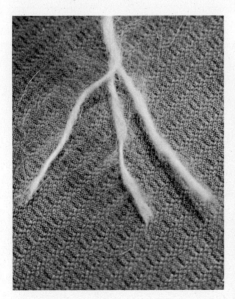

Fig. 1–11f. Velvet or velour yarn.

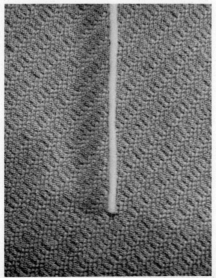

Fig. 1–11g. Pearl cotton.

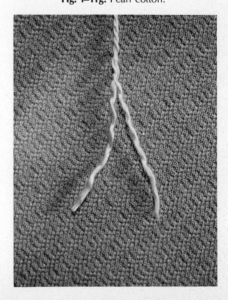

Persian yarn

Persian yarn is a loosely twisted 3-ply yarn. Each of these three plies is a tightly twisted 2-ply strand that is not meant to be separated (Figure 1–11b). Persian yarn's three plies are easily separated, compared to tapestry yarn. Persian comes in many, many colors. Its manufacturers seem to specialize in several colors (or shades and tints) in one family. These are great for Bargello patterns! Persian yarn is sold in 40-yard skeins and also by the strand, ounce, and pound. Watch for variation in quality. Cost is usually a good guideline.

Novelty yarns

Novelty yarns add interest and texture. Those used in this book include embroidery floss (Figure 1–11c), metallic yarn (Figure 1–11d), angora yarn (Figure 1–11e), velvet or velour yarn (Figure 1–11f), and pearl cotton (Figure 1–11g). Acrylic yarns are not recommended because they pill and because they are elastic. They have *memory*, which means that a piece cannot be straightened by blocking. However, when acrylic yarn is stitched on plastic, elasticity is no longer a problem. Novelty yarns do not wear well. Do not use them on objects that will get hard use.

How much yarn to buy

The question of how much yarn to buy seems to plague everyone at one time or another. The following table has the answer for you. Ideally one should figure the yarn needed by stitching one square inch of the stitch *to be used* on the canvas *to be used* with the brand and color of yarn *to be used*. Keep track of the amount of yarn used to stitch the sample and multiply that amount by the number of square inches in your design.

This is not always practical. So, I've come up with the following table. It cannot be perfectly accurate, as there are too many variables: stitch, canvas size, color, etc. (Remember, yarn that has been ripped should *never* be reused.) But this chart will give you a good idea of how much yarn you'll need to work a particular stitch on Mono or Penelope 10, 12, and 14 canvas. (There is only a 5% difference in yarn usage between 10 and 14 canvas, so this chart can be used for all three canvas sizes.) Ripping was *not* allowed for. A 5% Fudge Factor was added to compensate for the different brands and colors and tensions in yarn. All inches and centimeters were generally rounded to the next highest whole number; ounces and grams to two decimal places; yards to the nearest 1/16 of a yard. All measurements are for 3-ply Persian yarn. When more or less than 3-ply was used, adjustments have already been made. Stitches are listed in this table in the order in which they appear in Part Four of this book. Refer to the Stitch Index to find a particular stitch in the table.

NAME OF STITCH	Number of Ply used	Inches of Yarn/sq. in.	Yards of Yarn/sq. in.	Ounces of Yarn/sq. in.	Centimeters of Yarn/sq. cm.	Grams of Yarn/sq. cm.
Straight Gobelin	4	35	1	.0222	14	.0976
Interlocking Straight Gobelin	3	54	1½	.0343	21	.1507
Brick	3	27	¾	.0171	11	.0753
Giant Brick	4	36	1	.0229	14	.1004
Double Brick	4	34	1	.0216	14	.0949
Horizontal Brick	4	36	1	.0229	14	.1004
Parisian	3	26	¾	.0165	10	.0725
Double Parisian	3	26	¾	.0165	10	.0725
Pavillion	3	24	⅔	.0152	9	.0670
Hungarian	3	27	¾	.0171	11	.0753
Hungarian Ground	3	27	¾	.0171	11	.0753
Pavillion Diamonds	3	27	¾	.0171	11	.0753
Tied Pavillion	3	28	¾	.0178	11	.0781
Old Florentine	4	38	1¹/₁₆	.0241	15	.1060
Horizontal Old Florentine	4	38	1¹/₁₆	.0241	15	.1060
Beaty	4	38	1¹/₁₆	.0241	15	.1060
Wicker	4	40	1⅛	.0254	16	.1116

NAME OF STITCH	Number of Ply used	Inches of Yarn/sq. in.	Yards of Yarn/sq. in.	Ounces of Yarn/sq. in.	Centimeters of Yarn/sq. cm.	Grams of Yarn/sq. cm.
Horizontal Milanese	4	38	1 1/16	.0241	15	.1060
Vertical Milanese	4	36	1	.0229	14	.1004
Upright Oriental	4	36	1	.0229	14	.1004
Roman II	3	33	15/16	.0210	13	.0921
Pavillion Boxes	3	40	1 1/8	.0254	16	.1116
Triangle	3	30	7/8	.0190	12	.0837
F-106	4	38	1 1/16	.0241	15	.1060
Bargello	3	28	3/4	.0178	11	.0781
Basketweave	3	45	1 1/4	.0286	18	.1255
Continental	3	45	1 1/4	.0286	18	.1255
Half Cross	3	29	7/8	.0184	11	.0809
Irregular Continental	3	38	1 1/16	.0241	15	.1060
Petit Point	1	33	15/16	.0210	13	.0921
Rep	2	36	1	.0229	14	.1004
Slanted Gobelin	3	26	3/4	.0165	10	.0725
Slanted Gobelin 2 × 2	3	33	15/16	.0210	13	.0921

NAME OF STITCH	Number of Ply used	Inches of Yarn/sq. in.	Yards of Yarn/sq. in.	Ounces of Yarn/sq. in.	Centimeters of Yarn/sq. cm.	Grams of Yarn/sq. cm.
Slanted Gobelin 5 × 2	4	37	1	.0235	14	.1032
Interlocking Gobelin	3	55	1½	.0349	22	.1534
Oblique Slav	4	30	⅞	.0190	12	.0837
Encroaching Oblique	5	36	1	.0229	14	.1004
Kalem	3	59	1⅝	.0375	23	.1646
Lazy Kalem	3	45	1¼	.0286	18	.1255
Stem	3/1	36	1	.0229	14	.1004
Diagonal Stem	3	41	1⅛	.0260	16	.1144
Byzantine #1	3	35	1	.0222	14	.0976
Byzantine #2	3	36	1	.0229	14	.1004
Irregular Byzantine	3	36	1	.0229	14	.1004
Jacquard	3	42	1⅛	.0267	16	.1172
Irregular Jacquard	3	36	1	.0229	14	.1004
Diagonal Hungarian Ground	3	35	1	.0222	14	.0976
Staircase	3	35	1	.0222	14	.0976
Milanese	3	57	1⅝	.0362	22	.1590

NAME OF STITCH	Number of Ply used	Inches of Yarn/sq. in.	Yards of Yarn/sq. in.	Ounces of Yarn/sq. in.	Centimeters of Yarn/sq. cm.	Grams of Yarn/sq. cm.
Oriental	3	41	1 1/8	.0260	16	.1144
Mosaic	3	38	1 1/16	.0241	15	.1060
Mosaic Checker	3	40	1 1/8	.0254	16	.1116
Reversed Mosaic	3	38	1 1/16	.0241	15	.1060
Diagonal Mosaic	3	36	1	.0229	14	.1004
Mosaic Stripe	3	38	1 1/16	.0241	15	.1060
Cashmere	3	37	1	.0235	15	.1032
Tied Cashmere	3	39	1 1/16	.0248	16	.1088
Framed Cashmere	3	41	1 1/8	.0260	16	.1144
Elongated Cashmere	3	39	1 1/16	.0248	15	.1088
Horizontal Cashmere	3	38	1 1/16	.0241	15	.1060
Diagonal Cashmere	3	33	7/8	.0210	13	.0921
Scotch	3	39	1 1/16	.0248	15	.1088
Giant Scotch	3	36	1	.0229	14	.1004
Divided Scotch	3	36	1	.0229	14	.1004
Scotch Checker	3	41	1 1/8	.0260	16	.1144

NAME OF STITCH	Number of Ply used	Inches of Yarn/sq. in.	Yards of Yarn/sq. in.	Ounces of Yarn/sq. in.	Centimeters of Yarn/sq. cm.	Grams of Yarn/sq. cm.
Framed Scotch	3	41	1 1/8	.0260	16	.1144
Reversed Scotch	3	39	1 1/16	.0248	15	.1088
Framed Reversed Scotch	3	44	1 1/4	.0279	17	.1228
Diagonal Scotch	3	36	1	.0229	14	.1004
Moorish	3	36	1	.0229	14	.1004
Wide Moorish	3	39	1 1/16	.0248	15	.1088
Cross	2	36	1	.0229	14	.1004
Rice	3	65	1 3/4	.0413	25	.1813
Giant Rice	3	32	7/8	.0203	12	.0893
Double Cross Tramé	3	44	1 1/4	.0279	17	.1228
Raised Cross	3	39	1 1/16	.0248	15	.1088
Oblong Cross	2	36	1	.0229	14	.1004
1 × 1 Spaced Cross Tramé	2	38	1 1/16	.0241	15	.1060
1 × 3 Spaced Cross Tramé	2	21	5/8	.0133	8½	.0586
Alternating Oblong Cross	2	36	1	.0229	14	.1004
Flying Cross	3	28	3/4	.0178	11	.0781

NAME OF STITCH	Number of Ply used	Inches of Yarn/sq. in.	Yards of Yarn/sq. in.	Ounces of Yarn/sq. in.	Centimeters of Yarn/sq. cm.	Grams of Yarn/sq. cm.
Van Dyke	3	31	7/8	.0197	12	.0865
Tied Oblong Cross	2	43	1 1/4	.0273	17	.1200
Hitched Cross	3	35	1	.0222	14	.0976
Roman Cross	3	20	9/16	.0127	8	.0558
Double Stitch	2	34	1	.0216	13	.0949
Staggered Crosses	2	28	3/4	.0178	11	.0781
Woven Square	3	40	1 1/8	.0254	16	.1116
Bound Cross	3	38	1 1/16	.0241	15	.1060
Upright Cross	2	32	7/8	.0203	12	.0893
Long Upright Cross	3	35	1	.0222	14	.0976
Combination Crosses	2	32	7/8	.0203	12	.0893
Fern	3	42	1 1/8	.0267	17	.1172
Binding Stitch	3	20*	9/16*	.0127*	8**	.0558**
Diagonal Fern	3	32	7/8	.0203	12	.0893
Herringbone	2	38	1 1/16	.0241	15	.1060
Herringbone Gone Wrong	2	25	3/4	.0159	10	.0697

NAME OF STITCH	Number of Ply used	Inches of Yarn/sq. in.	Yards of Yarn/sq. in.	Ounces of Yarn/sq. in.	Centimeters of Yarn/sq. cm.	Grams of Yarn/sq. cm.
2-Color Herringbone	2	21	5/8	.0133	9	.0586
6-Trip Herringbone	2	38	1	.0241	15	.1060
Greek	2	22	5/8	.0140	9	.0614
Diagonal Greek	2	30	7/8	.0190	12	.0837
Waffle	2	29	7/8	.0184	11	.0809
Trellis Cross	4	31	7/8	.0197	12	.0865
Fancy Cross	3	44	1 1/4	.0279	17	.1228
Double Straight Cross	3	38	1 1/16	.0241	15	.1060
Double Leviathan	3	57	1 1/2	.0362	22	.1590
Triple Leviathan	2	42	1 1/8	.0267	17	.1172
Medallion	3	42	1 1/8	.0267	16	.1172
Triple Cross	2	24	2/3	.0152	9	.0670
Windmill	3	38	1 1/16	.0241	15	.1060
Tied Windmill	3	57	1 1/2	.0362	22	.1590
Butterfly	2	42	1 1/8	.0267	17	.1172
Lone Tied Star	3	47	1 1/3	.0298	18	.1311

NAME OF STITCH	Number of Ply used	Inches of Yarn/sq. in.	Yards of Yarn/sq. in.	Ounces of Yarn/sq. in.	Centimeters of Yarn/sq. cm.	Grams of Yarn/sq. cm.
Smyrna Cross	2	39	1¹/₁₆	.0248	15	.1088
Reversed Smyrna Cross	2	39	1¹/₁₆	.0248	15	.1088
Horizontal Elongated Smyrna	3	34	1	.0216	13	.0949
Vertical Elongated Smyrna	3	34	1	.0216	13	.0949
Alternating Smyrna	2	48	1¹/₃	.0305	19	.1339
Woven Cross	2	39	1¹/₁₆	.0248	15	.1088
Woven Band	3	38	1¹/₁₆	.0241	15	.1060
Knotted Stitch	2	34	1	0216	13	.0949
Periwinkle	3	32	⁷/₈	.0203	12	.0893
Fly	3	40	1¹/₈	.0254	16	.1116
Couching	4	22	²/₃	.0140	9	.0614
Diagonal Roumanian	3	43	1¹/₄	.0273	17	.1250
Wheat	3	36	1	.0229	14	.1004
Web	2	38	1¹/₁₆	.0241	15	.1060
Framed Star	3	36	1	.0229	14	.1004
Square Eyelet	2	41	1¹/₈	.0260	16	.1144

NAME OF STITCH	Number of Ply used	Inches of Yarn/sq. in.	Yards of Yarn/sq. in.	Ounces of Yarn/sq. in.	Centimeters of Yarn/sq. cm.	Grams of Yarn/sq. cm.
Diamond Eyelet	2	42	1⅛	.0267	16	.1172
Triangular Ray	3	28	¾	.0178	11	.0781
Ringed Daisies	2	39	1¹⁄₁₆	.0248	15	.1088
Diamond Ray	3	57	1⅝	.0362	22	.1590
Ray	2	36	1	.0229	14	.1004
Leaf	3	31	⅞	.0197	12	.0865
Diagonal Leaf	3	35	1	.0222	14	.0976
Roumanian Leaf	3	31	⅞	.0197	12	.0865
Diagonal Roumanian Leaf	3	38	1¹⁄₁₆	.0241	15	.1060
Close Herringbone	3	54	1½	.0343	21	.1507
Raised Close Herringbone	3	54	1½	.0343	21	.1507
Buttonhole	3	35	1	.0222	14	.0976
Buttonhole in Half-circle	2	40	1⅛	.0254	16	.1116
Chain	3	32	⅞	.0203	13	.0893
Open Chain	3	25	⅔	.0159	10	.0697
Diagonal Chain	2	24	⅔	.0152	9½	.0670

NAME OF STITCH	Number of Ply used	Inches of Yarn/sq. in.	Yards of Yarn/sq. in.	Ounces of Yarn/sq. in.	Centimeters of Yarn/sq. cm.	Grams of Yarn/sq. cm.
Woven Spider Web	3	80	2¼	.0508	31	.2232
Smooth Spider Web	3	83	2⅓	.0527	33	.2316
Ridged Spider Web	3	83	2⅓	.0527	33	.2316
Wound Cross	3	94	2⅝	.0597	37	.2623
French Knot	3	74	2	.0470	29	.2065
French Knots on Stalks	2	45	1¼	.0286	18	.1255
Bullion Knot	3	39	1¹⁄₁₆	.0248	15	.1088
Twisted Chain	3	43	1¼	.0273	17	.1200
Looped Turkey Work	3	90	2½	.0571	35	.2511
Cut Turkey Work	3	90	2½	.0571	35	.2511
Velvet	3	35	1	.0222	14	.0976
Loop	3	32	⅞	.0203	13	.0893
Lazy Daisy	3	40	1⅛	.0254	16	.1116
Needleweaving	3	35	1	.0222	14	.0976
Raised Cup	3	92	2½	.0584	36	.2567
Running Stitch	3	15	½	.0095	6	.0418
Stephens	3	32	⅞	.0203	13	.0893

NAME OF STITCH	Number of Ply used	Inches of Yarn/sq. in.	Yards of Yarn/sq. in.	Ounces of Yarn/sq. in.	Centimeters of Yarn/sq. cm.	Grams of Yarn/sq. cm.
Double Hungarian Ground	3	24	$^2/_3$	.0152	9½	.0670
Straight Stitch	3	30	$^7/_8$	.0190	12	.0837
Plaid	3	38	$1^1/_{16}$	.0241	15	.1060
Rainbow Plaid	3	38	$1^1/_{16}$	.0241	15	.1060
Staggered Cashmere	3	37	1	.0235	15	.1032
Framed Giant Cashmere	3	38	$1^1/_{16}$	.0241	15	.1060
Reversed Giant Cashmere	3	33	$^{15}/_{16}$	.0210	13	.0921
Rhodes	3	52	$1^1/_2$	.0330	21	.1451
Round Cross	3	50	$1^1/_2$	.0317	20	.1395
Chris Cross	3	42	$1^1/_8$	.0267	16	.1172

*per linear inch
**per linear centimeter

Easy project planner

"Now," you say, "that's well and good to know how much yarn I need per square inch, but it doesn't do me any good if I don't know how many square inches there are in my design!" True—but my Easy Project Planner will solve this problem (Figure 1–12). It is an acrylic sheet with a grid of square inches or centimeters. When it is laid over your design, you can count the number of square inches in each color. Estimate portions of one square inch and add together halves, thirds, or quarters of square inches.

Fig. 1–12 (*above*). Using the Easy Project Planner: Mother's hair is approximately 12 square inches; Mother's face is approximately 4 square inches; Baby's face is approximately 2 square inches.

To make the Easy Project Planner, buy two 1/16″ thick sheets of acrylic or Plexiglas from a shop that sells glass. Mine is 18″ × 18″ and I think it's a handy size. However, if scraps of another size are available to you, by all means consider using two of that size.

From an engineering-supply house purchase black tape 1/32″ wide. You will need 684 inches or 19 yards of tape to make an 18″ × 18″ Easy Project Planner ruled in square inches, and 1,692 inches or 47 yards of tape for the same size ruled in square centimeters. While you're at the engineering supply house, also buy a sheet of graph paper at least 18″ × 18″ with square inches (or square centimeters) marked off in dark lines.

To put the lines on the Plexiglas, tape the graph paper to a table. Place the Plexiglas on top of it. Line up the edges with the graph paper grid as well as you can. Lay the tape on the Plexiglas, using the graph paper grid as a guide (Figure 1–13). Put another sheet of Plexiglas on top of the first so that the tape is sandwiched between them. Bind the edges with duct tape.

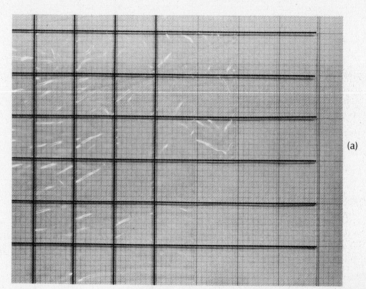

(a)

Fig. 1–13. (a & b—*right and below*) Lay black tape 1/32″ wide over lines on graph paper, which is underneath a sheet of acrylic. (c—*lower right*). The finished product.

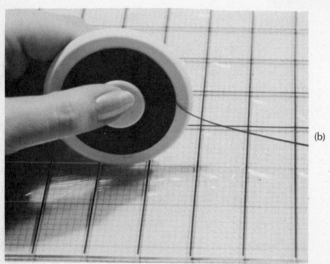

(b)

(c)

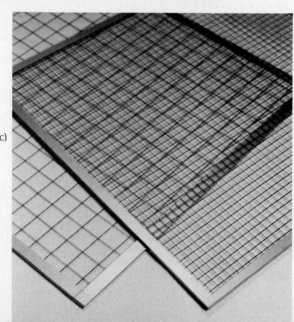

20

There are many uses for your Easy Project Planner besides figuring square inches. For example, you can use it to enlarge or reduce a drawing. It can help you to draw an item from real life (such as a vase of flowers) even if you cannot draw. (See page 61.)

Other equipment

Needlepoint doesn't require much in the way of supplies, as some hobbies do. The necessary supplies are shown in Figure 1–14.

Two pair of *scissors* are essential. One good pair of embroidery scissors is needed to cut yarn. The small points are a must for ripping stitches. A large, not-so-good pair of scissors is needed to cut canvas. Don't use your good fabric shears—nothing dulls scissors so fast as canvas. *Tweezers* also aid in ripping (see page 32).

Bind the raw edges of the canvas with masking *tape*, adhesive tape, or freezer tape.

You'll also need a *ruler* to measure the canvas. A *crochet hook* helps you to bury short ends of yarn in worked stitches.

A *frame* will help you get more even tension, and stitches will distort the canvas less if you use one. A frame that allows you to roll up excess canvas on two sides is easiest to work on. It is called a scroll or rotating frame.

Choose a *waterproof marker*—not one that is water-resistant—to draw on your canvas. Test the marker yourself on *every brand* of canvas that you buy. Write on a scrap of canvas with the marker. Let it dry thoroughly. Hold the canvas under running water. Blot with a white tissue. If any color runs, or bleeds, do not use that marker on that brand of canvas. It may work on another brand, so save it. *Never* take the manufacturer's word about a waterproof marker. Ink that runs can spell disaster in needlepoint. Often a marker will be permanent on many surfaces other than one that is highly sized, as is needlepoint canvas. *Test it yourself.*

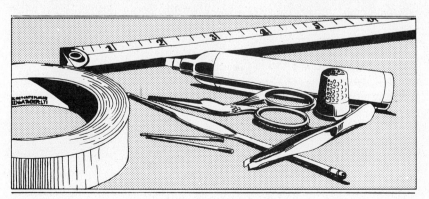

Fig. 1–14. Equipment needed for needlepoint.

21

2 Basic procedures

Keeping yarn

Keep the yarn for your current project looped around a plastic holder used for soda pop or beer (Figure 1–15). An embroidery hoop also works. When you store your yarn, it is easy to handle if it is tied as shown in Figure 1–16. It does not tangle easily and it unties readily. Simply pull the ends to untie it.

Keep track of color numbers or names, so that you can replace the yarn if necessary. Snip a piece of each color of yarn and tape it to the label.

Fig. 1–15. (a) Yarn for current project looped on plastic holder from soda or beer.
(b) Remove one strand for use.

(a)

(b)

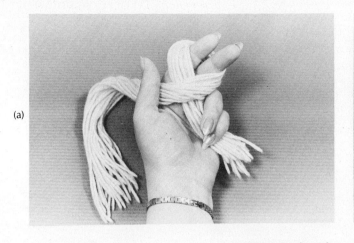
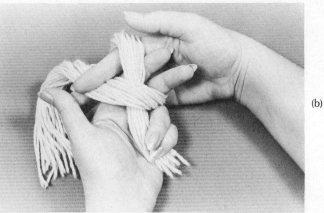

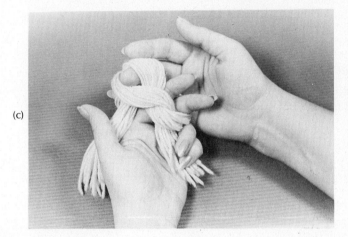

Fig. 1–16a, b, c, d. Knotting yarn for storage.

Preparing the canvas

You must take a few simple steps before you can stitch. Measure your canvas carefully. Cut between the mesh in a straight line. Even if your design is not a square or rectangle, cut one; squaring the corners makes blocking easier.

Bind the edges of your canvas with tape—masking, freezer, or adhesive (Figure 1–17). Rub the handle of your scissors across the tape after you've put it on the canvas. This will help it to stick better. Canvas ravels readily after the sizing on the canvas is softened with handling. Do *not* wait for the raveling to begin before you get out the tape. Even interlock Mono, which does not ravel readily, needs to be taped to keep the yarn from catching on the raw edges.

Fig. 1–17.
Bind canvas with masking tape.

Fig. 1–18. Roll canvas for easy access to working area; pin with large safety pins.

When stitching, roll your canvas to get to the area in the middle. *Never* crumple the canvas (Figure 1–18). Use large safety pins or the diaper pins that are lying useless in a drawer to pin the roll of extra canvas in place.

Handling the yarn

Generally, use yarn about 18 inches in length. The rough needlepoint canvas will soon wear the yarn thin. If you use a strand that is too long, the stitches at the beginning of your strand will be plumper than the stitches near the end of the strand. Novelty yarns must be even shorter.

So that you won't be tempted to use a too-long strand, pre-cut your yarn after you buy it. Persian yarn, which is sold by the ounce, usually comes 60 to 64 inches long. Cut these strands into thirds. Some kinds of Persian and tapestry yarns come by the skein. Untwist the skein and cut the circle once. Then cut that length into thirds. Knot as shown in Figure 1–16.

When tapestry yarn comes like the one pictured in Figure 1–19, simply cut the loops at *one* end. Leave the paper wrapper on. Pull just one strand from the other end of the skein.

Fig. 1–19. Cutting skein of yarn.

Some yarns come in skeins that do not lend themselves to any of the preceding methods. Wrap the yarn around a book or box that is approximately 18 inches in circumference. Cut the circle once and knot for storage.

Stitching with yarn

Yarn has *nap*, which means that the yarn will feel smoother one way than the other. (Some brands are hairier than others.) To determine the smooth way, hold a strand of yarn in one hand and run the other hand over it. Turn the yarn strand upside down and repeat with the same hand. Always stitch so that the smooth way goes through the needle and the canvas.

After you've threaded your needle, fold the yarn nearly in half (Figure 1–20). Move the needle along the yarn as you stitch. This keeps the needle from wearing a thin spot in the yarn.

Keep the twist of the yarn as it was when you removed it from the skein. When necessary, hold your canvas upside down, and let the yarn and needle dangle and untwist (Figure 1–21). If you don't do this, your stitches will be sloppy. As you become more experienced you will learn to give the needle enough of a twist to correct the kink in your yarn.

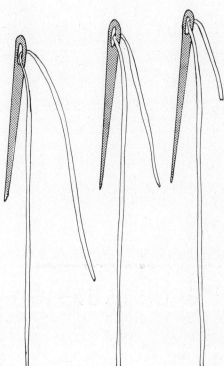

Fig. 1–20 *(above)*. Move the needle along the yarn as you use it.

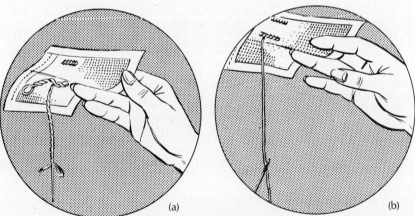

(a)　　　　　　　　　　　　　　(b)

Fig. 1–21. (a) When yarn becomes tightly twisted during stitching, turn canvas upside down. (b) Let needle dangle until yarn untwists.

Beginning and ending yarns

Do not knot yarn for needlepoint. To start your first stitches on a blank canvas, pull the needle through the canvas once, leaving about a one-inch tail. Take your next stitches over this tail until it is covered (Figure 1–22).

Fig. 1–22. Catch yarn tail on wrong side of canvas with needle and continue catching tail until completely buried.

25

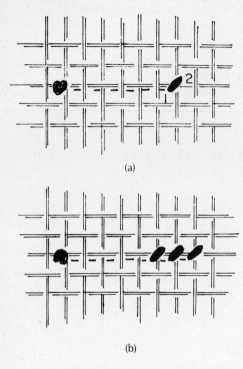

(a)

(b)

Fig. 1–23a & b. Waste Knot.

Many people like the *waste knot*. First, knot your yarn. (I know I said "never," but keep reading.) Put the yarn down into the canvas from the *front*, leaving the knot on the *right* side of the canvas. Come up to the right side of the canvas about an inch from the knot. Position this re-entry point so that the first few stitches will cover the tail. When you come to the knot, cut it off. (Thus the name, "waste-knot".) (Figure 1–23). You still don't have any knots in your finished needlepoint. Use this method when working on a frame.

To end the yarn, weave it over and under the wrong side of the stitches you've just worked (Figure 1–24a). Clip the excess yarn closely.

To begin subsequent yarns, bury the ends under stitches that have been worked—on the wrong side, of course. Don't bury a black yarn (or any other dark yarn) in an area of light stitches. It will show through on the right side.

The over-and-under weaving of the tail is not so secure with long stitches as it is with smaller stitches. For long stitches, take what is called a Bargello Tuck (Figure 1–24b). This is simply a backstitch, taken after you have woven the tail in, but before you bring the needle to the right side of the canvas.

Fig. 1–24a. Clip loose ends closely (after burying them) to produce a neat back. (Long ends look messy, can get caught up in other stitches, and produce lumps on right side of canvas.)

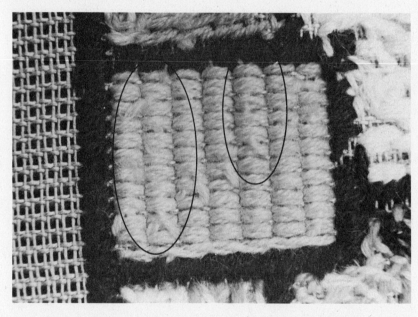

Fig. 1-24b. Bargello Tuck.

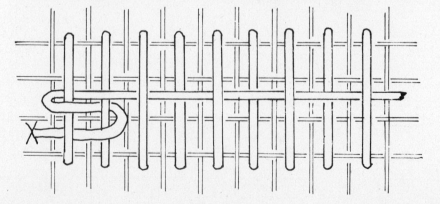

When a stitch has no backing to speak of, simply weave the yarn in and out of a few mesh of the blank canvas. Make sure that area will later be covered by your stitches.

If you can avoid it, do not stop or start your stitches in the same place. A definite lump or line will form.

Try not to carry a yarn from one area of stitching to another on the wrong side of the canvas for more than 1½ inches. When you do have to carry it that far, weave the yarn in and out of the backs of the stitches in the area you're skipping. Do not carry a dark yarn across a light area if you can help it. It will show through on the right side.

Stripping the yarn

Persian yarns can be plumped to make a fatter stitch that covers the canvas better. Simply separate the three plies and put them back together again. This process is called *stripping* the yarn. I find it's faster to hold the tip of the strand in one hand and run my fingers through the three plies, thus separating them. Anchoring one end saves having to put the plies back together evenly at the top of the strand.

When working diagonal stitches on Mono 14 canvas, only two plies of Persian yarn's three plies are used. Perhaps you've noticed that sometimes the yarn covers and sometimes it doesn't. This can be corrected by paying attention to which ply of the 3-ply strand you strip away.

Look at the three plies *closely*. Notice that in every strand there are a small, a medium, and a large ply that make up the strand. Chottie Alderson calls these a Baby, a Mamma, and a Daddy. In the past, when we used only two of the three plies, we laid the third aside and used it with the odd one from the next strand of yarn. Thus, we got three 2-ply strands from two 3-ply strands. If we would always pull the Mamma strand off when we separated or (thinned) the yarn, we would always have yarns of equal thickness (Figure 1–25 a and b). A strand made up of one Baby and one Daddy is equal in thickness to a strand made up of two Mammas. Now each strand will cover the canvas as well as the one before it.

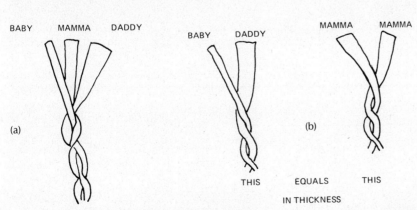

Fig. 1–25. (a) Baby, Mamma, Daddy. (b) One Baby and one Daddy=two Mammas.

27

Rolling the yarn

Oftentimes one stitch does not quite cover the canvas, even on the same strand of yarn. This may happen because the yarn has become overly twisted or it does not lie smoothly on the canvas. Either is especially true of yarn that has been thickened (Figure 1–26a). Rolling the yarn helps to correct the problem.

Use two hands—one on the bottom of the canvas and one on the top of the canvas—and a needle in each hand. The needle in your left hand helps to smooth the yarn as you pull the stitch through to the wrong side of the canvas with your right hand (Figure 1–26b). On large canvas, the fingers of your left hand can smooth the yarn as the right hand puts the needle into the canvas (Figure 1–26c).

The result is not only a smoother, more professional-looking stitch but also a stitch that covers better.

WRONG

(a) (b)

(c) (d)

(e)

Fig. 1–26. (a) Wrong stitches need rolling.
(b) Rolling yarn with needle.
(c & d) Rolling yarn with fingers.
(e) Correct results.

Continuous motion is like sewing—putting the needle into the canvas and bringing it out in the same motion (Figure 1–27). It gives an even tension when you are working without a frame and enables you to achieve rhythm and speed in stitching. It cannot be used with a frame because the canvas is too taut.

Fig. 1–27. Continuous motion.

Poking is used with a frame. Your dominant hand is constantly below the canvas and the other hand is on top of the canvas. Both hands work together.

When using a frame that you must hold with one hand—or if you wish to poke when not using a frame—use the method pictured in Figure 1–28. One hand holds the canvas or frame while the dominant hand pushes the needle into the canvas. The dominant hand also pulls the needle through on the wrong side.

Fig. 1–28a & b. Poking.

(a)
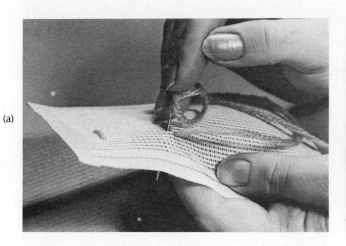
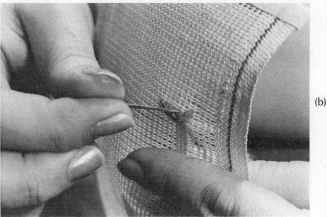
(b)

Direction of work

Try to stitch with the needle going *down* into a hole that has yarn in it. Bring the needle *up* in an empty hole. Bringing the needle up in a full hole makes it more likely that you will split the yarn of the already-worked stitches. You do not always have a choice, however.

Tension

Each stitch should be pulled as tight as the one before it. Each stitch should hug the canvas, but not choke it. Figure 1–29a shows correct tension. Too-tight tension ripples the canvas (Figure 1–29b). (Don't confuse this pulling with distortion of the canvas caused by various stitches. In that case, the canvas will lie relatively flat on a table.) Stitches that are too loose look sloppy (Figure 1–29c).

Note that long stitches will require slightly tighter tension than loose ones. See Mosaic Stitch (page 212) and Scotch Stitch (page 220).

Fig. 1–29a. Correct tension.

Fig. 1–29b. Too tight tension.

(a)

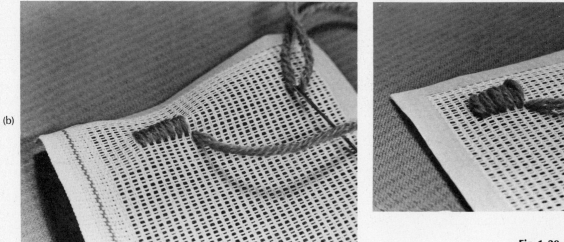

(b)

(c)

Fig. 1–29c. Too loose tension.

Thickening and thinning yarn

The thickness of yarn varies with its type (tapestry or Persian), brand, and color. Because of this we cannot just thread our needles with one strand of yarn and know it will cover the canvas.

Other factors that affect the covering ability of yarn are the size and brand of canvas and the stitch used (Figure 1–30).

Thickening and thinning of the yarn is much easier if you use Persian yarn, for its plies separate readily. To thicken, separate one 3-ply strand of Persian into its three plies. Add one (or two) of these to a 3-ply strand to make a 4-ply (or 5-ply) strand. Don't forget to strip your yarn (page 21). This makes the thickening almost invisible.

To thin, simply remove one or two plies.

To find out how thick (or thin) a yarn you will need, experiment on a piece of the canvas you will use for your project. Keep trying until you find the proper combination.

Beware of thickening too much. Sometimes a too-thick yarn will obliterate the stitch pattern or bulge the canvas. Yet, when stitched with one ply less, the canvas shows. What to do? Paint the canvas (page 64-67), and then this "grin-through" of canvas will be at least close in color to your yarn and not so noticeable.

The addition of some stitches can also help to cover the canvas. Consider using French Knots (page 284), Tramé (Figure 1–31), Frame Stitch (Figure 1–32), or Back Stitch (Figure 1–33).

There may even be times when this canvas showing through will enhance your design. (See page 189.)

If, when you've finished a section, you think the yarn could have been thickened more, don't cry or rip. Merely go over the stitches with one ply of yarn. This technique will not work on complicated stitches, however.

Fig. 1–30. Stitches on left show yarn so thin it does not cover canvas; stitches on right were worked with thickened yarn and cover properly.

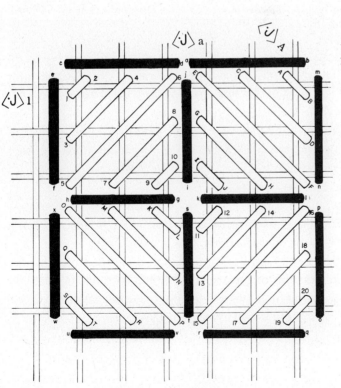

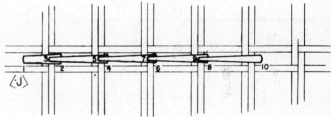

Fig. 1–31. Tramé.

Fig. 1–32. Frame Stitch around Scotch Stitch.

Fig. 1–33. Back Stitch.

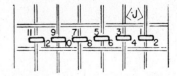

Direction of stitches

Stitch the design or lettering of a piece and then work the background. It must be done, generally, in one direction—top to bottom, right to left, etc. (The direction is determined by the stitch you use.) You cannot work in one corner and then work in another. In all probability, your stitch pattern then will not meet.

Compensating stitches

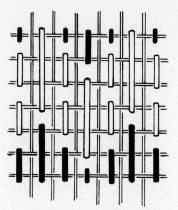

Fig. 1–34. Hungarian Stitch.

Decorative stitches never (it seems) fit into a design. Those places between the last whole motif of the stitch and the line of the design are filled with *compensating stitches*. They are so called because you must make do, or compensate, where the whole stitch motif does not fit.

Establish the stitch pattern in the largest part of your design. Work as many whole motifs as you can. Do not attempt to work a design's compensating stitches until you are quite familiar with the stitch.

When working compensating stitches try to work as much of the stitch motif as possible (Figure 1–34). If you are having trouble seeing just how much of the stitch you'll need, place the edge of a piece of paper over the drawing where your design's line cuts the stitch motif.

Sometimes the compensating stitches *must* be worked first.

Hold your needlepoint piece to the light to check for missed stitches.

Ripping and mending

It's unfortunate to have to rip, but even the best of us have to do it. With embroidery scissors cut the wrong stitches on the right side of the canvas. Use tweezers to pull out the incorrect stitches from the wrong side of the canvas (Figure 1–35).

Never reuse yarn that you have carefully ripped. The canvas roughs up the yarn too much to get a smooth stitch the second time around.

Do *not* cut the canvas.

You will have to rip a few good stitches to have enough yarn to work the ends in on the wrong side. A crochet hook makes quick work of this chore.

If you do cut the canvas, put a small piece of canvas under the cut, matching the mesh perfectly. Stitch through both thicknesses of canvas as if it were one. Be sure the patch is on the wrong side of the canvas (Figure 1–36).

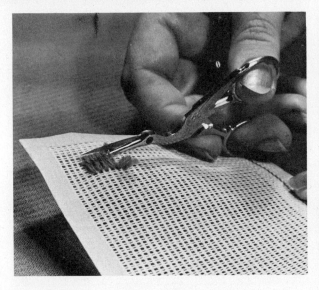

Fig. 1–35a. To rip, cut stitches on right side of canvas. (Be careful not to cut canvas.)

Fig. 1–35b. With tweezers, pull out incorrect stitches from wrong side of canvas.

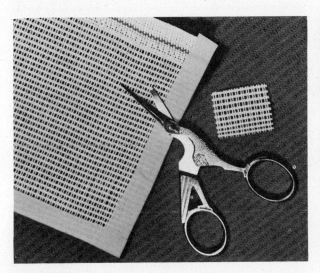

Fig. 1–36a. To mend canvas, cut patch slightly bigger than hole.

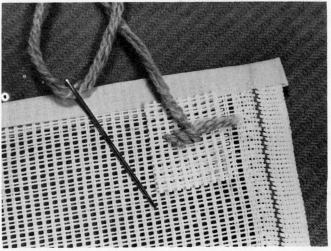

Fig. 1–36b. Work needlepoint stitches through both pieces of canvas as if they were one piece. (Wrong side of mended area shown.)

Cleaning needlepoint

Needlepoint can be cleaned. However, both of the available methods have drawbacks.

Washing with Woolite really gets the dirt out—and some sizing, too. So, it is no longer recommended for cleaning needlepoint. Mild soap and cold water is best. Rinse well. Roll in terry towels. Block immediately. (See page 293.)

A commercial needlepoint cleaner does not, in my opinion, get the needlepoint as clean as soap and water do. Also, the cleaning directions tell you to rub the needlepoint with a towel to remove the cleaner and dirt. Rubbing is not good for long stitches, which are prone to snagging. But these cleaners are handy for emergency touch-ups, spot removal, and cleaning things that cannot be washed (such as pre-finished leather articles, pages 76 and 90) and things that are a lot of trouble to take apart and clean (like a pillow).

Do not take your needlepoint to a dry cleaner. One touch of the presser can be fatal for the texture of needlepoint. Dirty cleaning fluid can dull your pretty colors.

Premature rotting of wool has been blamed on Scotchguard and other similar products. Foam rubber also rots wool. Put a piece of muslin between the foam rubber and the wool if you must have padding. Wool must have air to breath.

Instructions for left-handers

Left-handed people *can* do needlepoint. I've found, through teaching many left-handers, that they have learned to function in and interpret instructions from a right-handed world.

I've discovered that most left-handers find it easier to follow my stitch drawings if they turn the drawings upside down and reverse "right" and "left" and "up" and "down" in the written instructions. You may hold the canvas any way you wish as long as the final result is the same.

Use my hints or your own, but enjoy needlepoint and don't become discouraged because you're left-handed.

Part One has introduced you to the supplies and basic methods of needlepoint. Let's go on to Part Two and learn enough about Design and Color to work the tempting projects in Part Three.

COLOR
AND
DESIGN

Part Two considers color and design from the point of view of the needlepoint artist. Whether choosing yarn for a prepared canvas or creating an entirely new design, you should study the principles and techniques covered here. You will find both basic theory and many handy hints.

The color wheel and the five basic color schemes that you can make up by using it are described in Chapter 3. You will learn the importance of value in color schemes. You can determine the color values of your own designs by using an aid called a black glass. Directions are given for making a black glass with which to study your own designs.

The psychology of color is discussed to help you establish a mood appropriate to your design through the use of color. You may wish to create a realistic design or a decorative design. What color schemes are appropriate for the style you have chosen?

Putting all this together, a final section teaches you how to apply color theory step by step in painting your design. A checklist concludes the chapter to help you analyze your color scheme.

To create a successful needlepoint project, your design must suit the purposes of the final piece. Chapter 4 describes the use of line, composition, perspective, texture, and form in terms of needlepoint materials. You will learn to use both repetition and variety in stitches, so that you can draw on the collection of stitches presented in Part Four of this book: The Stitches.

3
Color

In most types of needlepoint you must choose the colors whether or not you have done your own design. If you have bought a kit that comes with yarn, this decision is made for you. Otherwise, the color choice is yours.

In doing needlepoint the design that you stitch can be done for you, or you may do your own.

A pre-worked canvas has the design stitched for you. All you have to do is choose the background colors and fill in the background. This may be plain or fancy or somewhere in between. Of course, how difficult the background is to stitch depends on how plain or fancy a background you choose.

Pre-worked canvas

A painted canvas has a design on the canvas, ready for you to stitch. You can buy this type of needlepoint canvas, or you can paint your own (page 45). The color choice is still yours. Sure, it's painted in color—but there are *lots* of reds and *lots* of blues, etc. So—which one?

Painted canvas

A charted design is a design worked out on graph paper; symbols are used to show different colors. To stitch, you start in the center of a blank piece of canvas and the center of the chart. Count the stitches and work them on your canvas; count, stitch; count, stitch; count, stitch . . . . If you can count, you've got it made! Again, the color choice is yours. Which red? blue?

Charted designs

Bargello	Bargello, also a charted design, begins with blank canvas. Here too, you begin in the center of your design and the center of the canvas. Work the main line or framework (page 185) to the right and to the left. Then all you have to do is repeat the pattern.
Four-way bargello	Four-Way Bargello is a little bit different from Bargello in spacing and putting the design on canvas. (It is discussed in more detail on page 188.) Its colors are similar to those of Bargello—usually in one family of colors with an accent color. Or the colors can blend from one to another, for example, orange to yellow with a touch of brown for accent.

Once you understand what color can do to make your design work, you will see why a brief study of color is important. Color can make mountains in the background of a landscape appear to be far away (Plate 17). It can make balls of yarn appear to be stacked on top of each other and then on top of a notebook (Plate 27). Color can give objects form or shape by shadows (Plate 4). Color can be used to develop a center of attention in a busy design (Plate 42). Color can also create moods, such as joy and warmth.

The color wheel

The Color Wheel (Plate 9) should be your guide to selecting and using color. There are three *primary* colors: red, yellow, and blue. The *secondary* colors are orange, green, and violet. The other colors are *tertiary* colors.

Warm colors are those colors on the color wheel from yellow to orange to red-violet. The colors on the other side of the color wheel from yellow-green to blue to violet are *cool*. The yellow-green and the violet are fairly neutral regarding warmth or coolness.

Even though red is considered a warm color, we can still have a cool red and a warm red. *Color relates to its environment.* When we compare two reds, the one that leans toward violet on the color wheel is cooler than the one that leans toward orange (Plate 5). By the same token, in considering two blues, you can see that the one that leans more toward violet is warmer than the one that leans toward green.

The warmth or coolness of color is an important point for you to learn. Warm colors come forward, and cool colors recede. This principle is what makes the balls of yarn in Plate 27 appear to be stacked on top of each other.

Adding grey to a color also makes it recede. This is the technique that is usually used to make mountains and far-away landscapes appear to be distant (Plate 17).

Color has three dimensions: hue, value, and intensity (chroma).

Hue is simply another word for color. Red, yellow, and blue are hues. Warmth or coolness is a part of hue.

Value refers to color's darkness or lightness. A light green leaf is higher in value than a dark green leaf (Plate 8).

Value is the *most* important of the dimensions of color. To change the value of a color, such as primary red, add white to make a tint. Add black to make a shade. Doing this does not change the hue—only the value changes.

Look at the black-and-white value scale (Figure 2–1). Primary red is at level 6, primary yellow is at level 2, and primary blue is at level 7. It takes only a little black added to red and blue to lower their value, but much white is needed to raise their value. Yellow is just the opposite: It takes very little white to raise the value of yellow and quite a lot of black to lower it. Primary yellow naturally starts out higher on the value scale than primary red and primary blue.

Fig. 2–1. Black and white value scale.

Some color schemes or designs will require you to work in a wide range on the value scale. Some color schemes will stay primarily at the top of the value scale. We call these *high key* or *high major* (Plate 4). A snow scene is also a high-key picture. Others will rest mainly in the middle of the value scale. These are referred to as *middle key* or *intermediate major*. Middle values are easiest for beginners to work with (Plate 3). Still others are at the bottom of the scale. These are called *low key* or *low major*. Imagine a dark stormy night scene; it, too, is low major.

To determine the key of a picture, consider the overall look. Dark colors can be found in a picture that is high key.

Some types of designs require colors of nearly equal value (Plate 32). See page 59, Oriental Perspective.

Value is easily seen when you compare black-and-white photographs and color photographs of the same thing. Even though colors are different, they will photograph as the same color if their values are equal.

Intensity

The *intensity* of a color is the strength of pure pigment. To change the intensity of a color add black or some other color (Plate 48). Colors of lower intensity recede. When the intensity is changed, the value is sometimes changed.

Color schemes from the color wheel

The color wheel can be—and should be—very useful in selecting color schemes for your needlepoint. We will discuss five kinds of color schemes in this book.

Complementary color schemes

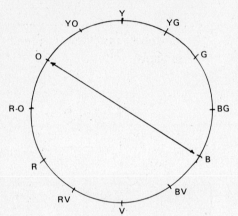

The *complementary* color scheme is the one we've all heard the most about (Figure 2–2). Complementary colors are the colors opposite each other on the color wheel (Plate 9). Knowing this doesn't seem to help, you say? Then use the following hint: When complementary colors are used in equal intensity, the result is jarring to the eye. However, when one color's intensity is changed the result is more pleasing. For example, a pink rose with bright green leaves is very pretty. A complementary scheme is more difficult to work with than the next two.

Fig. 2–2. Complementary colors.

Analogous color schemes

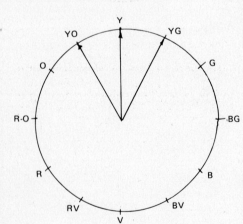

The *analogous* color scheme is the one most people prefer. It employs three colors that lie next to each other on the color wheel (Figure 2–3). Any group of three may be chosen, but the colors from green to yellow to red are the most popular.

Fig. 2–3. Analogous colors.

Monochromatic color schemes

The *monochromatic* color scheme lends itself readily to Bargello designs. It is several colors in the same family or, in other words, several tints and shades of one color. The Moon and Coyote project (pages 153-54) uses this color scheme. An accent color adds interest.

The *triadic* color scheme uses three colors that are an equal distance apart on the color wheel (Figure 2–4). A line drawn inside the circle from one color to the next forms an equilateral triangle. Red, yellow, and blue are one example; orange, green, and violet are another.

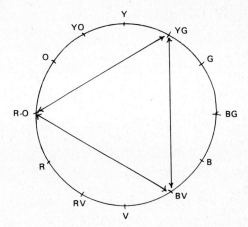

Fig. 2–4. Triadic colors.

The *split complementary* color scheme uses one color on one side of the color wheel and the two neighbors of its complement on the other side. For example, red-orange and blue-green are complements. The split complement would be red-orange, blue, and green, or blue-green, red, and orange (Plate 9 and Figure 2–5).

By sticking to a color scheme, you can avoid busyness in color. You are then limited to two or three colors and their shades and tints.

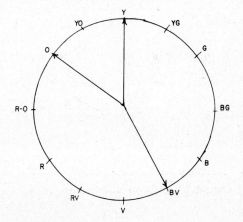

Fig. 2–5. Split complementary colors.

Creating moods from color

The psychology of color is important because color sets moods. You would not use explosive reds, yellows, and oranges for a quiet, somber mood. Blues and greys will not fit in a violent or exciting scene.

Use the following chart as your guide to color and mood:

Red	happy times, Christmas and Valentine's Day (a clear red is pleasing with other pleasing colors); anger, passion, danger
Orange	warmth, friendliness, harvest, Halloween
Yellow	happiness, warmth, sun, life, cowardice, deceit (gold is also harvest)

41

Green	nature, plants, outdoors, jealousy, envy, safety
Blue-green	distance, air, water
Blue	gloom, somberness (grey-blues), sky, water
Violet	dark, serious moods, royalty, mysterious feeling
Red-violet	cheapness, garishness
Cold colors	mold, decay
Warm colors	freshness and warmth

Colors are affected by their environment. *Never* choose colors for your needlepoint without placing them all together to see how they look (see page 46). A red that seems clear and warm may take a turn toward the cooler violets when placed next to a warm orange.

Colors appear bright, bold, and dramatic against a black or dark background. The very same colors will appear subdued when placed against a white or light background.

White makes dark colors stand out more.

Make certain that each area of your design will stand out against the background. A navy blue object will be lost against a black background.

A yellow surrounded by black will look much different when it is surrounded by red. See other color comparisons in Plate 5.

Local color

The *local color* of a piece is determined by the color that you've used the most. Usually this is the background color, but not always. Choose the local color first. Then all the other colors will fall into place more easily.

NOTE: When framing a picture (needlepoint or otherwise) the frame should match the local color. This way the picture is of primary importance, not the frame. Once in a while you'll want to emphasize the frame and the picture as a whole. Break this rule then (as in Figure 3–42, the Birth Sampler). Use the frame to pick up and thus emphasize a color used in small amounts (Plate 20).

Using color for style

The colors you choose for your design will help to determine its style. You should aim for either a realistic or a decorative overall effect.

Most people prefer *realism* in design. Several factors must be considered if one is to achieve this effect.

You must strive to get realistic hues, values, and intensities. The best way to do this is to observe nature and then try to match the *colors* you see with paint on paper and then with yarn on canvas.

Shadows should fall on the side opposite a light source. Try to match the color of the shadow. It has a little color from the object that casts the shadow (vase, Plate 4) and the object the shadow falls on (table, Plate 4). The red vase casts a shadow on the green table. The shadow is, thus, olive green. You can see this by shining a high-intensity lamp on the red yarn. Hold the green yarn so that the shadow of the red yarn falls on it. You will see the olive green.

Texture is created through the use of stitches. Imagine what the various parts of your design would feel like if you could not actually touch them. Try to match that texture to the feel and look of the stitches. For this reason it is handy to have a sampler (Plates 12, 14, and 28). Pieces with good texture will give you an overwhelming desire to touch them. Again, see Plate 4.

Modeling means that shadows give an object a round or three-dimensional look. Objects should be modeled. Highlights also add to this effect. (Plate 4)

Aerial perspective is another important feature of realism. Objects in the picture *must* appear to recede. A vase must sit *on* a table and the flower stems must be *inside* the vase. Perspective can be created with line as well as color (see Plate 4).

Nonrealistic (decorative) style

Oriental perspective is a prominent feature of decorative designs. No one item or design component seems to recede (Plate 32). This is achieved by using colors of the same value. Repeated colors in the foreground, middle ground, and background ensure a flat (not receding) design.

Colors need not be realistic; they may be imaginary, serving the purpose of the design. A tree may be red with violet leaves, yet everyone will know it's a tree. This kind of design is called *abstract*. Most people think of an abstract design as one that is geometric or the like, but in art circles such a design is called a *nonobjective design*.

A nonrealistic design may be textured or not, and objects are usually not modeled.

Triangle method

When you are trying to decide just where colors should go on a decorative piece, it helps to use the *triangle method* of coloring a design. Figure 2–6 shows how to place colors on a map of the United States. Arrange your colors in a triangle. For example, color Maine, Texas, and Idaho red; California, Minnesota, and North Carolina blue; and Nebraska, Michigan, and Florida yellow. The triangle method makes it easier to put a few colors on a large design.

Most of the designs in this book fall in the category of nonrealistic designs. They are easier to stitch than realistic designs.

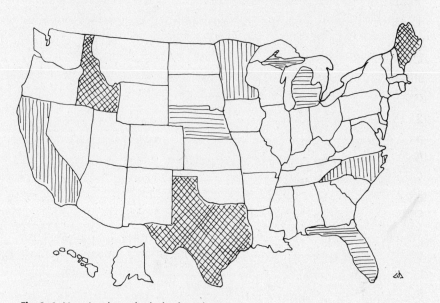

Fig. 2–6. Use triangle method of color selection to color many areas with only a few colors.

Applying color theory to needlepoint

In making the projects in this book, the designs are drawn for you. To a certain extent the colors are chosen, too. However, you must always feel free to change either or both design and color.

Let's assume for a moment that you wish to recreate one of the designs in this book exactly as it appears. The best way to choose colors is to take the book to your yarn shop and try to match the colors in the color photographs as closely as possible. As remarkable as color photography is, the photograph is still not quite like the real thing. So, you must re-evaluate the colors you have chosen when you see the yarn (see page 42).

If you decide to change the colors, you must make a colored drawing on paper. Enlarge your chosen design (page 62). Use construction paper to build basic areas of color. Cut pieces the approximate size and shape of each area of color and lay them on your design. Then paint the design on paper with crayons, colored pencils, markers, acrylic paints, or anything else that will color paper.

Painting the design

In painting your design, try to come as close as you can to the color of yarn you wish to use. The following are some hints that will make the painting of the design easier.

1. Tone your paper by using a light wash over the whole paper. This should be your background color (or local color). Use acrylic paint or water colors with a *lot* of water. You should still be able to see the guidelines of your drawing. Allow it to dry before going on.

2. Use a transparent palette. A side window from a car is perfect. You can get one free (or for a nominal charge) by asking for one at a junkyard. Put a piece of construction paper the color of your local color under your palette. When you choose and mix your colors you will then have a fair idea of what the color will look like before you get it on paper.

3. Buy the modular colors (pre-mixed) as well as the primary colors. There's really no need to spend hours learning to mix paint.

4. Except for the shadows that are cast, work from dark to light. It will be easier to find colors that fit together.

5. In using, for example, a split complementary color scheme of green, red-orange, and red-violet, you can use those colors *and* the colors that you get by mixing them. Red-orange and red-violet make a red. Red-orange and green make a sort of olive green.

6. Use warm colors next to cool colors and dark colors next to light colors.

7. Paint highlights and shadows last.

8. No color is as light as it seems or as dark as it seems.

Black glass

Step back and look at your design often to be sure the colors are falling into place as they should.

Value is the most important single point to consider. It must be right. A *black glass* (Figure 2–7k) aids you tremendously in determining whether your values are correct. It boils the values down to basics. To use it, look into the glass at the reflection of your drawing, yarn, or needlepoint piece. Colors that are high in value will stick out like the proverbial sore thumb. Colors that are low in value will recede and become lost.

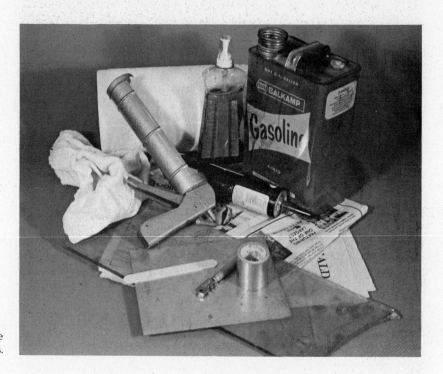

Fig. 2–7a. Materials needed to make a black glass.

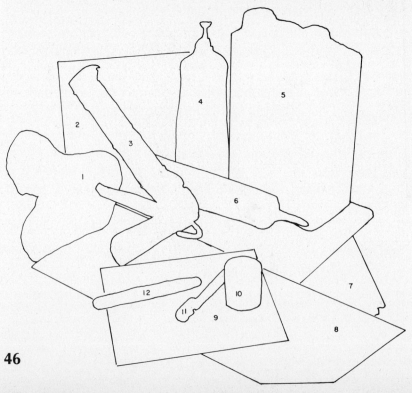

Fig. 2–7b. (1) rags, (2) paper towels, (3) caulking gun, (4) spray glass cleaner, (5) gasoline, (6) roofing tar, (7) newspaper—to protect working surface, (8) safety (car window) glass, (9) sheet metal, (10) duct tape, (11) glass cutter, (12) stick—to spread tar.

There will be times when you will want certain portions to come forward or to go back. The black glass will show just how much they do come out or go back. In Oriental Perspective (page 59) nothing should come forward or recede. The design elements should be flat.

The black glass also helps you with warm colors and cool colors. Remember that warm colors come forward and cool colors recede.

Also use the black glass to look at your skeins of yarn. I always take mine to the yarn shop to help me in choosing yarn.

It takes less than an hour to make this miraculous black glass. You will need to gather together these supplies before you start:

Constructing a black glass

1. A piece of car window glass (tinted or not) about 7" × 9". Get it from a junk yard.

2. A piece of sheet metal (any kind) the same size as the glass. (A sheet-metal place has scraps this size.)

3. Roofing tar. (Buy it for less than a dollar at a hardware store. If you do not have a gun to dispense it, you will need that, too. It's the same gun used for caulking.)

4. Duct tape (also available in a hardware store).

5. Gasoline (for clean-up).

6. Rags.

7. Scissors to cut the tape.

It's wise to have someone to help you whose hands will be clean. But on the other hand, maybe you need someone who doesn't mind getting his (or her) hands dirty! Figure 2–7 gives a complete guide to making the black glass.

Fig. 2–7c. Clean a piece of safety glass.

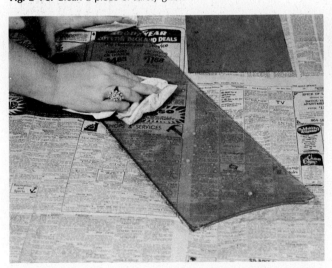

Fig. 2–7d. Mark and cut the glass to size.

Fig. 2–7e. Squeeze the tar onto the metal.

Fig. 2–7f. Spread the tar around with a stick, and eventually, your fingers.

Fig. 2–7g. Put a thick layer evenly on the glass.

Fig. 2–7h. Put the glass on top of the tar.

Fig. 2–7i. Smooth out the tar so that there are no bubbles. The bubbles shown in this photo must be eliminated.

Fig. 2–7j. Bind the edges with duct tape.

Fig. 2–7k. Use the reflection of your project in the black glass to help you choose the colors for your needlepoint.

Color checklist

Use the following checklist to be sure your color scheme works as you intend it to:

1. Have you stayed within the color scheme that you have chosen (analogous, complementary, etc.)?

2. Have you included some contrast of color (hues)?

3. Do you have a balance of light and dark areas?

4. Do areas of color intensity balance?

5. Are the values (lights and darks), intensities (brightness), and hues (analogous, complementary, etc.) in harmony?

6. Do you have warm colors next to cool ones?

7. Do you have dark colors next to light ones?

8. Do the colors take your eye around the design, just as lines do (page 57)?

9. Have you used areas of color to stop the action (page 57)?

4
Design

In the previous section covering color, for the purpose of discussion, we used the designs in this book as our vehicle for color. But if you wish to do your own designs, I have, in essence, given you a bushel of apples with no basket to put them in. Here comes the basket.

So, you want to do your own design? There are several decisions to make before you seriously begin to draw.

1. What will be the use of the finished needlepoint piece?

2. What will be the subject matter?

3. What will be the shape of the finished design—square, rectangular, round, irregular?

4. What kind of composition (arrangement of objects) are you considering?

5. Do you want aerial (realistic) or Oriental (decorative) perspective?

6. Do you wish the objects in your design to be modeled (realistic) or flat (decorative)?

7. Do you want shadows (realism)? If so, determine the source of light—from the right or left.

Once you have decided upon the answers to these questions, you have some kind of starting point.

Deciding the shape of the design gives a needed outer confinement. You may find later that this needs to be changed, but you have to start somewhere.

Form

Form is the basic shape or structure of *all* objects. Everything can be reduced to a sphere, a cube, a cone, or a cylinder (Figure 2–8).

Fig. 2–8. *All* things boil down to four shapes: sphere, cube, cone, and cylinder.

Every good design should have a variety of forms, yet some of them should be repeated. Constant repetition is boring, and constant variety is confusing. Repeated forms add texture. (Figure 2–9).

Fig. 2–9 a & b. Everything breaks down into four forms.

(a)

(b)

Texture

Texture is important to a design because it adds interest. It creates patterns of lights and darks; heavily textured areas appear darker (Figure 2–10). In needlepoint, most of the texture is added to the design by the use of stitches.

Texture is lost as the design moves farther from the viewer. In realistic designs, the stitches should be reduced in size for background objects. The individual bricks on a brick wall appear less and less distinct as you move farther away. Keep this in mind as you stitch a realistic design. This does not apply in a nonrealistic design.

Fig. 2–10. Texture.

Unity

Unity ties a design together and gives it a focus of thought (Figure 2–11). Such elements as focal point, point of entry, and proportion combine to create a unified design.

Fig. 2–11a. Unity—wrong.

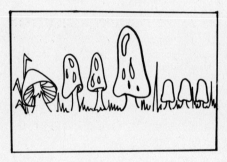

Fig. 2–11b. Unity—right.

Focal point

The focal point catches the eye and shows it something of interest. (Figure 2–12). Avoid putting it in the center of the picture. Things that are slightly off to one side are more appealing. A focal point can also be made with color (Plate 42).

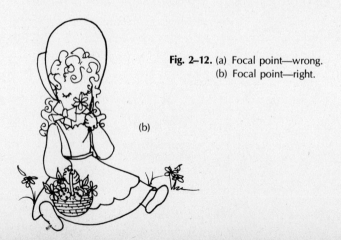

Fig. 2–12. (a) Focal point—wrong.
(b) Focal point—right.

(a)

(b)

A point of entry takes the viewer into the picture (Figure 2–13). A door, slightly ajar, invites the viewer inside a building. A path or sidewalk leads the viewer to a building, the focal point. A stream entices the viewer to follow it into the picture.

Fig. 2–13a. Point of entry—wrong.   **Fig. 2–13b.** Point of entry—right.

Proportion

Fill the space given with your design or focal point (Figure 2–14). A too-small object will be lost in a too-large area.

Fig. 2–14a. Proportion—wrong.   **Fig. 2–14b.** Proportion—right.

Balance

Your design should not violate the principle of balance. You can attain either a formal or an informal effect by the means you choose to balance the design.

Formal or symmetrical

In pictures that have formal balance, the right side of the picture is a mirror image of the left side (Figure 2–15). The two sides do not have to be exactly alike, but they should be very similar.

Fig. 2–15. Formal balance.

Informal balance

Informal balance is a little harder to see than formal balance. Visualize a picture of a circle hanging on a string (Figure 2–16).

Fig. 2–16a. Formal (symmetrical) balance.

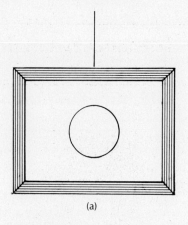

(a)

Fig. 2–17. Informal balance.

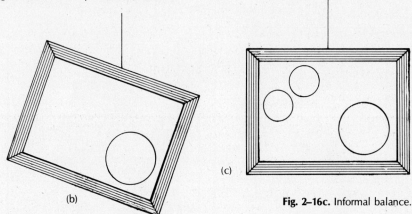

(b)

(c)

Fig. 2–16c. Informal balance.

Fig. 2–16b. Informal (asymmetrical) balance.

When the circle is in the center, the picture is formally balanced. Yet, when the circle is moved to the lower right corner, the picture seems to tilt because that corner looks heavier than the rest of the picture. Now add two smaller circles to the upper left corner. The picture straightens out because it is now informally balanced. It is easier to make an odd number of objects balance informally, although an even number can be made to work (see Figure 2–17).

54

Line

There are seven definitions of line. Only five apply to needlepoint:

1. Line carries its own inherent beauty (Hogarth's Line of Beauty) (Figure 2–18a).
2. Line divides or limits an area (Figure 2–18b).
3. Line defines forms (Figure 2–18c).
4. Line catches and guides the eye throughout the design (Figure 2–18d).
5. Line creates design or arrangement (Figure 2–18e).

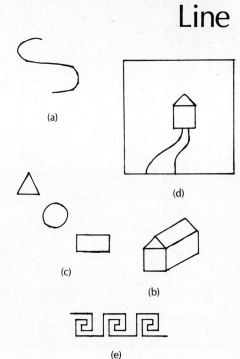

Fig. 2–18. (a) Hogarth's Line of Beauty.
(b) Line divides or limits an area.
(c) Line defines forms.
(d) Line catches and guides the eye throughout the design.
(e) Line creates design or arrangement.

The language of line

Lines, by themselves, tell many stories. Each type of line imparts a mood or feeling. Use the type of line you need for your design. Do not use conflicting types of lines. Lines that imply hate and war (conflicting diagonals) should not be used with lines that imply tranquility and calm (horizontal lines).

Fig. 2–19a. Horizontal lines are restful.

Fig. 2–19b. Vertical lines are stately.

Fig. 2–19c.
Curved lines are graceful.

Fig. 2–19d. Diagonal lines show action.

Fig. 2–19e. Hogarth's Line of Beauty.

Fig. 2–19f. Conflicting diagonals indicate war and hate.

Fig. 2–19g. Rhythmic curves mean joy and spaciousness.

Fig. 2–20. A *subjective line* is a broken one which the eye connects behind an object. The table continues on the other side of the vase. The rim of the vase is hidden behind the leaf. Can you find other subjective lines in this drawing?

The following chart and Figure 2–19 tell the language of line:

HORIZONTAL	≡	TRANQUILITY, REPOSE
VERTICAL	⎮⎮⎮	DIGNITY, STATELINESS
DIAGONAL	\\\	DYNAMIC MOVEMENT, INSTABILITY
CURVED	∿	GRACE, BEAUTY
CONFLICTING DIAGONAL	✕✕	HATE, WAR, CONFUSION
RHYTHMIC CURVES	3333	JOYOUSNESS, SPACE
HOGARTH'S LINE OF BEAUTY	∼	BEAUTY

Every design should have some curved lines, some straight lines, Hogarth's Line of Beauty, and at least one subjective line. A *subjective line* (Figure 2–20) is one which the eye connects behind an object to complete the line.

56

Avoid static points (Figure 2–21). Unless a static point is broken up, the eye will never leave that spot to continue to look at the rest of the picture. In the project on pages 153-54, the moon and its corona create a static point, but it is broken by the branch of the tree and, somewhat, by the coyote's muzzle. Never take a line into the corner of a picture, for the same reason.

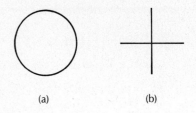

(a)   (b)

Fig. 2–21 a & b. Avoid these static points in your design.

The dynamics (or action) of line

The lines of a design can lead the eye out of the picture, never to return. This *must* be avoided at all costs (Figure 2–22). Avoid arrows, a road, or any other lines that point out of the picture. This applies to stitches, also. Oriental (page 209), for example, forms arrowheads. Make them point toward the center of the picture, not its edge. Reverse the stitch, if necessary.

There are many devices that you can use to stop the action. A dark spot of color just beyond the offending line will do the job. Curve a road or path back inside the picture. Use a hill, a curve, or a tree to stop the action. A house, a fence, or a hat on the end of the baseball bat are also effective in keeping the eye inside the picture. If you do use a fence, there should always be a gate that leads the viewer's eye around the inside of the picture. A building should always have an open door.

Fig. 2–22a. The horses, and your eye as well, go right out of the picture. This is wrong.

Fig. 2–22b. Your eye stays inside the picture. This is good composition.

Composition

Where you put the objects and lines in your design is considered as part of composition.

The *distribution of space* is very important. Figure 2–23 shows how space can be divided. NOTICE: As the focal point is removed from the center of the picture, the design becomes more interesting. As these lines are curved, even more interest is created.

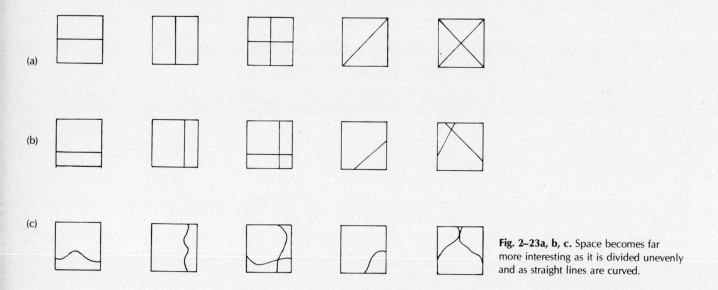

(a)

(b)

(c)

Fig. 2–23a, b, c. Space becomes far more interesting as it is divided unevenly and as straight lines are curved.

To find the best spot for the center of interest of your design, divide the length and width of your space into five equal parts (Figure 2–24a). Use any line, horizontally or vertically; but be sure there are two spaces between it and the closest boundary of the picture (Figure 2–24 b-e). Where these lines cross is the best place to put your center of interest.

Adding other things to a picture is easier when you have a starting point. Each object that you place in a picture should be tied in with or overlapped with the others. (See Plates 19, 27, 32, and 42.)

There are times when you can break all these rules and still achieve an effective design. Notice the bird to the right of St. Francis's shoulder on page 329. It is not tied in, but it works.

My mother always told me that I had to learn to make a cake from scratch before I could use a cake mix. You, too, must learn to design by the rules before you can break them.

Fig. 2–24a, b, c, d, e. Place the center of interest off-center.

 (a)
 (b)
 (c)
 (d)
 (e)

Perspective can be achieved with line. (The creation of perspective through color has been discussed on page 38.)

Aerial perspective

In *aerial perspective*, objects get smaller as they recede into the background. Figure 2–25 shows an imaginary vanishing point. As things approach this spot they get smaller. Proper perspective takes practice to perfect. I have merely introduced you to the subject here. If you want to go into it further, I suggest you study an art book that deals with perspective.

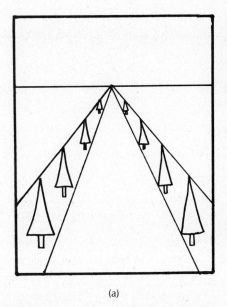

(a)

(b)

Fig. 2–25a & b. In *aerial perspective*, all things get smaller as they reach an imaginary vanishing point.

Oriental perspective

In the vest in Plate 32, all objects seem to be right up front. The size and shape of the objects, as well as the color (page 43), create this illusion, which is known as *Oriental perspective.*

Notice that the roulette table is just as wide at the far end as it is at the near end. In aerial perspective, the far end would have been smaller.

Ideas

If you wish to do your own design, there are many idea sources available to you. Sometimes you can copy directly from children's coloring books, stained-glass pattern books, and appliqué books.

Sometimes you can combine two or more designs to make one (page 137). To do this, trace all the design elements that you like and wish to include in your design. Cut them out. On another piece of paper, draw the outer boundaries of your design. Arrange all the loose pieces in a pleasing composition (Figure 2–26). Follow the Design Checklist that comes next to determine whether you have created a good design (artistically, that is). Tape the design in place before a breeze or a sneeze takes it away. See the final design in the bellpull, page 136.

Fig. 2–26a & b. Trace elements from these two designs and cut them out.

(a)

(b)

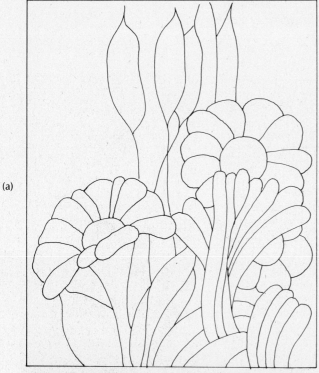

(c)

Fig. 2–26c. Arrange in a pleasing design.

Your Easy Project Planner (page 19) can be used to draw a picture from real life—even if you cannot draw. Figure 2–27 shows how it can be done. Have a groove sawed in a 4" × 4" piece of wood for a stand. The groove should be 2¾" to 3" deep and just wide enough for the Easy Project Planner to fit in it. Set it before the object(s) you wish to draw. On a blank sheet of paper, draw a grid. A one-inch grid will reproduce the object the same size as you see it through the Easy Project Planner. A smaller grid on your blank paper will reduce it, and a larger one will enlarge it. Don't forget to follow the design rules in the checklist in setting up your still life or landscape. Sometimes nature must be improved upon—so watch out for things that keep a design from following the rules.

Fig. 2–27(a) Slide the Easy Project Planner into a wooden stand.

(b) Draw the lines inside each square. This is the first rough drawing. Polish it and you have a design ready to stitch.

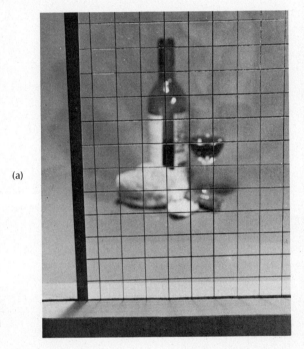

(a)

(b)

Does your design include the following points?

Design checklist

1. Space that has been pleasingly divided.

2. Lines that create an interesting design or arrangement.

3. Lines that define forms.

4. Aerial or Oriental perspective (not both).

5. Lines or objects that direct the eye through (not out of) the picture. Keep in mind that the pattern of stitches can lead the eye around, too.

6. Balance (turn your design upside down to check).

7. A variety of forms (spheres, cones, cylinders, and cubes), yet some repeated.

8. Objects that relate to their environment (e.g., no camels in the house; they should be in the desert).

9. No floaters. (Give solidarity by adding a dark line at the bottom of an object. Compare Plate 15 and Figure 3–48c.)

10. Objects that are tied together.

11. A variety of textures.

12. A predetermined source of light (if you're using shadows).

13. A subjective line.

14. Hogarth's Line of Beauty.

15. A combination of compatible lines (see Language of Line, pages 55-57).

16. No static points.

17. No parallel lines.

Remember that lines are much more than mere outline. They convey thoughts, feelings, and moods. Creative stitchery *must* begin with creative lines. These creative lines are simply those you choose to draw.

Have fun; enjoy! You will never know what you can do unless you try.

Enlarging or reducing a design

Once you have a design that you want to use, you must make it the proper size. Unless you like to work on very small canvas (16 or more mesh per inch), you will want broad curves and large areas. Don't have more than two or three areas smaller than a nickel, unless you plan to fill them with one motif of a decorative stitch.

Grid method

The *grid method* is the easiest way to change the size of a design by yourself. To do this draw squares on your design (or on a tracing-paper copy) and on a blank piece of paper. Simply copy the lines in each square and presto! Your design is larger (or smaller).

If you make the grid squares on your original design ¼" and the grid 1" on your blank paper, you will have increased your design by four times. If you make the grid on your original design in 1" squares and the grid on your blank paper ½" squares, you will have reduced the size of your design by half (see Figure 2–28a).

By changing the squares to rectangles, you can change the shape of your design, as well as enlarge it (Figure 2–28b).

Fig. 2–28a. To enlarge a design, draw squares on the original design.

Fig. 2–28b. On another sheet of paper, draw larger squares. Copy the contents of each square.

Fig. 2–28c. To change the shape of your design, draw rectangles instead of squares on the second sheet of paper.

Your Easy Project Planner (page 19) can help you do this. When you need one-inch squares on your original design, simply place the Easy Project Planner over your design. Now you only have to draw squares on one piece of paper. (It's easier on graph paper.) When you need one-inch squares on your blank sheet of paper, put the Easy Project Planner on a white sheet of paper on a table. Put a piece of tracing paper over it, and the black lines of the Easy Project Planner show through. Now you only have to draw squares on your original design.

The more complex your design is, the more work this grid method will be.

Photographic method

You could, also, take a picture of whatever real-life subject you wish to reproduce. Use film that makes slides. Put the slide in a projector and flash it up on the wall the size you want it to be. Tape paper to the wall and trace the projected image on the paper.

If you simply don't feel like enlarging or reducing your own design, you can always take your piece to a *lithographer*. The fee he charges will depend on the kind of equipment he has. There's a new gadget out that does the job in a couple of minutes. The lithographer merely dials the percentage of enlargement (or reduction) that you want. (He'll figure out what the percentage is; you only have to tell him about how big you want the final picture.) There will be a nominal fee for this.

On the other hand, if the lithographer has to do the job photographically, it will cost you three to four times as much. You may not consider this fee too much to pay for the service performed. Check into it before you discard this method of enlarging and reducing a design.

Transferring the design

Once your design is the right size, you can now put it on canvas.

Tracing the design

First you'll need to trace the lines of your paper design with a black felt-tip marker. If you use a broad tip and feel that it is too broad, your design is too small for needlepoint, unless you plan to use small canvas or do a lot of Petit Point.

Tape a large piece of white paper to a table top with masking tape. Tape your paper design to the blank paper. Put your needlepoint canvas over the design. There should be a 3" margin all the way around the design area. (Sometimes you will not need this much margin. Check Part 3: The Projects before you cut your canvas.) Tape the canvas in place.

Trace the design onto the canvas with a *waterproof* grey marker. Don't forget to trace the outside line, too. Not as hard as you thought, is it?

Painting the canvas

Next paint the canvas with *waterproof markers* or *acrylic paints* (Figure 2–29). The hints for painting the paper design also apply to painting the canvas. The following suggestions will also help you:

1. Thin your paint with water to make it the same consistency as liquid dishwashing detergent. An eye dropper keeps you from adding too much water. It is better for the paint to be too thick than too thin. Ideally the paint should not clog the canvas holes, nor should it come through on the other side of the canvas.

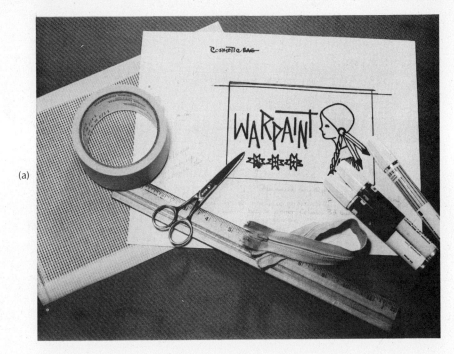

(a)

Fig. 2–29a. Supplies needed to ready a canvas for stitching.

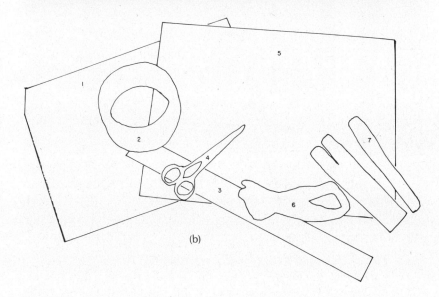

(b)

Fig. 2–29b. (1) canvas, (2) masking tape, (3) ruler, (4) scissors, (5) drawing of design, (6) zipper, (7) waterproof markers—if used instead of acrylic paints.

Fig. 2–29c. Bind the edges of the canvas with masking tape.

Fig. 2–29d. Rub the handle of a pair of scissors over the tape to make it stick better.

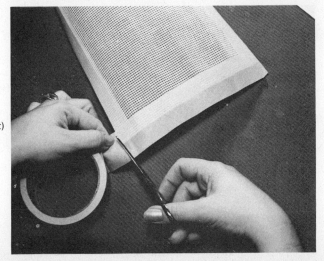

(c)

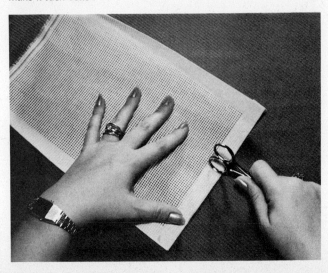

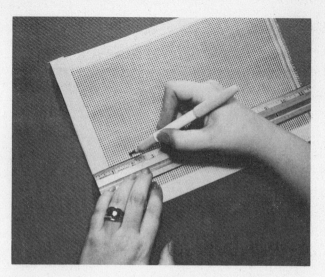

Fig. 2–29e. Mark two of the margins with a waterproof marker.

Fig. 2–29f. Be sure your needlepoint will be as long as the zipper you wish to insert.

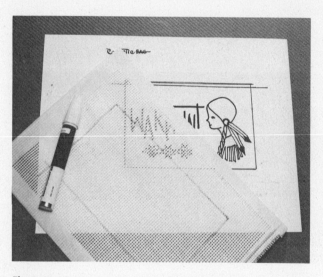

Fig. 2–29g. Trace your drawing with a black marker.

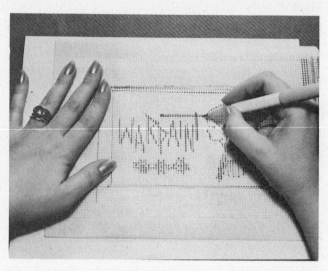

Fig. 2–29h. Lay the canvas over the design and trace it onto the canvas with a waterproof grey marker.

Fig. 2–29i. Your canvas should look like this.

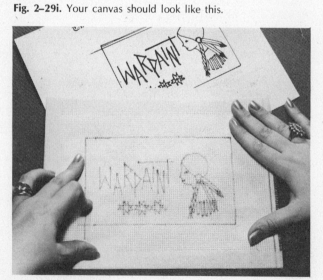

Fig. 2–29j. Paint the background. Let it dry.

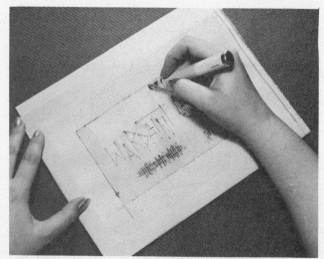

Fig. 2–29k. The canvas is now ready to stitch.

Fig. 2–29l. Painting with acrylic paints.

2.   Use a broad, stiff brush for large areas and a finer, yet still stiff, one for smaller areas. Brushes that are too wet will dissolve the sizing on the canvas.

3.   White (or tan) paint makes a good eraser. Cover your mistake with paint the same color as the canvas. Let it dry. Then you can paint right over it.

4.   Separate cans of water for each color save many trips to get clean water. Soup cans are ideal.

5.   Mix paint in throw-away containers to make clean-up much easier. Yogurt containers and plastic egg cartons work well.

6.   Clean-up with acrylic paints is easy—soap and water do the trick. But don't let the paint dry before you've cleaned the brushes.

7.   Spray with a fixative to set the paint. Acrylic paint is permanent once it has dried. *But test it yourself.* Run it under water and blot with a white tissue.

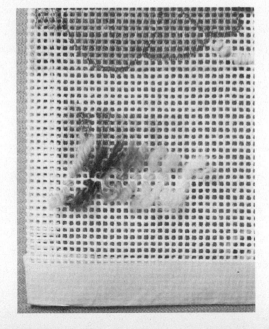

Fig. 2–29m. Paint a swatch of each color you use in the margin. Use it to match yarn colors.

Graph charts

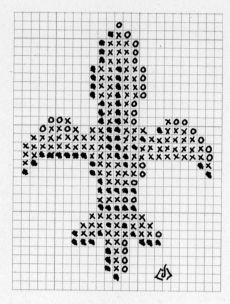

𝕏 DARK BROWN

O PALE YELLOW

X GOLD (ORANGE-GOLD)

Graph charts allow you precision in shading, detail, and geometric designs. Each X on the drawing is one Continental Stitch (see page 194).

If you want to make your own graph charts, you need to realize that the canvas is not absolutely square. If you need 100 mesh, don't measure 10 inches on 10 mesh canvas. Count out the exact number of mesh. To get an approximate idea of the size your needlepoint will be, use graph paper with the same number of squares per square inch as there are mesh per square inch on your canvas.

You can color your graph with colored pencils. Symbols are used in black and white drawings to represent different colors (Figure 2–30).

Fig. 2–30. Various symbols represent different colors in a graph chart.

Choosing stitches for your design

Choosing stitches for a design is the most fun—next to doing them. I like to use lots of stitches. This change makes the needlepoint more interesting to stitch. Without the variety in stitches, I'd never get through a big piece. However, never be afraid to repeat stitches if your design calls for them.

The decorative stitches can do the designing for you. But if you want to use them, you must choose a nonrealistic, or decorative, design (see page 43). Realism demands small stitches to get the proper shapes and shading. Use Basketweave (page 192) where you can. Petit Point gives you detail (page 199). Continental Stitch (page 194) gets in and out of tight places. Surface embroidery is good for very small things, such as people's faces.

Large stitches need large areas in a design to establish the pattern. Smaller stitches don't need such large areas.

Don't let the stitches take the eye out of the picture (page 57). Work the stitch so that it slants in the opposite direction if that will suit your purpose.

Do not use stitches that distort the canvas (see charts in Part Four) on projects that will not have something (like a frame) to hold the canvas permanently in place. The Diagonal Stitches are the worst offenders.

Rabbit skin glue will hold an out-of-shape piece in place without a frame, but it will make the piece very stiff. It is available in art supply stores. Rabbit skin glue comes in a powder form that must be mixed with water and cooked to form a gel. It takes several hours for it to set up after it has cooled. It will keep in the refrigerator for a few days, and after that it smells like a dead rabbit. So, make only what you think you'll use. Figure 2–31 shows you how to apply it.

(a)

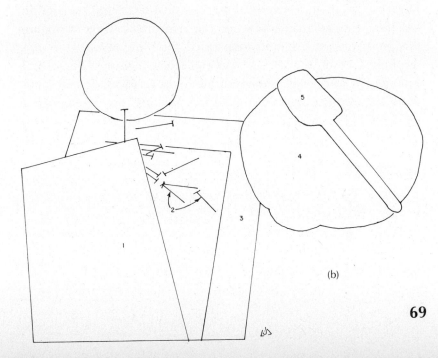

(b)

Fig. 2–31a & b. (1) canvas, (2) T-pins, (3) frame, (4) mixing bowl, (5) spatula.

(c)

(e)

(d)

Fig. 2–31c, d, e. Attach your needlepoint to a frame if it has decorative stitches, as this piece does. Use T-pins. Apply rabbit skin glue thinly.

Mixing diagonal stitches and vertical stitches

Diagonal stitches and vertical stitches do not go together easily, but they can be made to work out reasonably well. Work the diagonal stitches first and then stitch the vertical ones, sharing the hole (Figure 2–32a). Or you can stitch a row of Tent Stitch around the diagonal stitches in the background colors. Then work the vertical stitches in, sharing the hole.

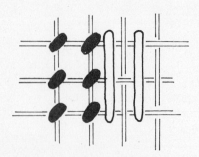

Fig. 2–32a. Diagonal stitches and vertical stitches share the hole when worked next to each other. Work the diagonal stitches first.

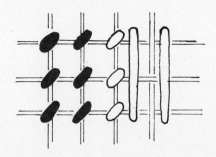

Fig. 2–32b. This alternate method of combining diagonal stitches and vertical stitches keeps the diagonal stitches from being swallowed whole. Work a row of tent stitches in the same color as the vertical stitches.

THE
PROJECTS

Because you're going to *Teach Yourself Needlepoint*, this book will take you to needlepoint school. Start in Beginners' and work your way through Expert!

The projects are arranged, more or less, in order of increasing difficulty. If you've done lots of charts, the charted projects later on in the Expert section may be easier for you than a painted canvas in Advanced Beginners'. Feel free to browse through these chapters to find a tempting project. Start with something on a level you feel you can handle easily. As you become familiar with the materials and techniques of needlepoint, you can go on to greater challenges.

In choosing a project, remember to consult the earlier chapters on color and design. You may wish to alter the color scheme or the size of a project. Techniques for these and other changes are given in the preceding chapters.

Finally, you will want to create your own designs. Don't be afraid to try! Have fun!

5

Projects for beginners

Christmas package

STITCH: Straight Gobelin

CANVAS: Mono 14, 6¾" × 10½" (1½" margins included)

YARN: Tapestry or Persian and gold metallic thread

NEEDLE: Size 20

SIZE OF FINISHED PROJECT: 3¾" × 3¾"

This attractive yet simple Christmas ornament is the ideal place for a beginner to start. Stitch 26 rows of Straight Gobelin across the narrowest part of the canvas. Leave rows #7 and #20 blank so that they can be stitched in gold thread. Also leave a space for two gold stitches in the middle of each row (Figure 3–1b).

Fig. 3–1a. Christmas Package. Designed and stitched by Needleworks, Ltd. *(Hagerty)*

(a)

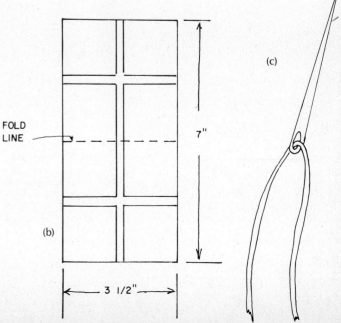

FOLD LINE

7"

(b)

(c)

3 1/2"

You may have to double the gold thread. Thicken it as much as you have to in order to cover the canvas. The metallic threads might prove to be a little harder to work with, but as you get into the project, you'll get the hang of it.

Metallic threads may ravel easily when cut. Try breaking the thread rather than cutting it. Should you have to double the thread to make it cover, just thread the needle with one end of the thread and double over as in Figure 3–1c. This way, both raw ends are buried right away and pose no raveling problems.

Attach a bow of gold thread. Block as explained on page 293. Fold on the line and stitch with the right sides of the needlepoint together as if it were a pillow (see page 306).

Bargello trivet

STITCHES: Bargello Line Pattern

CANVAS: Mono 14, 14″ × 14¼″ (3″ margins included)

YARN: Tapestry or Persian, five colors

NEEDLE: Size 20

SIZE OF FINISHED PROJECT: 8″ × 8¼″

Bargello is one of the most beautiful needlepoint stitches. Beginners as well as advanced stitchers love it. It is usually worked in a monochromatic color scheme (page 40), or its colors run from one color to another as they do here.

The chart in Figure 3–2b shows this particular design. It is called a line pattern because the design moves across one line and is then repeated in different colors. Other Bargello line patterns are easy to make. See page 185 for general instructions.

This trivet shows off the pattern beautifully. When it is in use, turn the needlepoint side down and put pots that are likely to be dirty or greasy on the cork side. Display your trivet on the wall or on a table under a figurine between uses.

(a)

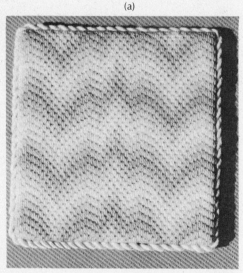

Fig. 3–2a. Bargello Trivet.
Designed and stitched by the author.
(Hagerty)

(b)

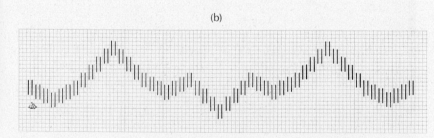

To start, fold your canvas in half and then in half again. Mark the center with a pencilled dot. Find the center of the drawing of the line pattern. Begin by stitching from the center to the left boundary line and then go back and stitch to the right boundary line. Once the line is established, the hard part is over! All you do now is repeat the line in each of your colors; then repeat the whole sequence of colors until your canvas is filled. Read page 32 to learn how to do the compensating stitches on the top and bottom rows.

Block your finished needlepoint (page 293). Lace over masonite as on page 300. Glue cork to the wrong side, and attach a twisted cord (page 308) with glue.

Pre-finished bargello evening purse

STITCH: Bargello Line Pattern

CANVAS: Mono 14 in a pre-finished faille evening purse

YARN: Silver and gold metallic thread (double thread)

NEEDLE: Size 20

SIZE OF FINISHED PROJECT: Depends on size of purse you buy. (This one's flap is 5¾" × 8".)

How elegant! *And* how *easy!*

Read the hints for Bargello on page 185 and those for working with metallic threads on page 74.

Pre-finished articles cannot be blocked. For this reason a stitch that does not distort the canvas has been chosen (see the charts at the beginning of the stitch chapters).

The only finishing needed is a lining on the inside of the flap. See page 310 for instructions on how to put it in. Sometimes a lining is provided for you, and this step can then be eliminated.

Fig. 3–3a. Bargello Evening Purse. Designed and stitched by Joan McMahon. *(Moats)*

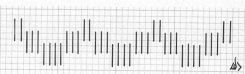

Pre-finished belt

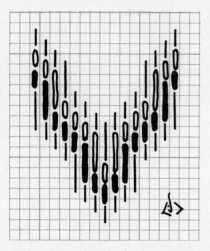

PATTERN REPEATS EVERY 5th ROW

(a)

STITCH: Hungarian Point Bargello Pattern

CANVAS: Mono 14 on a belt

YARN: Tapestry or Persian

NEEDLE: Size 20

A Hungarian Point Bargello Pattern is a little different from the ones we've just done. It is still a line pattern. In the others, all the stitches were over 4 mesh. This time some are over four, but others are over only two (Figure 3–4b). Notice that four different rows make up the pattern of lines. Repeat the group of four lines until you reach the end of the project.

Instructions for sizing will come with your belt. Follow them carefully.

Line the belt (see Chapter 19).

(b)

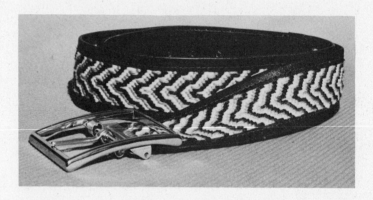

Bargello tie

(a)

STITCH: Bargello Pattern

CANVAS: Mono 14, 8½" × 25" (2" margins included)

YARN: Tapestry or Persian, five or six colors

NEEDLE: Size 20

SIZE OF FINISHED PROJECT: About 4" wide and 16¾" in length

This Bargello Pattern is different from those we've done before. It follows a design. The chart in Figure 3–5e shows you how to do the stitch.

The placement of colors depends on the look you want. Figure 3–5b shows the basic design. Figure 3–5c and d show how a color change makes the design look different.

If you wish to emphasize the letter C, choose the chart in Figure 3–5c. Stitch one C in white so that it will stand out. Put it toward the bottom and it will serve as a monogram.

76

If your name doesn't happen to begin with a C, you will want to stitch Figure 3–5d in five colors. It doesn't really matter where you begin to stitch, since it is an all-over design.

The colors should range in darkness the way they are shown on the chart. If I had it to do over, I think I would have chosen my colors with more contrast between the background color and the next darkest color. Only if you look closely can you see that there are two colors. Do not repeat my error.

This pattern will make a pre-knotted tie, which is necessary because the finished needlepoint is just too heavy to tie regularly.

Blocking and finishing instructions are in Chapters 18 and 19.

(b)

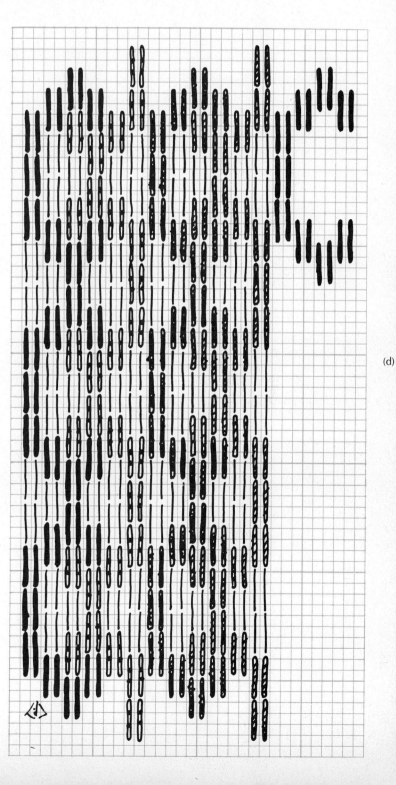

(c)

(d)

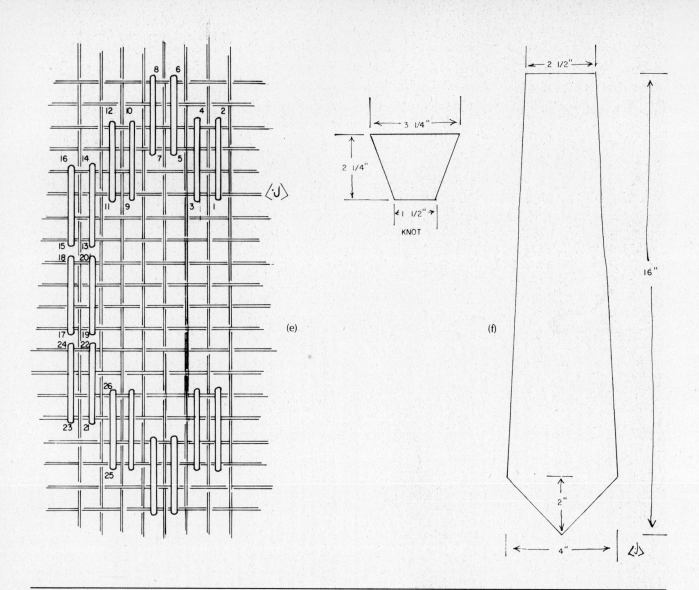

(e)

(f)

Eyeglass case

Fig. 3–6a. Velvet Eyeglass Case.
Designed and stitched by Needleworks, Ltd.
(Hagerty)

(a)

STITCHES: Bargello Line Pattern; Binding Stitch

CANVAS: Mono 18, approximately 4″ × 13″ (see below) or 7″ × 7″

YARN: Velvet yarn (It is nylon and thus washable.)

NEEDLE: Size 22

SIZE OF FINISHED PROJECT: Approximately 3″ × 6½″

To make this unusual eyeglass case, you'll first have to measure the glasses that will go into it. They come in too many sizes to guess. If your glasses are 2½″ × 5½″, add half an inch for ease. This means the area inside the dotted lines in Figure 3–6b will be 3″ × 6″ on each side of the solid line. (You may cut the canvas either way, depending on the shape of the piece of canvas you already have.)

   Leave two blank mesh along the solid line to put the Binding Stitch on after you block.

78

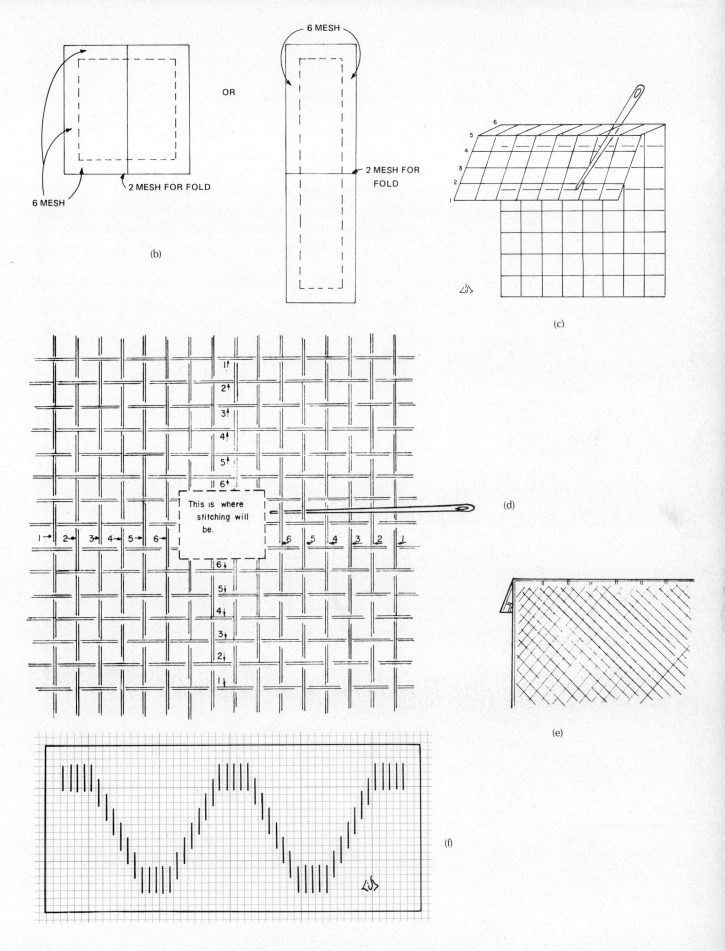

(b)

6 MESH

2 MESH FOR FOLD

OR

6 MESH

2 MESH FOR FOLD

(c)

(d)

This is where stitching will be.

(e)

(f)

79

The Two-Step Edge Finishing method that I use finishes raw edges as you stitch. It also prepares the canvas for the Binding Stitch (page 240). You must plan to do this before you take the first stitch.

You will need only six mesh (on Mono Canvas) all the way around your design, instead of the usual 3 inches that I recommend. Figure 3–6c shows you how to find those six mesh. Insert your needle under the 5th and 6th mesh. Fold the canvas so that four mesh will form a hem and two mesh (the 5th and 6th) will be on the edge (Figure 3–6d). The four mesh will fall into place if your needle is kept perpendicular to the canvas. Match the mesh exactly and baste in place. At the corners there will be four layers of canvas. Do the best you can. *Never* cut the canvas. It *will* ravel.

Stitch the Bargello Line Pattern in Figure 3–6f right through both thicknesses of canvas as if they were one. Also stitch right up to the mesh left for the Binding Stitch (Figure 3–6e). Block (page 293). Iron on a lining as described on page 310. There should be no lining over the fold. It would be too bulky.

Sew the seams together and finish the edges that are not a seam with the Binding Stitch (page 240).

Your needlepoint eyeglass case is now ready for use. You have finished it yourself and saved money!

Bargello credit card case

STITCHES:

☐ Double Hungarian Ground
☐ Continental Stitch
☐ Binding Stitch

CANVAS: Mono 14, 4¾″ × 12″

YARN: Tapestry or Persian

NEEDLE: Size 20

SIZE OF FINISHED PROJECT: 3″ × 3¾″

(a)

This handy credit card case is made with the same Two-Step Edge Finishing technique that was used in the preceding project. Prepare your canvas as described on page 78.

Stitch a border of Continental Stitches two mesh wide all the way around. Then fill in with the Double Hungarian Ground.

Block and line (page 208 and page 310).

Fold the canvas on the two outside lines as shown in Figure 3–7b. Sew the seams with the Binding Stitch. Finish the other edges of canvas with the Binding Stitch also. Hold a steam iron over it until it is slightly damp on both sides. *Do not touch* the iron to the needlepoint. Fold the whole thing in half. Place several heavy books on top of it and leave it overnight. After it dries it will stay folded.

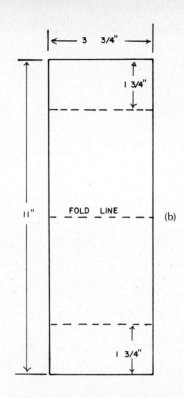

(b)

Wooden purse

STITCHES:

1 & 2. Bargello
3. Continental Stitch
4. Mosaic

CANVAS: Mono 14, 8½″ × 11″ (2″ margins included)

YARN: Tapestry or Persian

NEEDLE: Size 20

SIZE OF FINISHED PROJECT: 4½″ × 7″

This purse has a Bargello pattern that is worked into a design. Paint your design on canvas (page 64).

(a)

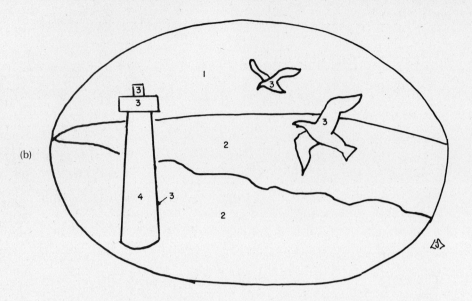

(b)

First stitch the seagulls and outline the lighthouse in Continental Stitch (see page 195). Fill in the lighthouse with Mosaic, using as many whole motifs as possible (Figure 3–8b).

Next work the sky in the stitch pictured in Figure 3–8c. End it as close to the horizon line as possible, without taking any compensating stitches.

Then stitch the water (Figure 3–8d), starting as close as you can to the horizon line without taking any compensating stitches. Once the first line of the water is established, go back and fill in with compensating stitches in the water color. Change to white yarn to stitch the foam at the water's edge. Stitch only the seven stitches at the lowest point of the pattern in white.

Note that the stitch for the sand is the same as the water. Only the color placement is different. There should be very few, if any, compensating stitches where the sand meets the water.

Block (page 293) and mount into a wooden purse as explained on page 318. Wooden purses can be bought at needlepoint and hobby shops.

(c)

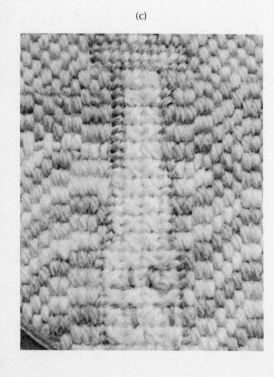

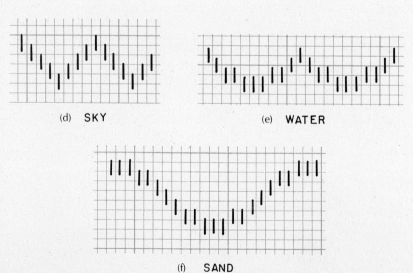

(d) SKY

(e) WATER

(f) SAND

82

Plaid floor pillow

STITCH: Chottie's Plaid.

CANVAS: Penelope 5, 36" × 36" (3" margins included)

YARN: Wool rug yarn, four colors

NEEDLE: Size 13

SIZE OF FINISHED PROJECT: 30" × 30"

Whether you put your pillow together yourself or have it done professionally, you will need two extra rows of stitches beyond the size of the pillow you want. These are called *sacrifice stitches* because they will be *inside* the seam allowance and they will not be seen (in essence, sacrificed). Needlepoint canvas is not strong unless it is stitched, so, the seam allowance must have these extra stitches to withstand pressure on the seam from stuffing and sitting on the pillow.

When the pillow is an all-over design such as this one, I don't worry about stitching extra sacrifice stitches; I just give up two on each side of my pillow.

I heartily recommend that you have your pillow professionally finished—unless you are an expert seamstress. The size alone makes this pillow difficult to finish. Then the buttons and stuffing add more problems.

Rainbow plaid pillow

STITCH: Rainbow Plaid

CANVAS: Mono 14, 18" × 18" (2" margins included)

YARN: Persian (Use 2-ply)

NEEDLE: Size 20

SIZE OF FINISHED PROJECT: 14" × 14"

Chottie's Rainbow Plaid is worked exactly the same way as the Plaid. Only the arrangement of colors is different (see page 195).

Block and finish as on pages 293 and 306.

Placemat and coaster

STITCHES:

☐ Continental Stitch
☐ Binding Stitch
☐ Staggered Cashmere (background)
☐ Cross

CANVAS: Plastic: placemat, egg—10½" × 13½"; bacon—3" × 10½"; coaster—3" × 3"; napkin ring—3" × 5¼" (could be made to match bacon strip)

YARN: Acrylic knitting worsted (2 strands) (for ease in washing)

NEEDLE: Size 16

SIZE OF FINISHED PROJECT: Coaster—3" × 3"; placemat—10½" × 16½"; napkin ring—3" × 5¼"

Plastic canvas has its advantages and its disadvantages. There are no raw edges of canvas to contend with. That is a definite plus. Also, plastic canvas keeps its shape, which is an important factor in a tote bag (Plate 26). Plastic canvas can be easily cut to any size you wish. Stitches will not distort it. It can be washed in mild soap and water as often as necessary, and there is no sizing to wash out. When a stitch does not quite cover, the canvas does show through; but since the canvas is translucent, the color of the yarn you're using is what shows through. Finally, *no* blocking is needed.

On the minus side, however, are also a few items. First, when plastic canvas is used in 5 or 7 mesh per inch, projects are thus limited to broad, bold designs. (It now comes in 10 mesh per inch.) Continuous-motion stitching is not possible. Poking is slow; but if that's all you do anyway, you won't mind. It is possible to bend the canvas to take a continuous motion stitch, but that causes a tendency to pull too tightly. This causes the canvas to warp. It is also hard to get to the middle comfortably.

The chart in Figure 3–11b is graph paper filled with X's. Each X represents one Continental Stitch, even though the X is *in* a square, rather than over the lines. Symbols are often used to indicate other colors. Each symbol is treated as if it were an X.

Each bacon strip is a separate piece of canvas. It is attached by taking Cross Stitches over two mesh (instead of one) that have been butted together. Cover the edges (the last mesh all the way around) with the Binding Stitch.

When you are through stitching, all you have to do is line the back of the placemat with fabric (page 310) and glue ⅛" cork sheeting to the back of the coaster.

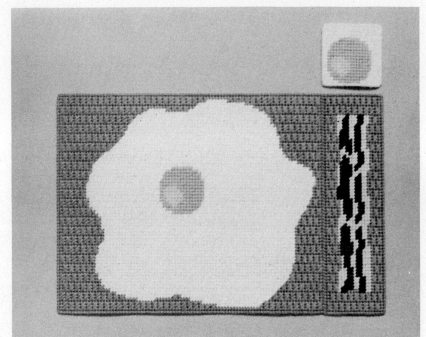

(a)

(b)

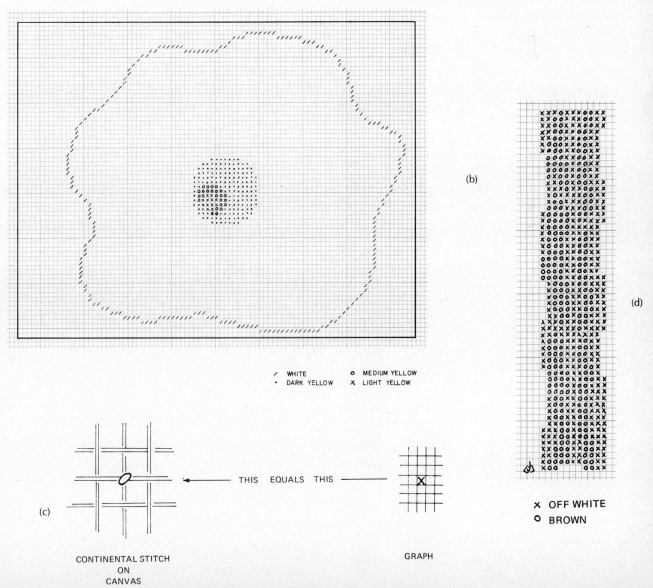

/ WHITE   o MEDIUM YELLOW
• DARK YELLOW   x LIGHT YELLOW

(d)

THIS EQUALS THIS

(c)

CONTINENTAL STITCH
ON
CANVAS

GRAPH

x OFF WHITE
o BROWN

Plastic key chain

STITCHES:
☐ Continental Stitch (key)
☐ Mosaic (background)
☐ Binding Stitch

CANVAS: Plastic canvas, 2 pieces, 10 mesh × 21 mesh

YARN: Persian (thickening required, use 5-ply)

NEEDLE: Size 16

SIZE OF FINISHED PROJECT: About 1½″ × 3″

Stitch the key design first. Then work the background. Stitch the same pattern, your initials, or another stitch on the other piece of plastic.

 With the wrong sides together, sew the two pieces of plastic canvas together with the Binding Stitch. Attach a key chain (available at craft and hobby shops) with the last few stitches you take.

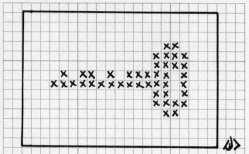

Reversed giant cashmere pillow

STITCHES: Reversed Giant Cashmere, Cut Turkey Work

CANVAS: Mono 12, 18½″ × 23″ (3″ margins included)

YARN: Tapestry or Persian, three colors

NEEDLE: Size 20

SIZE OF FINISHED PROJECT: 12½″ × 17″

(a)

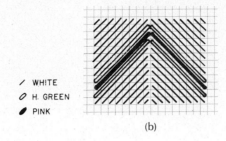

/ WHITE
O H. GREEN
● PINK

(b)

Cover the canvas in Reversed Giant Cashmere Stitch. Figure 3–13b shows where to substitute colors in the Reversed Giant Cashmere Stitch.

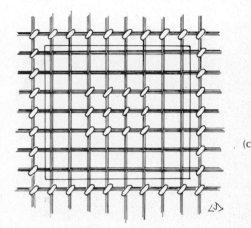

(c)

Leave two mesh blank and then stitch two rows of sacrifice stitches (page 83). The two blank mesh will be filled with Turkey Work after the needlepoint pillow has been stitched to a backing fabric (see Figure 3–13c).

Block and stitch the backing fabric onto the needlepoint. Then stitch Turkey Work around the edges in two rows. Work the outermost row first. Hold the canvas so that the outermost row is at the bottom. When you get to a corner, simply turn the canvas so that the outermost row is still on the bottom. Continue around the canvas. Stitch the next row, which is between the first row of Turkey Work and the Reversed Giant Cashmere Stitch. Leave the fringe about 1¼" to 1½" long. Finish making the pillow (page 306).

JOY Christmas banner

STITCH: Continental Stitch

CANVAS: Plastic, three squares, 30 mesh × 30 mesh

YARN: Gold metallic and Persian (thickening required, 5-ply)

NEEDLE: Size 16

SIZE OF FINISHED PROJECT: Approximately 7" × 21"

Using the Continental Stitch, work each letter in Persian yarn on one square of plastic canvas. It will take *about* 5 ply to cover the canvas. It may take as many as 4 strands of metallic yarn to cover. This will depend greatly on what kind of metallic thread you buy.

Bind the edges (the last mesh all the way around) with the Binding Stitch.

Finish according to the directions on page 312.

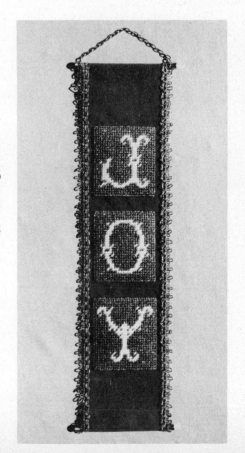

87

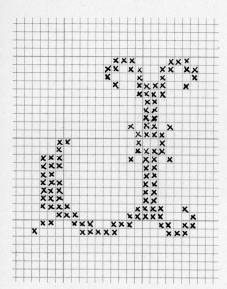

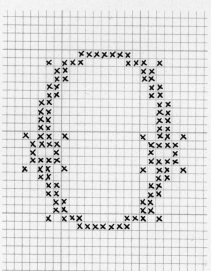

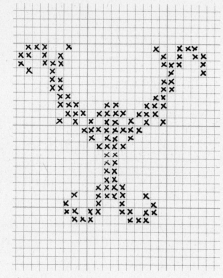

Christmas ornaments

STITCHES: Continental Stitch, Binding Stitch

CANVAS: 4 plastic squares, 21 mesh × 21 mesh

YARN: Persian (about 5-ply)

NEEDLE: Size 16

SIZE OF FINISHED PROJECT: 3″ × 3″

Following the charts (Figure 3–15 b–e), stitch the designs on squares of canvas. Stitch as much as you can in one color before you go on to the next color. Finish the edges with the Binding Stitch.

Make a Twisted Cord for hanging loops (page 308). Line as described on page 310. (Don't iron a lining onto plastic—the canvas will melt!)

(a)

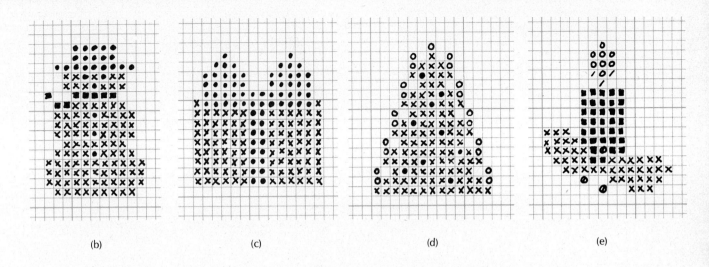

(b)   (c)   (d)   (e)

Soldier and drum Christmas ornament

STITCHES:
1. Continental Stitch
2. Brick (background)
3. Straight Stitch

CANVAS: Mono 14, 6″ × 6″ (2″ margins included)

YARN: Persian (2-ply)

NEEDLE: Size 20

SIZE OF FINISHED PROJECT: 2″ in diameter

Stitch the drum onto canvas from the chart in Figure 3–16b.

Block and finish as described on pages 293 and 317.

This project makes a lovely gift for a party's hostess, the kids' teachers, neighbors, etc. It doesn't take long to work, yet it looks so very special.

(a)

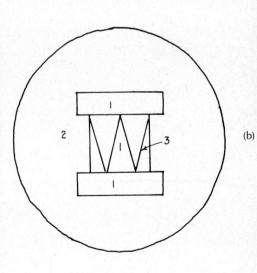 (b)

89

Checkbook cover

STITCHES: Continental Stitch; Basketweave

CANVAS: Mono 14 in pre-finished leather checkbook cover

YARN: Persian (2-ply)

NEEDLE: Size 20

SIZE OF FINISHED PROJECT: Needlepoint portion is 3¾" × 5½"

Before you buy the checkbook cover, try your checkbook in it to be sure it fits. I didn't try mine until *after* I'd stitched it—of course it didn't fit!

(a)

(b)

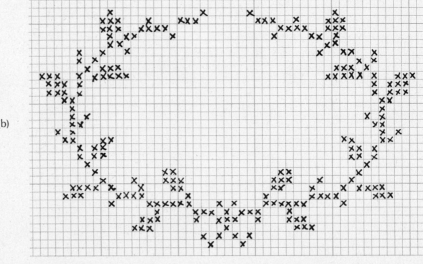

(c)

Carefully count to center your design (Figure 3–17b) and monogram (Figure 3–17c). Often you can make up for a one-mesh or two-mesh error as you finish an article. When an item is pre-finished, it's got to be right or forever be crooked. When counting to center a design like the wreath, it's easier to count the leftover mesh around the design and put an equal number on the top and bottom and on the right and left, than to find the center of the design. Use the same method to center the monogram.

Stitch the background. Line as described on page 310.

Mouse

STITCHES:
☐ Basketweave
☐ Stephens Stitch (background)
☐ Continental Stitch (around design)

CANVAS: Mono 12, 17″ × 17″ (3″ margins included)

YARN: Tapestry or Persian

NEEDLE: Size 20

SIZE OF FINISHED PROJECT: 11″ × 11″

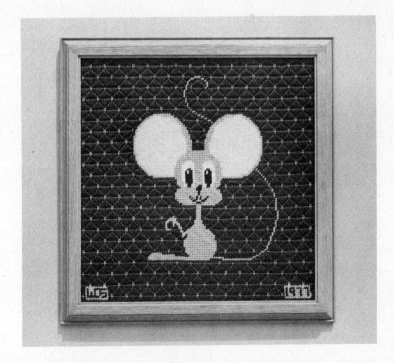

● BLACK
□ WHITE
× GREY
⁄ PINK

SURROUND ENTIRE DESIGN WITH TENT STITCH IN BACKGROUND COLOR

It is more difficult to work Basketweave in a design, but it can be done. You have to count the number of stitches in a diagonal row instead of in a horizontal row. Work Tent Stitches (in the background color) around the design before doing Straight Stitches. Finish the background in the Stephens Stitch. This is one of those occasions when letting the canvas show through helps the design. If you don't like it, fill in the space as in Figure 3–18b, above.

Block (page 293). If you frame (or mount) the needlepoint yourself, you'll save a lot of money. See framing instructions on page 300.

STITCHES:

☐ Continental Stitch

☐ Couching

☐ Straight Stitch

CANVAS: Mono 18, 7½" × 11", each (2" margins included)

YARN: Full strand embroidery floss

NEEDLE: Size 22

SIZE OF FINISHED PROJECT: 3½" × 7", each

Stitch one of the designs onto canvas. Use Couching to make the twig and Straight Stitches for the bird's wing.

Block and finish as on pages 293 and 313.

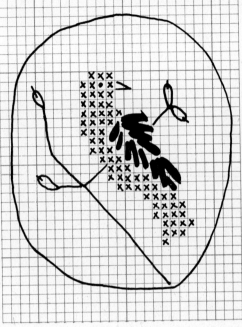

- DARK BROWN
× BROWN
/ GREEN

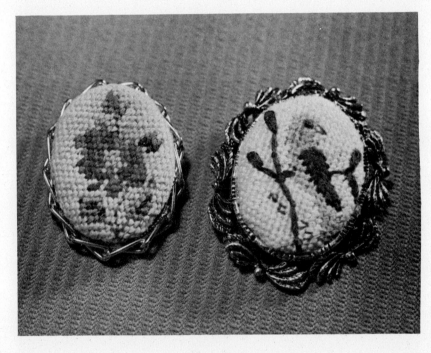

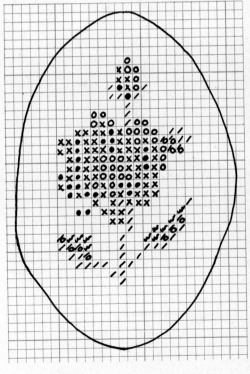

• DARK RED	⅙ DARK GREEN
× RED	/ GREEN
○ LIGHT RED	⥟ LIGHT GREEN

Footstool

(a)

STITCHES:
1. Mosaic
2. Roman II
3. Continental Stitch (for leaves)
4. Lazy Daisy (for tops of strawberries)
5. Running Stitch (for seeds)

CANVAS: Penelope 10, 18″ × 18″ (3″ margins included)

YARN: Tapestry or Persian (seeds 2-ply Persian)

NEEDLE: Size 20

SIZE OF FINISHED PROJECT: Needlepoint 12″ in diameter to fit on a stool 10″ diameter

First, buy the braid used to finish the stool. *Then* buy the yarn to match it. There are many more colors of yarn than there are of braid.

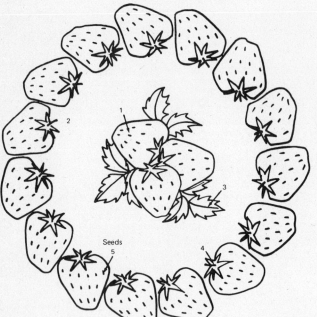

(b)

(c)

Paint your design on canvas (page 64). Stitch the strawberries and leaves first. Then work the background. After the canvas is covered work the embroidery stitch, Lazy Daisy, for the tops of the strawberries—right over the other stitches (Figure 3–20c). Disregard the mesh and stitch as if the needlepoint were fabric. Use a Running Stitch (also an embroidery stitch) for the strawberry seeds.

Block and assemble as demonstrated on pages 293 and 313. The extra 2 inches of needlepoint will give the poof.

STITCH: Continental Stitch

CANVAS: Mono 14, 2 pieces, 6½″ × 6½″ (2″ margins included)

YARN: Pearl cotton #3

NEEDLE: Size 20

SIZE OF FINISHED PROJECT: 2⅝″ × 2⅝″

Stitch the same design on two pieces of canvas. Pearl cotton is delightful to work with and the finished product is very pretty. However, if you use a too-long yarn, the pearl cotton will lose its sheen. As soon as you notice any dulling, stop stitching and start a new thread.

Block and finish as a pillow (pages 293 and 306). Use a pearl cotton loop to hang it by.

ALL CONTINENTAL STITCH

6
Projects for advanced beginners

The projects in this section are a little more difficult than those for beginners, but they still are not hard. They require more of an understanding of the intricacies of the stitches used.

Four-way bargello pillow

STITCH: Four-Way Bargello

CANVAS: Mono 14, approximately 18″ × 18″ (2″ margins included)

YARN: Tapestry or Persian, eight colors (here, there are three reds, four blues, and one white), you may use more or less

NEEDLE: Size 20

SIZE OF FINISHED PROJECT: 14″ × 14″

Four-Way Bargello can be made from any line pattern. The most important step in making a Four-Way Bargello project is marking the diagonal lines on the canvas. Your stitching will be off if the line is wrong. First draw the top and left-side boundary lines. Using a pencil with a sharp point, start a diagonal line in the upper left corner and work toward the opposite corner. Let the pen-

(a)

cil bump across the canvas from hole to hole as you draw the line (Figure 3–22b). This line must be *perfect*. Do not try to stitch until it is. It is almost impossible to correct it as you stitch unless you've had quite a bit of experience with needlepoint.

Stitch the line in Figure 3–22b, starting from the upper left corner. When you finish stitching that line, draw the other diagonal line. Start it where the line of stitching ends and go to the lower left corner to meet the left boundary line. Finish by extending it to meet the top boundary line, thus making the upper right corner. Draw the right-side and bottom boundary lines. Be sure the lines are exact.

(b)

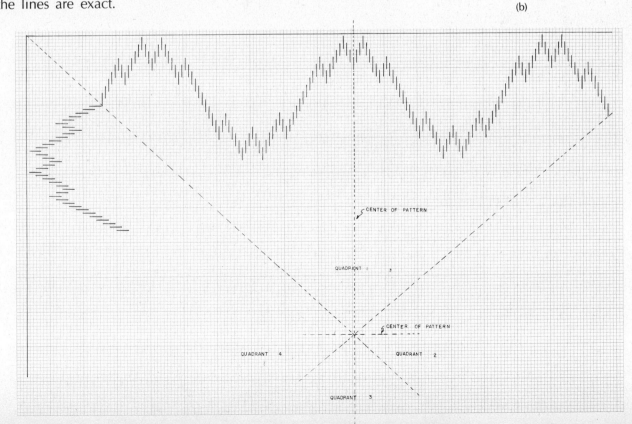

If you start with the outermost whole line when you stitch your own design or the one I've shown here, the compensating stitches will be *much* easier to do. Just keep repeating the line all the way to the center. When the line reaches one of the diagonal lines, you've drawn on the canvas, just *stop*. It will come out right automatically. Work a row in quadrant one. Turn the canvas 90° and work the same row in quadrant two. Turn the canvas 90° and work the same row in quadrant three. Turn the canvas 90° and work the same row in quadrant four. You now have one row all the way around the outside of your canvas, near the boundary lines. Turn the canvas 90° and stitch a second row just below the first one you stitched, going toward the center of the canvas. Work all the way around the canvas, turning after stitching each quadrant until you reach the center.

Then finish stitching the space between the outermost whole line and the boundary line with as much of the row as you can and with compensating stitches (see Figure 3–22b).

If you do turn your favorite line pattern into a Four-Way Bargello, don't worry about what it will look like in the center. If you like the basic line, you'll like the way it turns out. Be surprised—and you'll be so anxious to see what the center looks like that you'll keep working until it's done!

If you want a particular design in the center or mid-way, draw it out on graph paper. Still work the pattern to the outermost row and stitch from the outside in.

Block and put the pillow together as on pages 293 and 306.

Diagonal bargello pillow

STITCH: Diagonal Bargello

CANVAS: Mono 12; 16″ × 16″ (2 ″ margins included)

YARN: Pearl cotton (doubled), variegated

NEEDLE: Size 20

SIZE OF FINISHED PROJECT: 12″ × 12″

With a little bit of experimentation, almost any Bargello line pattern can be worked on the diagonal. This pattern is over four junctions of the canvas.

Pearl cotton must be stitched from one end only if you don't want it to twist. (You don't.) Try threading the needle from one end of the thread and then a second from the other end. Always thread the needle from the end that produces the smoothest, untwisted stitches. When more than one strand of yarn is stitched through one hole, each strand must lie smoothly beside the others. See Rolling the Yarn (page 28).

Block (page 293) and finish (page 306).

Fig. 3–23a. Diagonal Bargello Pillow. Designed by the author; stitched by Jackie Beaty, John Christensen, and the author. *(Moats)*

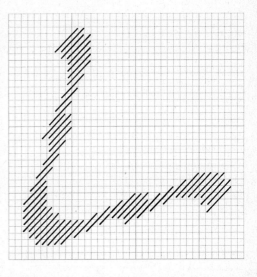

Mushroom picture

(a)

STITCH: Continental Stitch

CANVAS: Penelope or Mono 10, 11″ × 14″, (3″ margins included)

YARN: Tapestry or Persian

NEEDLE: Size 20

SIZE OF FINISHED PROJECT: 5″ × 8″

This modern treatment of mushrooms is worked all in Tent Stitch. First paint the design on canvas. The caps of the mushrooms are then outlined. Figure 3–24 c-e shows outlining in Tent Stitch. Notice that diagonal lines that slant to the right are made from stitches that connect to make a straight line. Those that slant to the left are made up of stitches that do not connect, thus making a dotted line.

After the outlining is complete, fill in the design areas. Stitch the background.

Block and frame (pages 293 and 300).

(b)

(b)

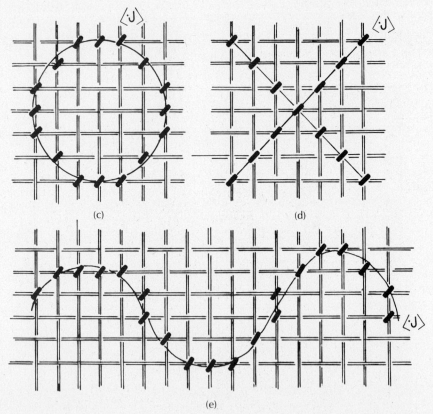

(c)

(d)

(e)

Fig. 3–25a. Oriental Seasons.
Designed and stitched by Kay Kendall.
(Hagerty)

STITCHES:

☐ Bargello
☐ Basketweave (characters and narrow border)
☐ Brick (background)

CANVAS: Mono 14, 14½″ × 16½″ (3″ margins included)

YARN: Persian

NEEDLE: Size 20

SIZE OF FINISHED PROJECT: 8½″ × 10½″

In this Oriental-style piece, each character represents one of the four seasons: spring (green), summer (yellow), fall (red), and winter (blue). The Bargello border uses the same colors.

See page 70 for mixing vertical stitches and diagonal stitches.

Block and frame (pages 293 and 300).

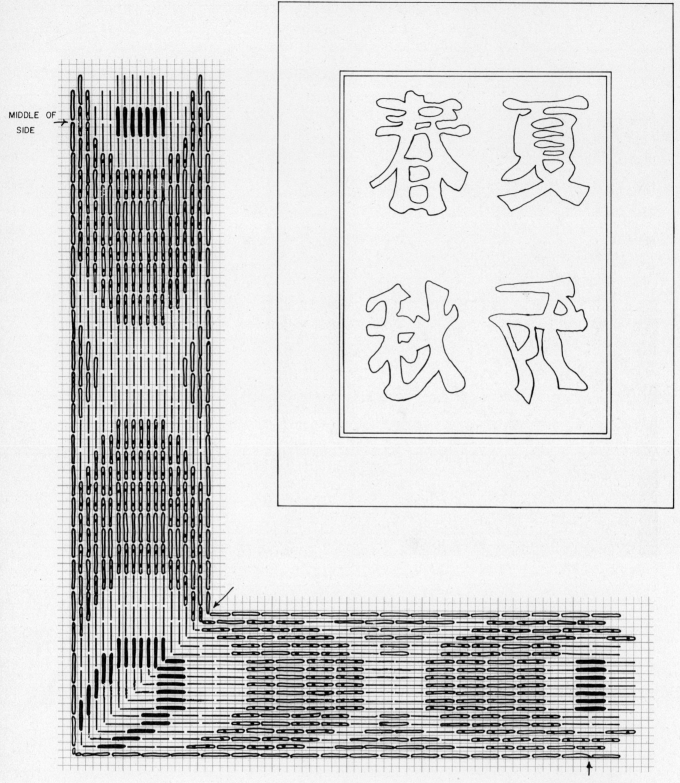

MIDDLE OF
SIDE

MIDDLE OF BOTTOM

102

STITCHES:
1. Chain Stitch
2. Basketweave
3. Double Straight Cross
☐ Continental Stitch (in small places)

CANVAS: Penelope 5, 25″ × 44″

YARN: Persian—6 strands or 18-ply

NEEDLE: Size 13

SIZE OF FINISHED PROJECT: 23″ × 42″

(a)

Fig. 3–26a. Rug.
Designed and stitched
by Lois Ann Necaise. *(Moats)*

(b)

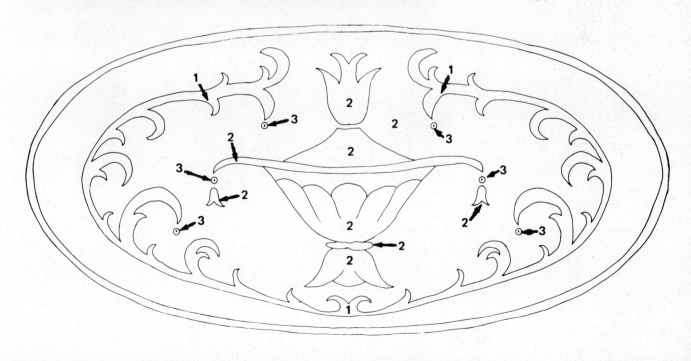

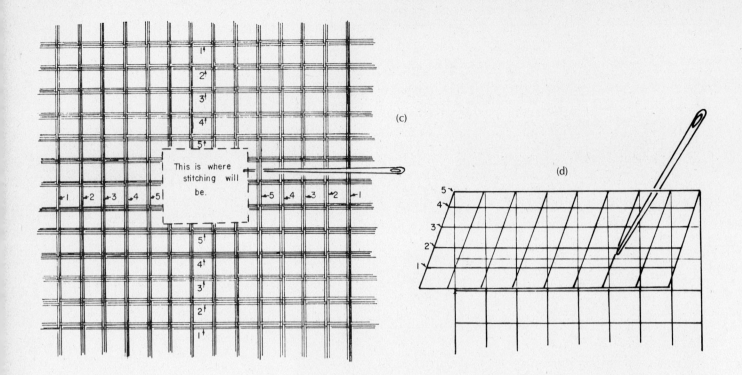

(c)

This is where stitching will be.

(d)

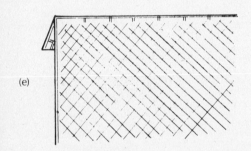

(e)

Use the Two-Step Edge Finishing technique. Turn four mesh under and leave one on the edge (Penelope canvas) (Figure 3–26 c and d) for the Binding Stitch. Baste. Stitch the design in the chart in Figure 3–26h. As you work the background, stitch through the two thicknesses of canvas as if they were one. Stitch right up to the edge (Figure 3–26e).

Block (page 293). Stitch the Binding Stitch (page 240) on the edge. Line (page 310).

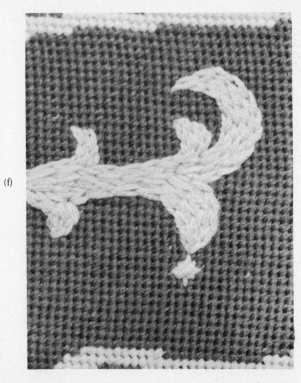

(f)

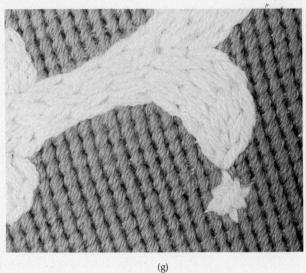

(g)

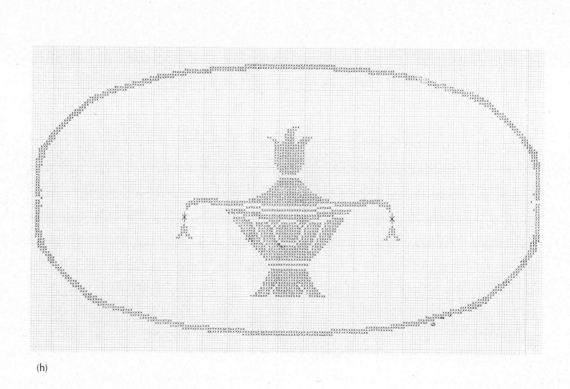

(h)

Flowers in vase

STITCHES: Continental stitch; Herringbone Gone Wrong (vase)

CANVAS: Mono 14 (Mono 10 was used here, but a smaller canvas would give prettier curves.) 15″ × 18″ (3″ margins included)

YARN: Persian (2-ply)

NEEDLE: Size 20

SIZE OF FINISHED PROJECT: 9″ × 12″

Fig. 3–27a. Flowers in Vase. Designed by the author; stitched by Ruth Ippolito. (*Moats*)

Judgment plays a part in stitching this vase of flowers. When the line falls between the junction of two mesh, you must decide which mesh to stitch (see page 100, c-e). Sometimes one stitch in the wrong place will ruin the line of the object you are stitching. Until you can learn to judge without actually taking the stitch, you will put in and take out a lot of extra stitches. Even the most experienced needlewoman (needleperson?) will misjudge once in a while.

This is a good practice piece for this lesson; if you do decide later that one stitch in particular would have been better left out (or added), it is not as disastrous as it might have been on another design, like a geometric.

Block (page 293) and frame (page 300).

(b)

(c)

STITCHES:

1. Continental Stitch
2. Basketweave
3. Petit Point
4. Chain Stitch
5. Round Cross
6. Fancy Cross
7. Reversed Scotch
8. Couching
9. Straight Stitch

CANVAS: Penelope 10, 8″ × 11″ (2″ margins included)

YARN: Tapestry or Persian (Persian 1-ply) for Petit Point, embroidery floss (one 6-ply strand) for Petit Point face

NEEDLE: Size 20, size 22 for Petit Point

SIZE OF FINISHED PROJECT: 4″ × 7″

(a)

(b)

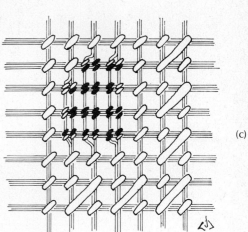

(c)

The Reversed Scotch Stitch always leaves a bit of canvas that shows. Here, the background was painted yellow and deliberately allowed to show. The colors of the blue background yarn and the yellow canvas are mixed by the eye, so that the spot seems green.

To achieve detail in one or two particular areas, use Penelope canvas and split the mesh for Petit Point (page 199). Here the Indian maiden's face and braids were done in Petit Point. It's easier to stitch these tiny stitches if you first poke your needle between the mesh, thus separating them. When your design in Petit Point does not come out even, in terms of mesh, just stitch the surrounding area in Petit Point with the background color (Figure 3–28c). If you're working a decorative stitch (other than Tent), you may want to work Tent Stitches or Petit Point up to the next whole motif of your decorative stitch. This will prevent the decorative stitch from overpowering the hardworked Petit Point.

The feathers were worked in 1 ply of Persian yarn in two rows of Chain Stitch. One row (in 1 ply of Persian yarn) of Couching was worked in another color to indicate a shaft in the feather. Straight Stitches were used for the tips of the feathers. This means you just slant a stitch the way you want it and take one stitch for one line on a drawing.

The Fancy Cross was separated and worked as motifs that stand alone (Figure 3–28 d and e).

Block and assemble according to the directions on pages 293 and 317.

(d)

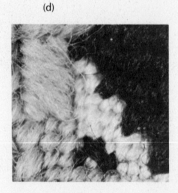

(e)

(f)

108

Fig. 3–29a. Long Stitch Landscape. Designed and stitched by the author. *(Moats)*

STITCH: Long Stitch (see Straight Stitch)

CANVAS: Mono 14, 30″ × 30″
(3″ margins and 4″ mat included)

YARN: Persian or tapestry

NEEDLE: Size 20

SIZE OF FINISHED PROJECT: 16″ diameter

The Long Stitch is what many manufacturers are calling a Straight or Satin Stitch. All or nearly all the picture is worked in this stitch.

   This project *must* be worked on a frame. It is impossible to keep the tension of the yarn even and the canvas straight without a frame.

   Stripping and rolling the yarn is very important here (see pages 27 and 28). Don't forget the Bargello Tuck (page 26).

   Block (page 293) and frame (page 300).

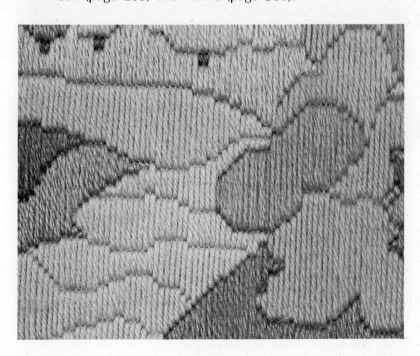

Eyeglass case with initials

STITCHES:
☐ Bargello (Hungarian Point)
☐ Continental (letters and background behind them)
☐ Binding Stitch

110

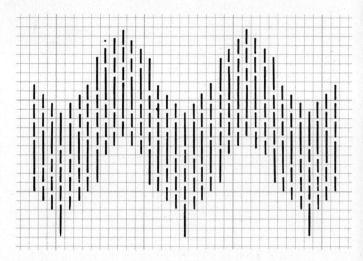

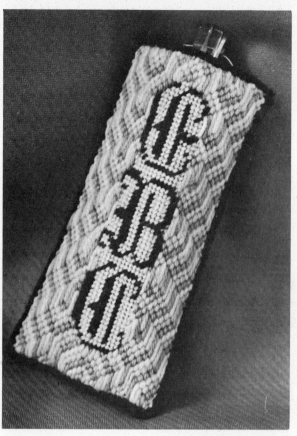

CANVAS: Mono 14, 4" × 13" or 7" × 7"

YARN: Persian (2-ply used)

NEEDLE: Size 20

SIZE OF FINISHED PROJECT: 3" × 6"

Chart the letters you'll need on graph paper. Draw the boundaries you want, centering the initials. Transfer the initials to canvas by counting and stitching. There is no need to draw them on the canvas. Fill in behind them in Continental Stitch. It is *impossible* to get Bargello behind these letters—I know: I tried! And I ripped!

Work the same Bargello pattern for the other side of the case.

Block (page 293) and line (page 310). Sew together with the Binding Stitch (page 240).

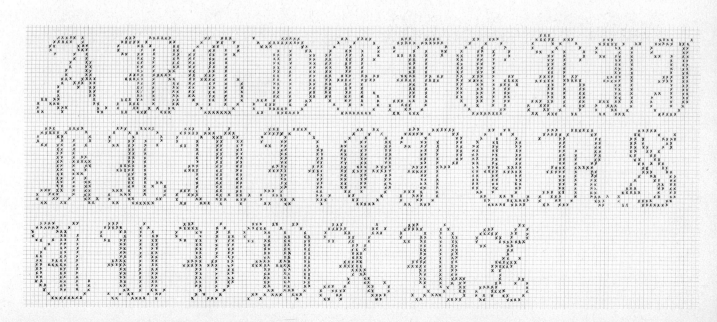

Don't hurry, don't worry . . .

Fig. 3–31a. "Don't Hurry, Don't Worry. . ." Designed and stitched by Wayne Stephens. *(Moats)*

STITCHES: Continental Stitch; Basketweave (background).

CANVAS: Mono 12, 16″ × 18″ (approximately 3″ margins included)

YARN: Tapestry or Persian, embroidery floss (two full 6-ply strands) for flowers and their centers

NEEDLE: Size 20

SIZE OF FINISHED PROJECT: 10⅜″ × 12″

Proper placement of letters and design on canvas is the lesson to be practiced with this project. Work the motto first and then work the border. No repair will be needed if you make an error in placing the first row of the motto. The border can simply be placed in the correct spot when it comes time to stitch it.

Block (page 293) and frame (page 300).

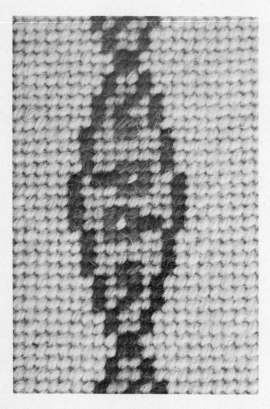

STITCHES:

1. Continental Stitch
2. French Knots
3. 2 × 2 Slanted Gobelin (reversed)
4. Straight Stitch
5. Oriental (background)

CANVAS: Penelope 10, 16½″ × 17½″ (3″ margins included)

YARN: Tapestry or Persian, embroidery floss for wings (9-ply)

NEEDLE: Size 20

SIZE OF FINISHED PROJECT: 10½″ × 11½″

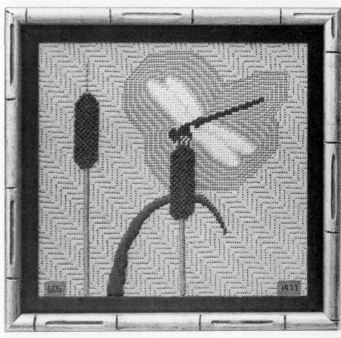

Fig. 3–32a. Dragonfly. Designed and stitched by Wayne Stephens. *(Moats)*

(a)

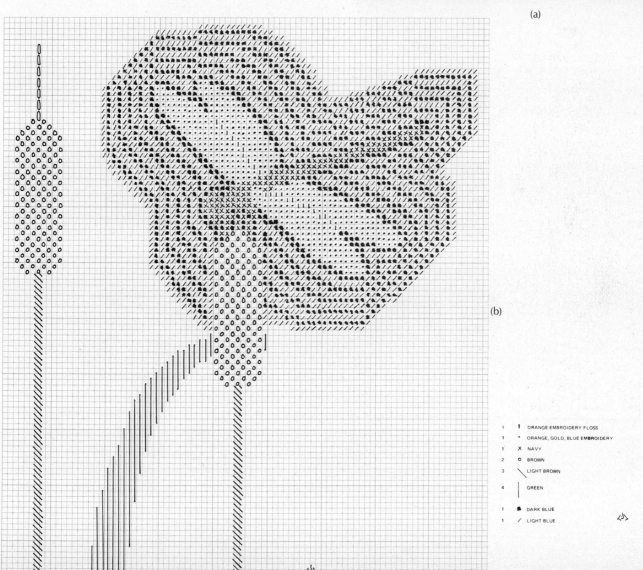

(b)

1	❘	ORANGE EMBROIDERY FLOSS
1	•	ORANGE, GOLD, BLUE EMBROIDERY
1	X	NAVY
2	O	BROWN
3	\	LIGHT BROWN
4	❘	GREEN
1	◾	DARK BLUE
1	/	LIGHT BLUE

This project gives you an opportunity to work different stitches from a chart. The wings, body, and area around the dragonfly are stitched in Continental Stitches. Embroidery floss of three colors was used to give the wings an iridescent look—3 ply of light gold, 3 ply of light blue, and 3 ply of light green.

The French Knots are made according to the directions on page 284, except that the needle goes back into the same hole it came up in. You may go into the next hole, but watch to make sure you stagger the French Knots.

The grass is stitched with a Straight Stitch as charted in Figure 3–32b.

The background is then stitched. Block (page 293) and frame (page 300).

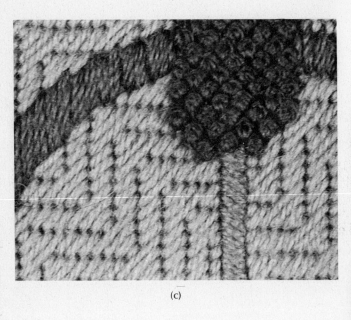

(c)

(d)

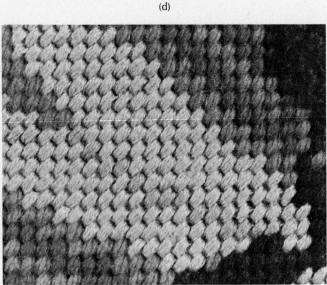

Mirror case

STITCHES:

1. Double Cross Tramé
2. Cut Turkey Work
3. Smyrna Cross
4. Continental Stitch
5. Triple Leviathan
6. Diamond Eyelet with Backstitch
7. Tied Windmill
8. Ridged Spider Web

9. Double Leviathan
10. Framed Star
11. Ringed Daisy
12. Medallion
13. Alternating Smyrna
14. Diamond Ray
15. Looped Turkey Work
☐ Basketweave (background)
☐ Binding

(a)   (b)

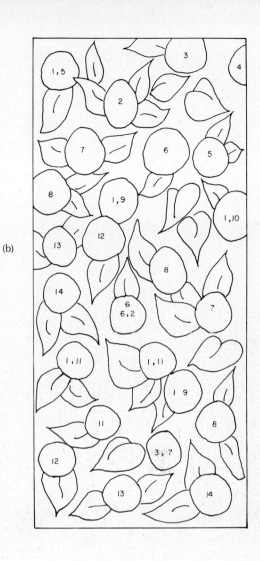

CANVAS: Penelope 10, 5″ × 16½″

YARN: Tapestry or Persian

NEEDLE: Size 20

SIZE OF FINISHED PROJECT: 4″ × 6″

Improvisation is the lesson learned here. The case is basically techniques we've used before. The Two-Step Edge Finishing sews its hem as it goes. The design is painted on the canvas. Outline the leaves in dark green Continental Stitch. They are next stitched in Basketweave.

Many decorative stitches stand alone in a single motif and can easily represent a flower. The circles on the drawing in Figure 3–33b represent one of these decorative stitch motifs. Be sure that the decorative stitch motifs are at least the same size as the circles, or the leaves will overpower the design. It's all right if the flowers are bigger than the circles.

If the circle is not covered by one decorative stitch motif, then you must improvise. Use a Back Stitch (Figure 1–33), French Knots (see page 284), or one row of Turkey Work (see page 286). Perhaps two or three motifs of a small stitch will do the trick. Improvise!

Block (page 293) and line (page 310). Sew together with the Binding Stitch (page 240), catching the lining as you go (photo, page 241).

115

Striped sampler pillow

STITCHES:

1. Triangle
2. Fern
3. Horizontal Elongated Smyrna
4. Double Brick
5. Leaf #1
6. Wicker
7. Wheat
8. Straight Gobelin (over 5)
9. Waffle
10. Tied Pavillion
11. Raised Cross
12. Upright Oriental
13. 2 × 2 Slanted Gobelin

CANVAS: Mono 14, 18″ × 18″ (2″ margins included)

YARN: Persian (generally use 2-ply; straight stitches use 3-ply)

NEEDLE: Size 20

SIZE OF FINISHED PROJECT: 14″ × 14″

Stitching a sampler pillow is fun; it serves not only as a decorative addition to your home, but also as your reference to the stitches. Stripes of varying width were chosen for interest. The exact width was determined by the number of mesh needed for a decorative stitch to come out evenly, in whole motifs.

The 2 × 2 Slanted Gobelin Stitch is an excellent stitch to separate decorative stitches.

Block (page 293) and make into a pillow (page 306).

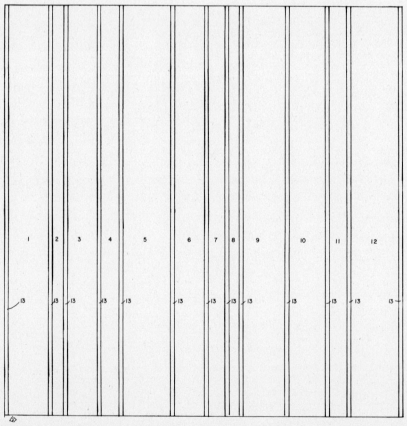

STITCHES:
1. Straight Gobelin, varying heights
2. Horizontal Elongated Smyrna Cross, varying sizes
3. Rhodes
4. Horizontal Milanese
5. Roman Cross, varying sizes
6. Smyrna Cross
6. Double Leviathan
6. Waffle (mix the three ''6's'' as needed to fill area)
7. Continental Stitch
☐ Binding Stitch

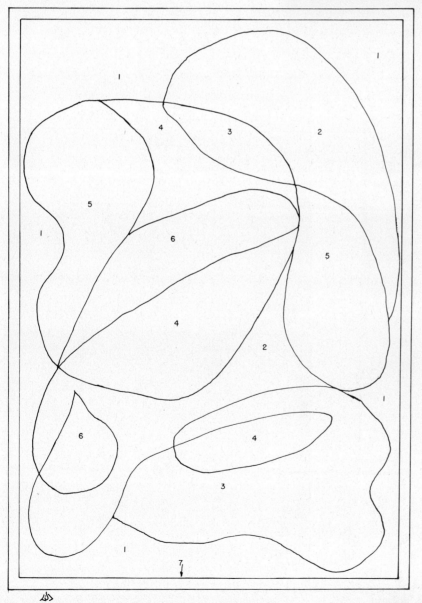

CANVAS: Mono 14, 8¾" × 12"

YARN: Gold and bronze metallic thread and black embroidery floss (one full 6-ply strand)

NEEDLE: Size 20

SIZE OF FINISHED PROJECT: 4" (approximately) × 7¾" (depends on where you fold it)

This project offers a lesson of another kind in improvisation. The Rhodes, Roman Cross, and Straight Gobelin Stitches were varied in height, width, or both. This was done to add interest and also to make the stitch fit the area as best you can. When compensating stitches were not possible, the Continental Stitch was used.

It was also used to stitch the outline and the border. It's easier to stitch this first. Remember the Two-Step Edge Finishing method on page 80? Use it here.

Block with T-pins (page 298) and line (page 310). Sew the seams and finish the edges with the Binding Stitch (page 240) in black embroidery floss.

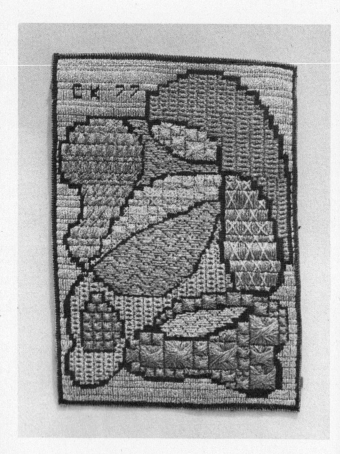

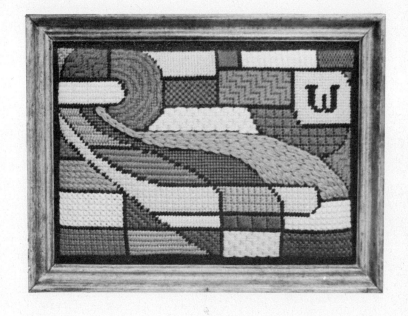

STITCHES:

1. Diagonal Mosaic
2. Milanese
3. Horizontal Cashmere
4. Couching
5. Continental Stitch
6. Chain Stitch
7. Interlocking Gobelin
8. Scotch
9. Elongated Cashmere
10. Interlocking Straight
    Gobelin
11. Brick
12. Byzantine # 1
13. Basketweave
14. Horizontal Brick
15. 2 × 2 Slanted Gobelin
16. Greek
17. Mosaic
18. Cashmere
19. Double Cross Tramé
20. Giant Scotch (over 5)
21. Smyrna Cross
22. Horizontal Brick
23. Parisian
24. Fly
25. Knotted Stitch
26. Giant Scotch (over 7)

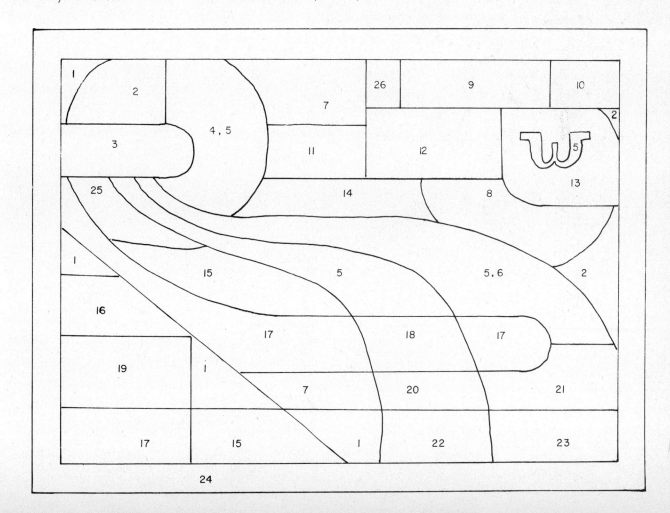

CANVAS: Mono 14, 10⅛″ × 12¾″ (2″ margins included)

YARN: Persian (mostly 2-ply; use 3-ply for Straight Stitches) or Elsa Williams tapestry yarn (a skinny yarn)

NEEDLE: Size 20

SIZE OF FINISHED PROJECT: Finished needlepoint, 6⅛″ × 8¾″, is to be wrapped around a board, 5¾″ × 8⅜″

Stitch the outline first in Continental Stitch. Then fill in with the stitches. Continental Stitches under the Chain Stitch give it added height. It also helps to cover the canvas where the Chain Stitch doesn't quite make it.

The stitches were carefully chosen to fit into small areas. The box top can serve as a sampler of small stitches. Weeding through a long list of stitches looking for a small stitch to fit a small area can be tedious. Now it's done for you!

Block and finish as on pages 293 and 319.

Christmas tree skirt

STITCHES:
1. Basketweave
2. Continental Stitch (all outline)
3. Mosaic
4. Brick
5. Pavillion

Fig. 3–37a. Christmas Tree Skirt. Designed by Cindy Pendleton; stitched by the author. *(Moats)*

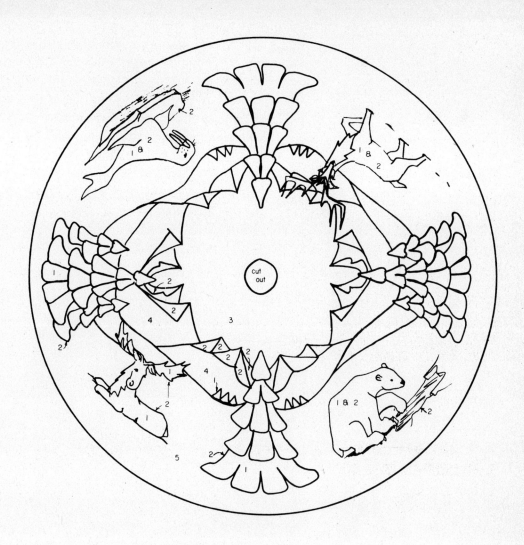

CANVAS: Penelope 3½, 60″ × 60″ (3″ margins included)

YARN: Persian—five 3-ply strands

NEEDLE: Size 13

SIZE OF FINISHED PROJECT: 54″ diameter

Don't let the size of this project scare you. It really isn't that big when you consider the number of stitches involved—very few on such large canvas.

It is *vital* that the stitches *do not distort* the canvas. Quickpoint canvas goes out of shape more readily and more drastically than smaller canvases. The stitches were therefore chosen with care. Even though the Mosaic Stitch of the sky distorts, it was reversed in the adjacent quadrants to offset or equalize the distortion. See Stripping the Yarn (page 27).

Put your design onto canvas so that the straight of the mesh runs through the centers of the big trees. Stitch so that the vertical mesh for each quadrant are going vertically through the big tree on the right each time. This gives you a place toward which you can orient your stitches. It also helps to equalize the stress of distorting stitches.

121

A Christmas tree skirt lies on the floor under the Christmas tree, covering the base of the tree. The hole in the middle is large enough for the center post of an artificial Christmas tree to fit through. If you want to use this with a real tree, you'll have to cut a seam from the center to the outer edge. This seam will, of course, lie on the back of the tree.

This piece was too big for my frame, so I held it in my lap. It's easier to work from the center out on each quadrant and then turn the canvas 90° and repeat the process.

Because this piece is so large to work with, I recommend strongly that you have it professionally blocked and finished.

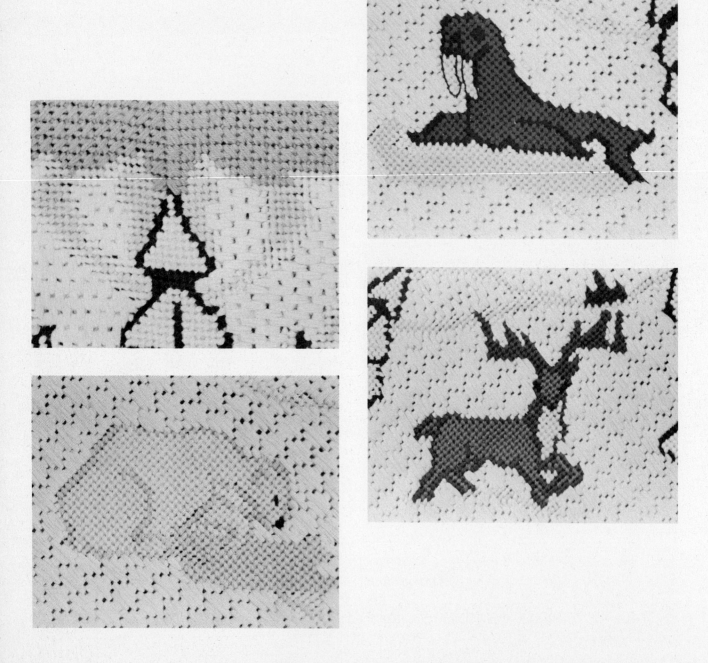

Intermediate projects

The projects for Intermediate stitchers do not introduce many new techniques. They are merely more difficult exercises in procedures we've already learned. Several new stitches are presented, however.

Christmas stocking

STITCHES:
1. Reversed Smyrna
2. Upright Cross
3. Cross
4. 1 × 3 Spaced Cross Tramé
5. Flying Cross
6. Chain
7. Oblong Cross
8. Smooth Spider Web
9. Cut Turkey Work
10. Mosaic Stripe
11. Ridged Spider Web
12. Couching

CANVAS: Penelope 7 (use the heavyweight; the lightweight does not hold up well to the increased thickness of yarn), 14″ × 21″ and 8″ × 11″ (2″ margins included)

YARN: Persian (usually 5-ply), gold metallic (thickened)

NEEDLE: Size 16

SIZE OF FINISHED PROJECT: Stocking—10″ × 17″; Cuff—4¼″ × 7″

123

This stocking is stitched in two pieces: the stocking itself and the cuff. The stocking is stitched up far enough so that blank canvas will not show underneath the cuff. So, there are about 2½" of blank canvas at the top of the stocking. Stitching this area takes extra time and money (for yarn used) and adds extra bulk.

Stitch the design on both pieces of canvas. (Don't forget the sacrifice stitches, page 83.) Block (page 293).

Face the points of the cuff with fabric. Lay the cuff on top of the stocking, matching the mesh perfectly. Stitch two rows of Cross Stitches through both thicknesses of canvas as if they were one, as shown in Figure 3–38c. Continue with Cross Stitch or Continental Stitch as sacrifice stitches. Finish as described on page 317 (Cosmetic Bag), except for the zipper.

(b)

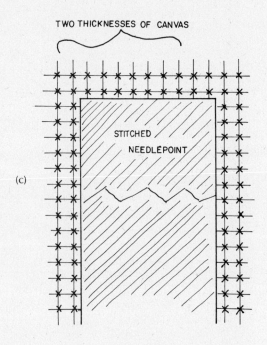

(c)

TWO THICKNESSES OF CANVAS

STITCHED NEEDLEPOINT

(d)　　　(e)

STITCHES:
1. Cross
2. Long Upright Cross
3. Upright Cross
4. Old Florentine
5. Horizontal Brick
6. Buttonhole in Half-Circle
7. Diagonal Cashmere
8. Continental Stitch
9. Vertical Milanese
10. Hungarian
11. Cashmere
12. Mosaic
13. Diagonal Mosaic
14. Double Stitch
15. Giant Scotch
16. Byzantine #1
17. Diamond Ray
18. Giant Brick

CANVAS: Penelope 7 (heavyweight, see page 1), 24″ × 30″ (3″ margins included)

YARN: Persian (usually 5-ply)

NEEDLE: Size 16

SIZE OF FINISHED PROJECT: 18″ × 24″

This is a lesson in outlining in Cross Stitch. Everything is outlined but the tree's leaves. The Cross Stitch outline eliminates the Continental Stitch's dotted line to the left (page 195).

The Horizontal Brick and the Brick Stitches were stitched with the same color yarn; the turning of the stitches makes it look as if two colors were used.

The Buttonhole Stitch must be stitched to fit the outlined area. The diagram on page 278 gives you only an idea of how to work the stitch.

Block and frame (pages 293 and 300).

ALL OUTLINE - CROSS STITCH

126

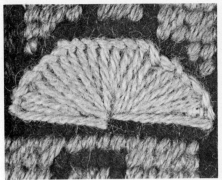

Charted Christmas ornament

STITCHES: Because stitches have been combined here so precisely, I have not listed them. Just follow the chart exactly.

CANVAS: Mono 18, 6″ × 6″

YARN: Embroidery floss (one 6-ply strand) or silk; gold and silver metallic

NEEDLE: Size 22

SIZE OF FINISHED PROJECT: 3″ × 3″

Stitch according to the chart. The red and green are embroidery floss or silk and the gold and silver are metallic, of course.
Block and finish (pages 293 and 317).

Fig. 3–40a. Charted Christmas Tree Ornaments. Designed and stitched by Needleworks, Ltd.
(Hagerty)

Sampler pillow

STITCHES:

1. Scotch Checker
2. Diagonal Scotch
3. Basketweave
4. Moorish
5. Framed Scotch
6. Irregular Jacquard
7. Mosaic Checker
8. Staircase
9. Encroaching Oblique
10. Waffle
11. Mosaic Stripe
12. 2 × 2 Slanted Gobelin
13. 1 × 1 Spaced Cross Tramé
14. Reversed Mosaic
15. Scotch
16. Oblique Slav
17. Reversed Scotch
18. Tied Cashmere
19. Petit Point
20. Brick
21. Jacquard
22. Diagonal Cashmere
23. Cashmere
24. Pavillion Boxes
25. Framed Scotch
26. Interlocking Gobelin
27. Half-Cross
28. Continental Stitch
29. Framed Reversed Scotch
30. Hungarian Ground
31. Bargello Framework Pattern
32. Upright Cross
33. Straight Gobelin
34. Triangle
35. Web
36. Chain
37. Fly
38. Rep
39. Diagonal Hungarian Ground
40. Mosaic
41. 2-Color Herringbone
42. Oriental
43. Diagonal Mosaic
44. Byzantine #1
45. Cross
46. Fern
47. Milanese
48. Old Florentine

CANVAS: Penelope 10, 21″ × 27″ (3″ margins included)

YARN: Tapestry or Persian (for Petit Point and Rep)

NEEDLE: Sizes 20 and 22 (for Petit Point and Rep)

SIZE OF FINISHED PROJECT: 15″ × 21″

The main lesson learned here is, obviously, how to work many kinds of decorative stitches. You don't have to use the same stitches in the same places I did, if you don't want to. Just stitch one in one corner and put another stitch next to it. Place the next stitch area adjacent to the one just completed.

Do stitch the 2 × 2 Slanted Gobelin border on two sides. Don't try to put the next stitch in until the outside border of the preceding stitches has been stitched. Complete the border after you work each stitch. When you've reached the other two opposite sides with stitches, finish working the border.

Stitch letters and numbers in Continental and work the background behind it in Basketweave.

I cannot stress strongly enough the importance of working the outside border before you put stitches in that area. It is *so* easy to miss by one mesh. Stitching the border keeps you on the right track.

Block and finish (pages 293 and 306).

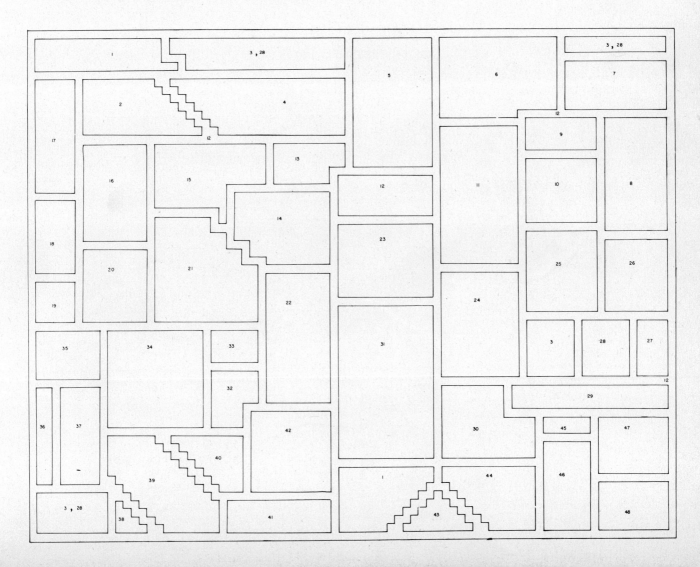

Birth sampler

STITCHES:

1. Oblong Cross
2. Lazy Daisy
3. Diamond Ray
4. Smyrna Cross
5. Double Leviathan
6. Close Herringbone
7. Triple Leviathan
8. Needleweaving
9. Upright Cross
10. Horizontal Elongated Smyrna
11. Continental Stitch
12. Bound Cross
13. Cross
14. Woven Cross
15. Woven Spider Web
16. Trellis Cross (alone)
17. Long Upright Cross
18. Woven Square
19. Double Cross Tramé
20. Rice Stitch
21. Lone Tied Star
22. Roumanian Leaf
23. Alternating Oblong Cross
24. Diamond Eyelet
25. Double Stitch
26. Medallion
27. Staggered Crosses
28. Raised Cup
29. French Knots
30. Oriental

CANVAS: Mono 10, 14″ × 16″ (3″ margins included)

YARN: Tapestry or Persian

NEEDLE: Size 20

SIZE OF FINISHED PROJECT: 8″ × 10″

Some improvisation is necessary here. Figure 3–42c shows you how to chart your own letters. You'll have to do this unless you happen to be making this for a child named Anne Katharine, born on July 6, 1974! Neatly write the words you wish on graph paper. Then mark the Continental Stitches as shown.

Fig. 3–42a. Birth Sampler. Designed and stitched by the author. *(Moats)*

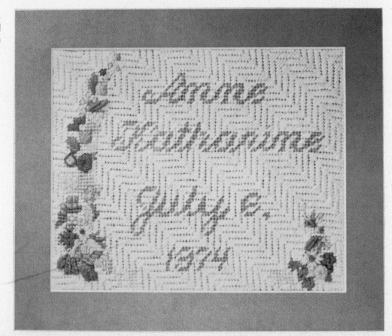

Because flowers overlap, there will be compensating stitches to take. Leaves must be worked in and around flowers. This is another one of those projects that is good to practice on. If you put a stitch for a leaf or a flower in the wrong place or you blow a compensating stitch, it will never be noticed by anyone but you.

Block and frame (pages 293 and 300).

(c)

Wallet and credit card case

STITCHES: Continental Stitch (letters); Basketweave

CANVAS: Mono 14 in pre-finished wallet and credit card case

YARN: Persian (2-ply)

NEEDLE: Size 20

SIZE OF FINISHED PROJECT: Needlepoint in this wallet—2¼"
× 6"; in this credit card case—1⅝" × 3⅛"

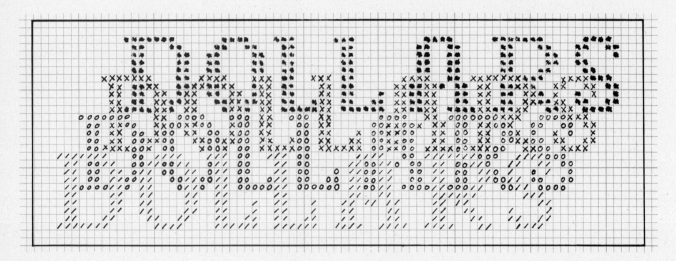

In working this, take care not to pull your Continental Stitch too
tight, for the canvas will distort. The wallet came with an iron-on
lining that helps to keep it in shape.

Be sure the values (page 39) of your colors run from light to
dark; otherwise, the effect is ruined.

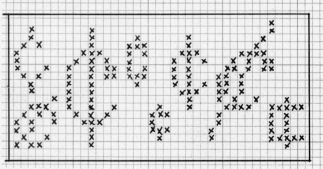

STITCHES: Contintental Stitch (outline); Basketweave

CANVAS: Penelope 10, 18″ × 21″ (3″ margins included)

YARN: Tapestry or Persian

NEEDLE: Size 20

SIZE OF FINISHED PROJECT: 12″ × 15″

This unusual design offers you more practice with a chart and Basketweave. Block and frame (pages 293 and 300).

• GOLD	✗ TURQUOISE
∕ BLUE	◣ CREAM
○ RED	6 COTTON FLOSS OVER BLUE
◑ DARK RED	

STITCHES:

1. Double Leviathan	12. Mosaic
2. Chain	13. Diagonal Mosaic
3. Double Brick	14. Slanted Gobelin
4. Pavillion Diamonds	15. Divided Scotch
5. Double Parisian	16. Diagonal Scotch
6. Pavillion	17. Scotch
7. Upright Cross	18. Cashmere
8. Smyrna Cross	19. Horizontal Cashmere
9. Alternating Smyrna	20. Cut Turkey Work
10. Roumanian Leaf	21. Binding Stitch
11. Diagonal Leaf	22. Continental Stitch

(a)

CANVAS: Mono 10, 8″ × 54″

YARN: Persian (4-ply for Straight Gobelin)

NEEDLE: Size 20

SIZE OF FINISHED PROJECT: 7″ × 48″

After you've painted your design on canvas, outline all the flowers and leaves with a color a shade or two darker than the object. Then fill in with the stitches listed.

Use the Two-Step Edge Finishing method described on page 80 on the two long sides. Leave the ends with a 3″ margin (Figure 3–45b).

Block (page 294). Bind the edges with the Binding Stitch and apply rabbit skin glue (page 299). Attach bell-pull hardware (page 312) and line (page 310).

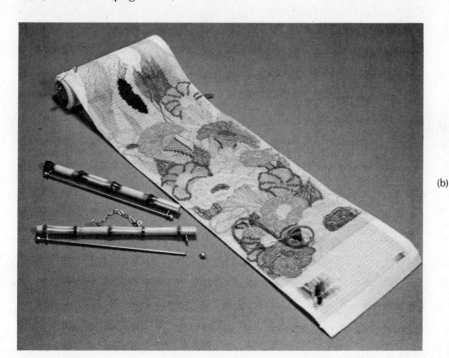

(b)

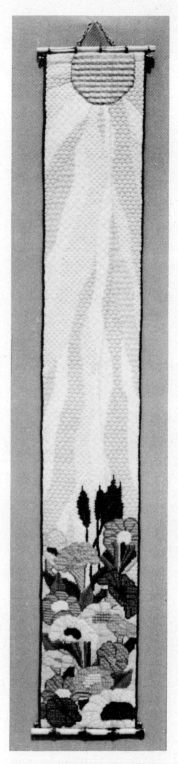

Fig. 3–45a. Floral Bell Pull. Adapted from two designs by Ed Sibbett, Jr. and the author; stitched by Betty Powers. *(Moats)*

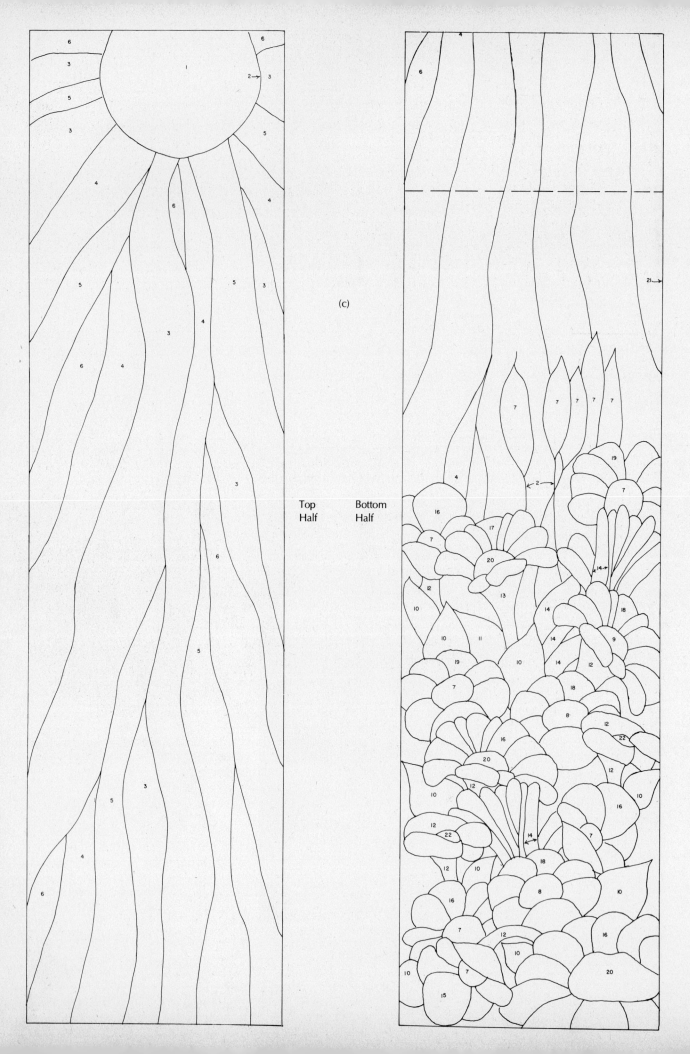

(c)

Top Half   Bottom Half

(d)

(e)

(f)

Hassock

STITCHES:

1. Cross
2. French Knots
3. Petit Point
4. Twisted Chain
5. 2 × 2 Slanted Gobelin
6. Couching (for outlining pole)
7. Reversed Mosaic
8. Framed Cashmere
9. Diagonal Mosaic
10. Lazy Kalem
11. Staggered Cross
12. Tied Oblong Cross
13. Staircase
14. Continental Stitch
15. Upright Cross
16. Elongated Cashmere
17. Cut Turkey Work
18. French Knots on Stalks
19. Kalem
20. Smyrna Cross
21. Ringed Daisy (half of circle)
22. Woven Spider Web
23. Ridged Spider Web
24. Smooth Spider Web
25. Velvet
26. Looped Turkey Work
27. Chain
28. Open Chain Stitch (on top of background)
29. Double Stitch
30. Round Cross
31. Reversed Scotch
32. Diagonal Greek
33. Diamond Ray
34. Van Dyke
35. Periwinkle
36. Tied Oblong Cross
37. Scotch
38. Loop
39. Mosaic
40. Diagonal Fern
41. Knotted Stitch
42. Brick
43. Buttonhole

Fig. 3–46a. Hassock. Designed by Cindy Pendleton; stitched by Marlene Meek. *(Moats)*

137

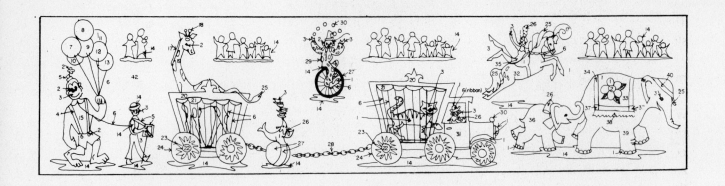

CANVAS: Penelope 7, top, 24″ × 24″ (for round top 18″ in diameter); sides 20½″ × 64″ (3″ margins included)

YARN: Persian (usually 5-ply)

NEEDLE: Size 16

SIZE OF FINISHED PROJECT: Top 18″ in diameter, side 14½″ tall and 56 9/16″ in circumference

138

This project is a major exercise in painting the canvas and in stitching a large number of stitches in a design.

Work all three Spider Webs on the same spokes. Change methods (and colors if you like) in midstream.

Stitch the top and block (page 294). Stitch the side pieces to within 1″ of the line on either end. Block. Take the top and the sides to an upholsterer. Ask him to stitch them together with cording in the seam. He should lap the two ends of canvas over each other, so that the margin marks match. There will be two thicknesses of canvas about 3″ wide. The mesh must match. Have him trim the rest away.

When the upholsterer is through with this top seam, take it home. Put glue on the raw edges thinly—just enough to hold the canvas. Stitch the area of blank canvas through both thicknesses of canvas. Be sure that the yarn covers the ends of the canvas. The seam should be invisible if you stitched carefully.

Take the needlepoint back to the upholsterer and have him finish it by stitching a durable fabric to the bottom. There should be cording in this bottom seam, too. Have him stuff the hassock, also.

Stamp

STITCHES:
1. Byzantine #1
2. Mosaic
3. Continental
4. Scotch
5. Diagonal Mosaic
6. Jacquard
7. Petit Point
8. 2 × 1 Slanted Gobelin
9. Ridged Spider Web (in two colors)
10. Chain (all small circles)
11. French Knot (center of all small circles)
12. 3 × 1 Slanted Gobelin
13. Couching (outlines of striped resistors and light orange contacts on row on left)
14. Diagonal Cashmere
14. Diagonal Cashmere
15. Straight Stitch

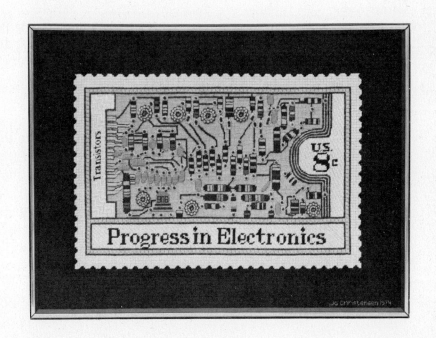

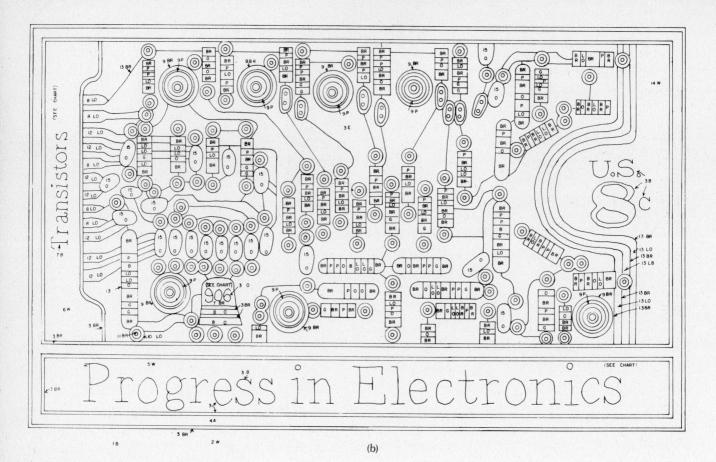

(b)

LO—LIGHT ORANGE (OUTSIDE OF ALL
    SMALL CIRCLES)
W—WHITE
B—BLACK
BR—BROWN (ALL FRENCH KNOTS AND ALL
    COUCHED LINES EXCEPT BY U.S. 8¢)
LB—LIGHT BROWN
P—PINK
O—ORANGE
G—GREEN

CANVAS: Penelope 10, 26″ × 34″ (3″ margins included)

YARN: Tapestry or Persian (for Petit Point)

NEEDLE: 20 and 22 (for Petit Point)

SIZE OF FINISHED PROJECT: 20″ × 28″ (including 3″ black border)

This project combines two techniques: painted canvas and a charted design. Figure 3–47b shows the overall design. Figure 3–47c shows a chart of the detailed areas.

    The design is an artist's rendering of what a printed circuit board looks like. Neither the design nor the colors are true to life. Because my husband is a stamp collector as well as an electronics engineer, he wanted the needlepoint exactly like the stamp. So, I let *him* choose the colors of yarn with a magnifying glass and the real stamp. To achieve greater accuracy in color, you may want to do the same yourself. Buy the stamp from a stamp dealer.

    In case you'd like to do another stamp, have a photographer or a lithographer blow up the stamp to a workable size as I did. This size will vary with the design on the stamp. Work out the details on graph paper.

    Then paint your design on canvas and stitch.

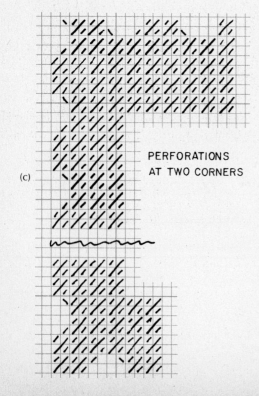

(c)

PERFORATIONS
AT TWO CORNERS

140

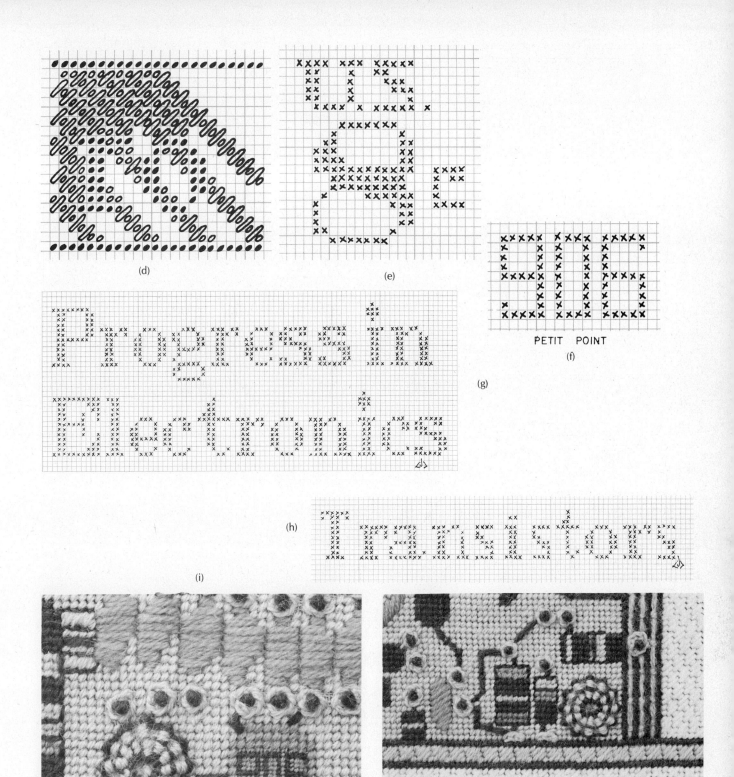

(d)

(e)

PETIT POINT

(f)

(g)

(h)

(i)

(j)

When working a decorative stitch behind letters, I've found it easier to figure the compensating stitches for every other row. It's half the work. (See Figure 3–47d.) Now all you need to do is fill in the blank spaces between the worked rows.

Block and frame (pages 294 and 300).

8 Advanced projects

By the time you get to advanced projects you should be adding your own creative touches to the work you're doing. Now you should not be copying exactly.

Although enough information is given for copying the following projects, they should serve as examples only of the lessons learned. Apply your newly gained knowledge to your own designs.

Mushroom and butterfly

STITCH: Continental Stitch

CANVAS: Mono 10 and 14, 7½" × 7½" (2" margins included)

YARN: Tapestry or Persian (2-ply Persian on Mono 14)

NEEDLE: Size 20

SIZE OF FINISHED PROJECT: 3½" diameter

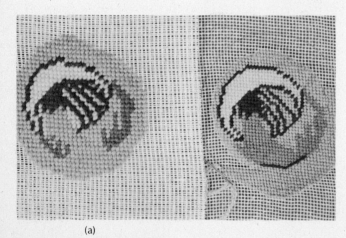
(a)

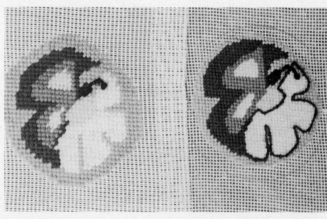
(b)

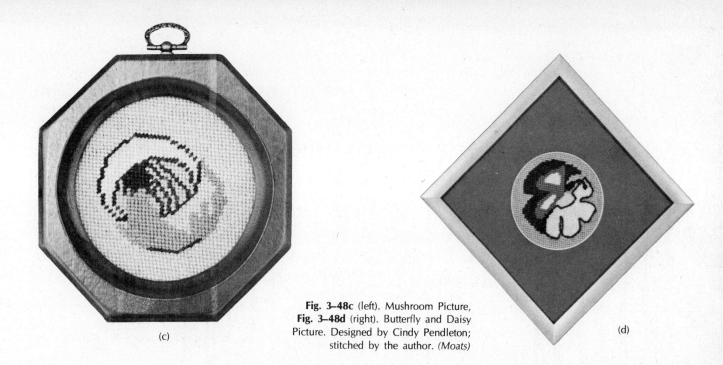

Fig. 3–48c (left). Mushroom Picture,
Fig. 3–48d (right). Butterfly and Daisy
Picture. Designed by Cindy Pendleton;
stitched by the author. (Moats)

(c)

(d)

Two major lessons in color and design are presented here. The mushroom on the left in Figure 3–48a seems to float. The other one, however, has solidarity, created by adding a dark line at the bottom of the mushroom. This dark line is actually a shadow.

The butterfly on the left in Figure 3–48b seems to overpower the white flower, because of a lack of color balance. Actually, the color of the flower should have been darker—enough to support the weight of the butterfly. In order to salvage the project, the error has been corrected, somewhat, by outlining the flower in navy blue. This adds substance to the white flower.

Fig. 3–48f. Butterfly and Daisy
Pincushion. Designed by
Cindy Pendleton; stitched by
the author. (Moats)

(e)

(f)

(g)

(h)

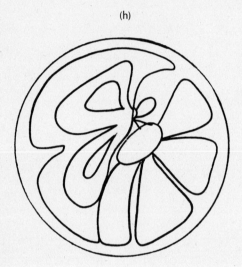

When I took my finished needlepoint to the professional framer, he told me his mat cutter would cut a circle only 3½" in diameter. Of course, my needlepoint was 3" in diameter! So I had to go home and stitch half an inch more all the way around. You can still see (in spots) where I added. The moral of the story is: check on details like this with professional finishers *before* you start to stitch!

These two small round designs and the others in Figure 3–48 are excellent gift ideas. They work up quickly and can be finished in a variety of ways: as in Plate 15 (pillow), as pictures, or as a pincushion. Block first (page 294). Making a pin cushion is like making a pillow (page 306). Framing with a mat is described on page 306 and framing without a stretcher frame is on page 300. On page 309 are the instructions for inserting needlepoint into fabric. Finish as a pillow (page 306).

Each design was stitched on two different sizes of canvas to illustrate what a difference can be made in your design by using smaller or larger canvas. Figures 3–48a and b show the two designs stitched on Mono 10 (left) and Mono 14 (right). Notice the curves in each picture. Those stitched on Mono 14 are smoother. This is because there are 100 stitches per square inch (10 × 10=100) on Mono 10, and 196 per square inch (14 × 14=196) on Mono 14. You may think that although Mono 14 is just 4 mesh per linear inch smaller that it won't make that much difference. But actually, it's twice the work.

Tiger

STITCHES:
1. Straight Stitches
2. Kalem
3. Diagonal Mosaic (reverse for tree on left)
4. Cut Turkey Work
5. Continental Stitch
6. Mosaic
7. Velvet
8. Roumanian Leaf
9. Diagonal Cashmere
10. Byzantine #1

CANVAS: Mono 14, 17" × 22" (3" margins included)

YARN: Persian (2-ply, mostly)

NEEDLE: Size 20

SIZE OF FINISHED PROJECT: 11" × 16"

(a)

(b)

OUTLINE – CONTINENTAL

If you look only at the black-and-white photograph (Figure 3–49a) or at the line drawing (Figure 3–49b), you might say this is a drawing of a jungle, not a tiger—but one quick look at the color photograph (Plate 42) will show you why I call it "Tiger" and not "Jungle."

Color has created a center of interest in a busy design. All of the other objects are stitched with more subdued colors than the tiger.

Outlining was done with Continental Stitch in a color a shade or two darker than the object.

Block (page 294) and frame (page 300).

145

Pussy willows

STITCHES:
1. Cut Turkey Work   4. Wide Moorish
2. Continental Stitch   5. Diagonal Mosaic
3. Chain   6. F-106

CANVAS: Mono 10, 12½″ × 23¼″ (3″ margins included)

YARN: Tapestry or Persian

NEEDLE: Size 20

SIZE OF FINISHED PROJECT: 6½″ × 17¼″

This picture presents another color problem: The pussy willows must appear to be *in* a vase, which is *on* a table, which is *in front of* the wall. (See Chapter 3.)

    Stitch shadows in the same stitch; change only the colors. See color of Shadows (page 43).

    Block (page 294) and frame (300).

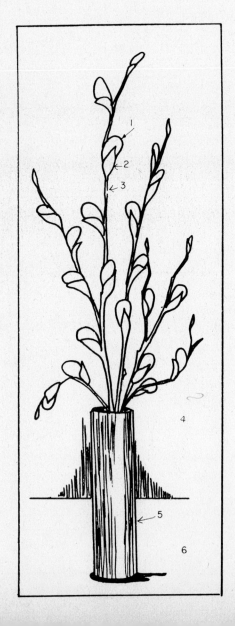

146

STITCHES:

1. Binding
2. Woven Band (4-ply tapestry strands)
3. Cross
4. Greek (two 4-ply tapestry strands)
5. Triangular Ray (4-ply Persian)
6. Double Leviathan (4-ply tapestry strands)
7. 2-Color Herringbone (stitched in one color)
8. Reversed Scotch (Two 4-ply tapestry strands)
9. 6-Trip Herringbone
10. Buttonhole (two 4-ply tapestry strands)
11. Cashmere
12. 2 × 2 Slanted Gobelin (two 4-ply tapestry strands)
13. Giant Rice (4-ply Persian)
14. Butterfly
15. Diagonal Mosaic (4-ply Persian)
16. Beaty (4-ply Persian)
17. Diagonal Cashmere
18. Continental Stitch (4-ply Persian)
19. Milanese (4-ply Persian)
20. Mosaic (4-ply Persian)
☐ 3 × 3 Slanted Gobelin (handle)
☐ Triangle Stitch (two 4-ply tapestry strands) (bottom and sides)

(a)

(b)

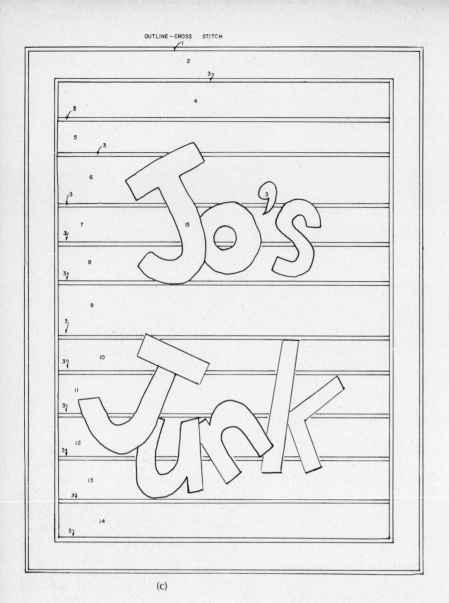

(c)

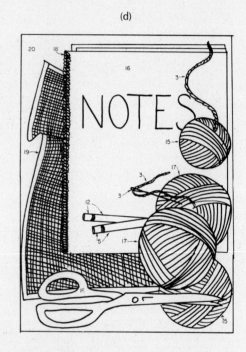

(d)

CANVAS: Plastic canvas (see Figure 3–51e)

YARN: Tapestry or Persian (one whole 4-ply or 3-ply strand used unless otherwise noted)

NEEDLE: Size 16

SIZE OF FINISHED PROJECT: 3″ × 10½″ × 13½″

The color exercise in this project is illustrated in Plate 27. The balls of yarn must appear to be stacked on top of each other. The scissors must be in front of the bottom ball of yarn and on top of the canvas. The pencils must be underneath the orange ball of yarn, yet on top of the notebook, and so on.

(e)

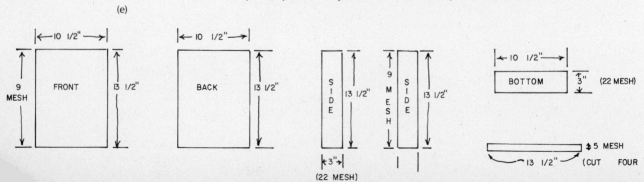

In order to do this the warmest colors must be in front and the colors must get cooler and greyer as they go back. So, the whole dark orange ball is the warmest; the scissors come next; and then comes the bottom ball of yarn. The next coolest ball of yarn is the yellow-orange one (half of a ball) and then the yellow one. Even though the notebook is still yellow, it is somewhat greyer than the yellow ball of yarn and so it recedes behind all the balls of yarn. Orange is a warm color, but that means the pure orange of the color wheel. The canvas is stitched in a greyed orange, so it appears to be underneath the notebook. The brown background must be behind all of these things.

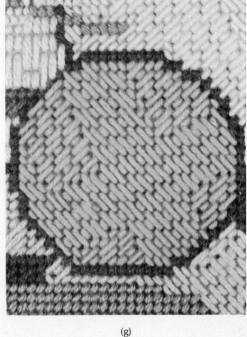

(g)

(h)

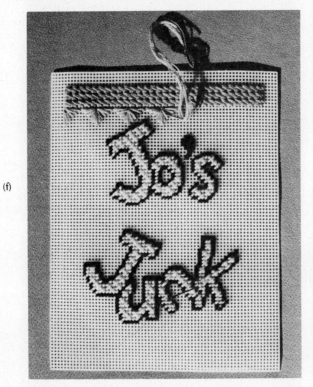

(f)

Stitch the gussets (sides) and the bottom in the Triangle Stitch. It'll come out even except for one mesh. Compensate. It's hardly noticeable. Don't sweat the small stuff.

Stitch the handles in 3 × 3 Slanted Gobelin. Leave the last 5 or 6 mesh on each end blank. Sew the handles together with the Binding Stitch as you did the key chain on page 86. Stop it where the other stitches stop.

Baste the handles in place on the wrong sides of the blank sheets of plastic for the front and back of the tote bag. When you work these areas, stitch through all three thicknesses of canvas as if they were one. The handles will be securely attached.

Stitch each piece of the tote bag separately. The Diagonal Cashmere Stitch was turned so that it resembled yarn wound in a ball (Figure 3–51f). Sew the pieces of the tote bag together with the Binding Stitch.

Line as on page 310.

Farm scene

STITCHES:

1. Cross
2. Divided Scotch
3. Fly
4. Combination Crosses
5. Alternating Oblong Cross
6. Diagonal Mosaic
7. Roumanian Leaf
8. Diagonal Chain
9. Mosaic Stripe
10. Milanese
11. Byzantine #2
12. Diagonal Roumanian
13. Diagonal Greek (reversed)
14. Horizontal Cashmere
15. Elongated Cashmere
16. Continental Stitch
17. Horizontal Brick
18. Mosaic
19. Couching
20. Diagonal Cashmere
21. Oriental
22. Diagonal Stem
23. Moorish
24. Rice
25. Diagonal Fern

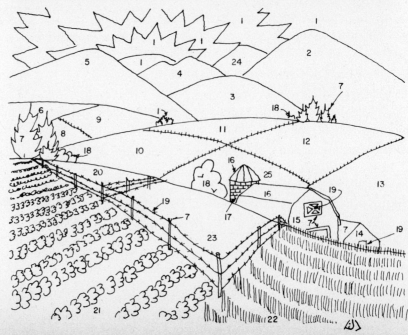

CANVAS: Penelope 7, 23″ × 29″ (3″ margins included)

YARN: Persian (mostly 4-ply and 5-ply)

NEEDLE: Size 16

SIZE OF FINISHED PROJECT: 17″ × 23″

Line and color make aerial perspective evident in this picture. In the original needlepoint, some colors were out of value—the yellow field and two light green fields were the worst offenders. Plate 17 shows how the picture looks after it was doctored. I used permanent markers to color the yarn right on the finished needlepoint. Although the colors in Plate 17 are not perfect, they certainly are a lot better. I cannot work on it any more for fear of ruining the yarn. Avoid this by getting your painted paper picture perfect before you start to stitch. Remember, in aerial perspective, the colors must recede (page 43).

The area stitched in Oriental Stitch takes the eye out of the picture. The Oriental Stitch should have been reversed as the Diagonal Greek Stitch was. The sky is done by a simple, yet pretty, shading method. The color is merely changed at the lines on the drawing.

Block and frame (pages 294 and 300).

City skyline

STITCHES:
1. Stem
2. Horizontal Old Florentine
3. Framed Giant Cashmere
4. Alternating Oblong Cross
5. Couching
6. Mosaic
7. Continental Stitch (outline)
8. Cashmere
9. Irregular Continental

CANVAS: Mono 10, 15¾″ × 26½″ (3″ margins included)

YARN: Tapestry or Persian (for shading)

NEEDLE: Size 20

SIZE OF FINISHED PROJECT: 9¾″ × 20½″

The shaded sky is the new technique in this project. The Irregular Continental Stitch is made to fit the area and color conformation that you need.

Fig. 3-53a. City Skyline Designed by Cindy Pendleton; stitched by Carole Key. (Moats)

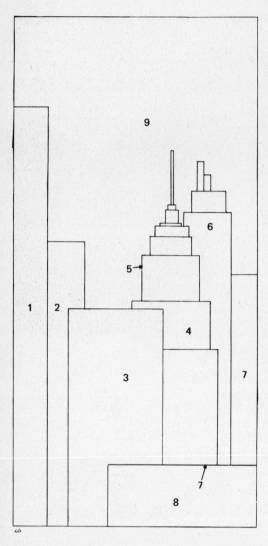

The placement of color is, as you can see, graduated from light to dark at the top of the picture. However, the color that was started near the buildings was determined by the rule of alternating light and dark colors. So the lightest blue was put beside a dark building and the next darkest was put beside a light building.

The more colors you can find in your range of colors, the more effective the shading will be. If you cannot get the right color range, *do not even try to shade.* The results will be disastrous. Here, five colors were used. Let's call them A, B, C, D, and E. It's easier to shade with Persian yarn because it is easily separated. It takes three areas of each color to advance to the next color. The last one needs only one area. The five colors used here will need 13 areas to finish the shading process. Draw lines on your canvas (with a waterproof marker) that divide it into 13 fairly equal sections.

Start stitching with the lightest color; this will be 3-ply, or AAA, of color A. In the second area, stitch with a strand that's made up of two plies of A and one ply of B, or AAB. In the next area, use one ply of A and two plies of B, or ABB. Continue following this pattern (see following chart) until you've worked up to a 3-ply strand of the last color. Tapestry yarn can be used, but it is more difficult to separate it into strands.

3-PLY YARN	4-PLY YARN
Area	Area
1. AAA	1. AAAA
2. AAB	2. AAAB
3. ABB	3. AABB
4. BBB	4. ABBB
5. BBC	5. BBBB
6. BCC	6. BBBC
7. CCC	7. BBCC
8. CCD	8. BCCC
9. CDD	9. CCCC
10. DDD	10. CCCD
11. DDE	11. CCDD
12. DEE	12. CDDD
13. EEE	13. DDDD
	14. DDDE
	15. DDEE
	16. DEEE
	17. EEEE

Some of the buildings did not stand out enough when the stitching was finished. A Couching Stitch was added in the way of outline to achieve this desired end.

A needlepoint piece with stitches that distort and with straight lines in the design is a bear to block! Use T-pins (*stainless steel*) to make the lines straight within the boundaries. Sometimes

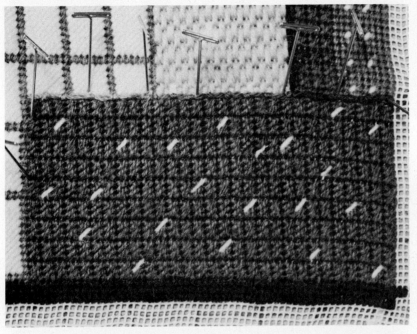

even that won't work, and rabbit skin glue must be used. But if you can't get it straight long enough to put the rabbit skin glue on, even that won't work. The lines may have to be forever crooked. Frame (page 300).

The moon and the coyote

STITCHES:
1. Continental Stitch
2. Straight Stitch (pine needle)
3. Double Stitch (tree)

CANVAS: Mono 10, 12¾" × 19½" (3" margins included)

YARN: Persian (for shading)

NEEDLE: Size 20

SIZE OF FINISHED PROJECT: 6¾" × 13½"

This project uses a different method of shading. The preceding chart is still followed, but you take two or more rows of Continental Stitch in colors AAA and then scatter a few stitches out beyond that line (see Figure 3–54c). Fill in two or more solid

(a)

Fig. 3-54a. Moon and Coyote (or Wolf). Designed by Cindy Pendleton; stitched by the author. *(Moats)*

153

(b)

rows in colors AAB. Scatter a few of those stitches in the next area. Continue until you've reached a strand made up of three ply of the background color. Usually it's easiest to start with the color that occurs in your design in the smallest amount.

There are two things I'd change about this if I were to stitch it again. First, the background color (the darkest one) would not be so dark. The tree and the coyote do not show up as well as I think they should. The highlights do help to bring them out somewhat, though. The frame, which is the color of the coyote, helps also.

Second, I would make the corona around the moon larger, with a light blue hitting as far down (at least) as the coyote's throat. Someday . . . But we all learn from our mistakes; if we don't they are for naught.

Block and frame (pages 294 and 300).

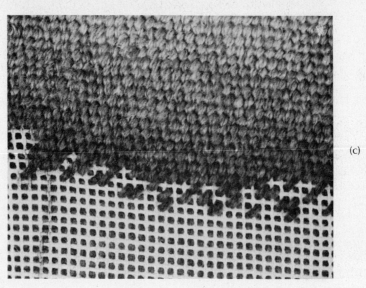

(c)

Flower purse

STITCHES:

1. Cross
2. Double Straight Cross
3. Buttonhole in Half Circle
4. Double Stitch
5. Bullion Knot
6. French Knots
7. Chris Cross
8. Triple Cross
9. Ridged Spider Web
10. Combination Crosses
11. Double Leviathan
12. Ray
13. Fancy Cross
14. Smooth Spider Web
15. Looped Turkey Work
16. French Knots on Stalks
17. Wound Cross
18. Square Eyelet
19. Diagonal Cashmere
20. Continental Stitch (for initials and date)
21. Triple Leviathan
22. 2 × 2 Slanted Gobelin (4-ply)

(a)

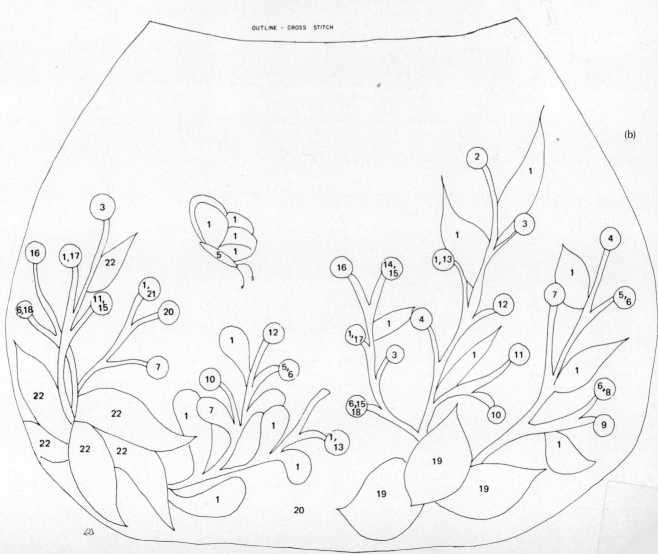

OUTLINE - CROSS STITCH

(b)

(c)

CANVAS: Penelope 7, 16½" × 20½" (2" margins included)

YARN: Persian (mostly 3-ply to 5-ply)

NEEDLE: Size 16

SIZE OF FINISHED PROJECT: 12½" × 16½"

Many of the flower stitches in this purse are one or more stitches put together, or they are parts taken from a stitch with an overall pattern (such as Double Stitch). The circles on the diagram in Figure 3–55b merely suggest where you might put a flower. Try to come up with stitch combinations of your own.

Buy your backing fabric before you select the yarn colors and also buy your handle before you cut the canvas.

Block (page 294) and finish according to instructions on a commercial pattern.

(d)

(e)

9
Expert projects

Now that you've learned the basics, it's time to put them together, work harder versions, or try new media or new procedures. This chapter only introduces you to the infinite kinds of needlepoint that can be done. Don't just copy the pieces given here; create your own designs, stitches, and even techniques!

World map

STITCHES:
1. Continental Stitch
2. Diagonal Mosaic
3. Brick
4. Scotch
5. Petit Point

CANVAS: Penelope 10, 24" × 20" (3" margins included)

YARN: Tapestry or Persian (for Petit Point)

NEEDLE: Size 20 and 22 (for Petit Point)

SIZE OF FINISHED PROJECT: 18" × 24"

Each of the techniques involved in making this needlepoint map is not particularly difficult, but putting them all together into one project takes some expertise.

The canvas is first painted with the basic map design and then stitched. After that, the charted designs must be placed into the picture in the appropriate places. The outlines drawn on your canvas will help you get them right. The background is worked in a trellis effect, as charted. It too must be put into the piece, as well as the letters and the border.

Precision is a must in the trellis background, border, letters, and the placing of the two fleurs-de-lis.

Each of the countries is outlined twice: once in its own color.

Block and frame (pages 294 and 300).

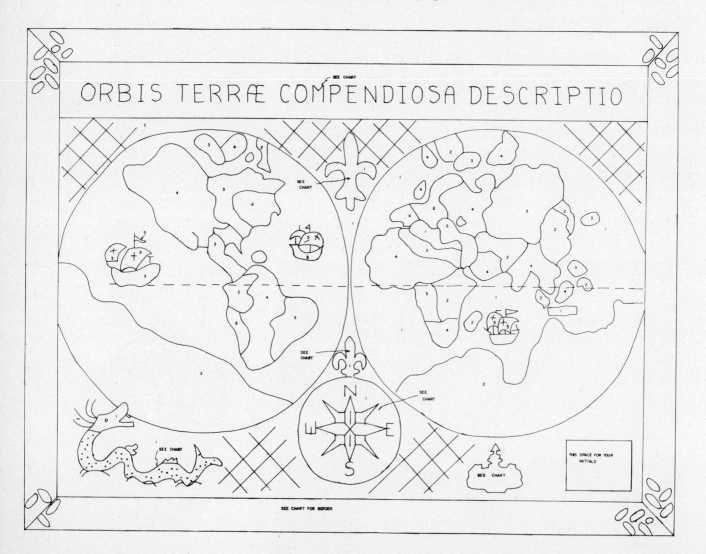

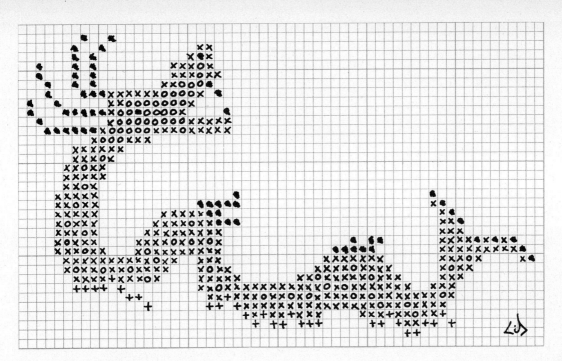

      🐾 DARK BROWN
      ✗ GOLD
      O LIGHT YELLOW
      + BLUE-GREEN

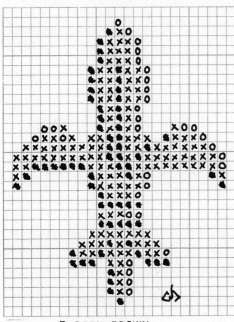

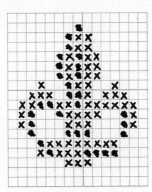

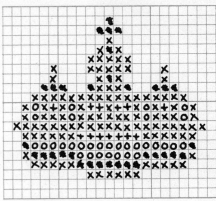

🐾 DARK BROWN
O PALE YELLOW
✗ GOLD (ORANGE-GOLD)

🐾 DARK BROWN   🐾 DARK BROWN   + RED
✗ GOLD   O WHITE   ✗ GREEN

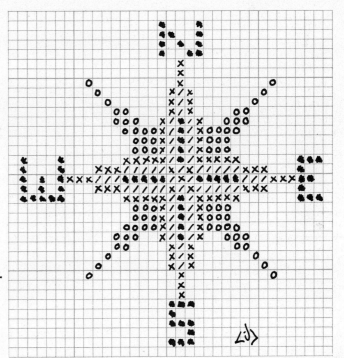

🐾 DARK BROWN
✗ BLUE
/ WHITE
O RED

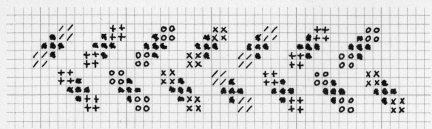

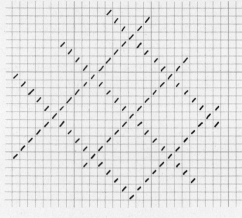

- ● BROWN
- / BEIGE
- + GREEN
- ○ RED
- ✕ BLUE

/ LIGHT COFFEE BROWN

ORBIS TERRE COMPENDIOSA
DESCRIPTIO.

Ukrainian wedding picture

STITCHES: Basketweave; Continental Stitch (where Basketweave won't fit)

CANVAS: Mono 14, 17" × 20" (3" margin included)

YARN: Persian (2-ply)

NEEDLE: Size 20

SIZE OF FINISHED PROJECT: 11" × 14"

When working with black yarn and white yarn, you must do your best to keep them separate and to keep the white yarn white. If you work the black first, you get black fuzzies in the white. If you work the white first (as many experts advocate), the white yarn gets dirty from excessive handling. And there you sit—between a rock and a hard spot!

In stitching this project, you have no choice. The chart is simply too difficult to work the white first, so work the black first. It will help to choose a yarn that is less hairy than others. Yarns do differ.

Be sure your hands are clean when you stitch with white yarn. Stitched-in dirt is harder (if not impossible) to get out than surface dirt. I know; I have tried!

This picture was on the front of a wedding invitation. I had it enlarged, charted it, and stitched it for the wedding gift.

Block and frame (pages 294 and 300).

Mississippi river-boat gambler vest

STITCHES:

1. Basketweave
2. Double Cross Tramé
3. Chain
4. Straight Stitches
5. Reversed Mosaic
6. Brick
7. Reversed Scotch
8. Diagonal Mosaic
9. Greek
10. Slanted Gobelin
11. Fly
12. Smooth Spider Web
13. Diamond Ray
14. Bargello
☐ Continental Stitch (outline)
☐ Hitched Cross (background)

CANVAS: Mono 10, nylon canvas made for clothing, 27″ × 28″ (3″ margins included)

YARN: Tapestry or Persian

NEEDLE: Size 20

SIZE OF FINISHED PROJECT: Depends on size of pattern used; this one is men's size 40, 22″ high by 18″ wide (front only stitched).

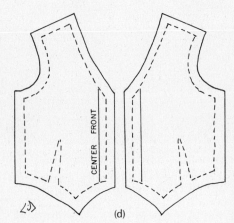

ALL OUTLINE—
CONTINENTAL

BACKGROUND—HITCHED CROSS

Bargello pattern for stitch 14 on vest.

The first thing you need to do when stitching clothing is to get a commercial pattern the proper size. For a vest, all you'll need to stitch in needlepoint is the two front pieces. Take the front pattern piece out of the pattern envelope and press it with a hot *dry* iron. Trace it onto a piece of canvas as shown in Figure 3–58d. Flip the pattern and trace the pattern's mirror image onto the canvas, also. Leave 3" all the way around the outside. It's all right if the two center cutting lines are close together. You won't cut the pattern pieces apart until it's time to assemble the vest. Then trace the design onto the canvas. Move the design so it continues on the other side of the dart. Fold the dart together to make sure that your design lines meet. (Mine don't—I hope you do better!) You might have to fudge a bit, but make the lines meet.

One 3-ply strand of Persian or one 4-ply strand of tapestry yarn doesn't *quite* cover the canvas, yet thickening the yarn makes a too-bulky stitch. So, when I painted the canvas, I knew it would show. The background was painted blue. The red yarn and the blue paint are mixed by the eye, and the red vest picks up a purplish cast.

The nylon canvas *must* be stitched on a frame or in an embroidery hoop. It really has no body of its own. This soft feel is what makes it so nice for needlepoint clothing. But it's not nice to stitch on. Getting smooth tension is difficult; if you pull too tightly, the canvas just buckles under your needlepoint stitch.

Do not stitch the area inside the dart. Remember to stitch sacrifice stitches. Iron-on interfacing is needed to keep the canvas from puckering if you pulled your stitches too tightly. But interfacing adds the bulk you avoided by using the nylon canvas.

When you trace the design onto canvas, there will be portions of the design duplicated. The area to the right of the center front line on the left piece, and the area to the left of the center front line on the right piece will be traced twice. This means there will be two watch fobs. Stitch the one that will be on top when the vest is worn and snapped closed in Smooth Spider Web. Stitch the watch fob underneath in Basketweave to avoid bulk.

Have it put together professionally for a really tailored look. Or, if you wish to do it yourself, follow the directions on the commercial pattern.

STITCHES:

1. Irregular Byzantine
2. Roumanian Leaf
3. Raised Cup
4. Needleweaving
5. Chain

Fig. 3-59a. Three-Dimensional Flowers in Vase. Designed and stitched by the author. *(Moats)*

CANVAS: Interlock Mono 14, 12″ × 16″ (3″ margins included)

YARN: Persian (2-ply), velvet yarn (vase), angora yarn (flowers), and pipe cleaners (leaves and stems)

NEEDLE: Size 20

SIZE OF FINISHED PROJECT: 6″ × 10″

This project utilizes several techniques not usually associated with needlepoint.

Paint only the three leaves and the outline of the vase on the canvas. Stitch the leaves and the background. Block (page 294).

Now cut the canvas out of the inside of the vase (Figure 3–59b). Apply a thin layer of white glue to the raw edges. Let it dry. Tape (with masking tape) the bottom third of a 5-ounce paper cup to the inside hole in the canvas. The cup should be bottom up (Figure 3–59c). This cup will serve as a form over which you can stitch the vase with shape.

Work the vase in Needleweaving, making up a pattern of holes as you go. Secure the tails of the Needleweaving stitches in the background stitch. Remove the cup. (It probably has fallen out by now anyway!)

If you do not have green pipe cleaners, paint white ones with a permanent green marker. Shape *basically* as shown in Figure 3–59d. Work Needleweaving over the pipe-cleaner form. Bury the yarn tails as well as you can.

Work the Chain Stitch over straight pipe cleaners. These will be the flower stems. The pipe cleaners *should* show through. It is somewhat awkward to hold the pipe cleaner and work the stitch, but you will soon get the hang of it, I'm sure.

Make the flowers from the Raised Cup Stitch, right on the pipe cleaner.

Stick the pipe cleaners through the Needleweaving of the vase, *very* near the top. Secure the ends with sewing thread by stitching yarn to yarn. Bend and arrange the stems and leaves any way you like.

Stuff the vase with a layer of fabric first and then with polyester fiber-fill. Sewing by hand with sewing thread, whip a piece of fabric to the back of the needlepoint to hold the stuffing in.

Frame in a shadow box frame (see page 300).

165

(b)

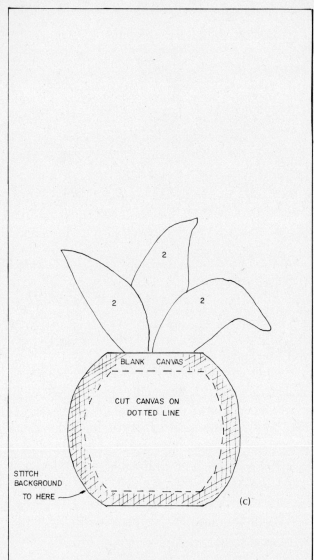

BLANK CANVAS

CUT CANVAS ON
DOTTED LINE

STITCH
BACKGROUND
TO HERE

(c)

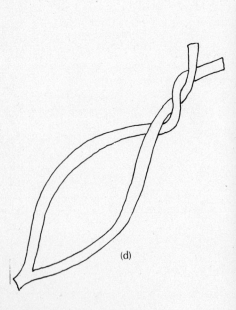

(d)

166

THE
STITCHES

Before you even start to stitch, you will need to know the definitions of the symbols used in the drawings. The artist's signature ⟨J⟩ shows the location of the beginning of the stitch. In stitches that are done in steps, the starts are identified by ⟨J⟩1, ⟨J⟩A, ⟨J⟩a, ⟨J⟩AA, and ⟨J⟩aa, in that order.

Arrows alone indicate a row change with no turning of the canvas. Arrows accompanied by a clock show a turning of the canvas:

T⟨🕐⟩ means, "Turn 90° to the right."

T⟨🕕⟩ means, "Turn 180°."

T⟨🕘⟩ means, "Turn 90° to the left."

Where they would complicate things, these arrows and clocks have been omitted. You can still tell where to turn the canvas. Simply turn the book so that the numbers are upright. Turn your canvas the same way and stitch.

When several stitches go into the same hole, the numbers have been omitted because there simply is not room for all of them. (See the chapter on Eye Stitches.)

The numbering has been arranged to create the best possible backing. Economical use of yarn usually creates a poor backing. This poor backing reduces the durability of needlepoint.

A change of color is indicated by darkening the stitches, but the use of a second color is not absolutely necessary. This darkening also helps you to see the next row more clearly. Other colors (third, fourth, etc.) are indicated by different designs within each stitch. When working with two colors that cross each other, put the darker on the bottom. Work the lighter colors last.

The canvas pictured is the canvas used for the particular stitch. Generally, all stitches can be worked on Penelope canvas; Regular Mono canvas does have some restrictions on the types of stitches that can be used. These have been pictured on Penelope canvas. (These restrictions do not exist on Interlock Mono canvas.) The rest of the stitches have been drawn on Mono canvas for simplicity and clarity.

10 Straight stitches

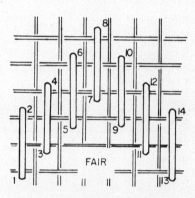

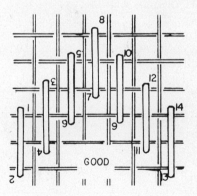

Straight Stitches are those stitches that cover the canvas vertically or horizontally. A vertical stitch covers two to six horizontal mesh and lies entirely between two vertical mesh. A horizontal stitch covers two to six vertical mesh and lies entirely between two horizontal mesh.

A single strand of both tapestry and Persian yarn, when worked in Straight Stitches, covers Mono 14 canvas well. On Penelope or Mono 10 or 12 you will have to thicken your yarn.

Straight Stitches make beautiful patterns and make a good background (as a rule). They work up quickly and can give a good backing if you plan on it.

Most of the Straight Stitches depend on color for their splendor. (See pages 40-41.)

Straight Stitches do not distort the canvas when you stitch. I recommend Straight Stitches for beginners.

Take a Bargello tuck as you bury the tail (page 26).

If you wish to mix Straight Stitches with Diagonal Stitches, you can refer to page 92, the Mouse project, for directions.

Making good backing

STRAIGHT STITCHES	Border	Good Backing	Poor Backing	Background	Design	Accent	Fast	Slow	Geometric Pattern	Shading	Yarn Hog	Snags	Snag-Proof	Little Texture	Medium Texture	High Relief	Flower Stitch	Weak Pattern	Medium Pattern	Strong Pattern	Distorts Canvas
Straight Gobelin	•	•		•	•				•				•	•				•			
Straight Stitch																					
Interlocking Straight Gobelin		•		•	•			•		•	•			•				•			
Brick		•		•	•				•	•			•	•				•			
Giant Brick		•		•	•		•		•	•		•		•					•		
Double Brick		•		•	•		•		•					•					•		
Horizontal Brick		•		•	•		•		•	•		•		•					•		
Parisian		•		•	•		•		•	•				•					•		
Double Parisian		•		•	•		•		•					•					•		
Pavillion	•	•		•	•		•		•					•					•		
Hungarian	•	•		•	•	•	•		•					•					•		
Hungarian Ground		•		•	•		•		•					•					•		
Double Hungarian Ground		•		•	•		•		•					•					•		
Pavillion Diamonds	•	•		•	•	•	•		•			•		•						•	
Tied Pavillion	•	•		•	•	•	•		•			•		•						•	
Old Florentine		•		•	•		•		•			•		•					•		
Horizontal Old Florentine		•		•	•		•		•			•		•					•		
Beaty	•	•		•	•		•		•			•		•					•		
Wicker		•		•			•		•			•		•					•		
Horizontal Milanese		•		•	•	•	•		•			•		•						•	
Vertical Milanese		•		•	•	•	•		•			•		•						•	
Upright Oriental		•		•	•		•		•			•		•						•	
Roman II		•		•	•			•	•					•					•		
Pavillion Boxes		•		•	•		•		•			•		•						•	
Triangle	•	•		•	•	•			•			•		•						•	
F-106	•	•		•	•	•	•		•			•		•						•	
Bargello Line Pat.		•		•	•		•		•	•		•		•						•	
Bargello Framework Pattern		•		•	•		•		•	•		•		•						•	
Four-Way Bargello		•		•	•		•		•	•		•		•			•			•	
Stephens Stitch		•		•	•		•		•					•						•	

This stitch can be worked over any number of mesh, up to six.

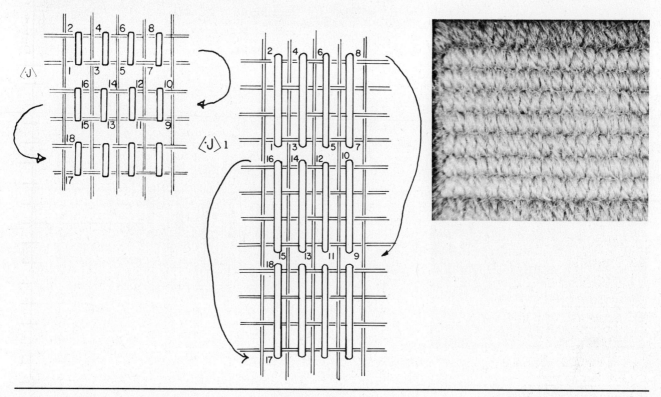

Straight stitch

I've used this term to indicate any stitch that is taken by placing thread or yarn between point A and point B. It may take several stitches, laid side by side, to fill the area (actually Satin Stitch) (see Figure 3-29a and figure b below); or it may take several stitches in different directions to create the desired effect (figure a below).

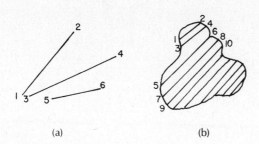

(a)   (b)

Interlocking straight gobelin

This Gobelin Stitch may be worked over two to five mesh. Thicken your yarn if your stitch is over two mesh tall. It is particularly good for shading.

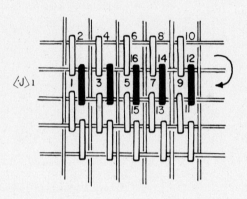

Brick

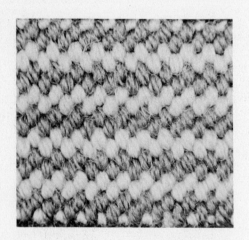

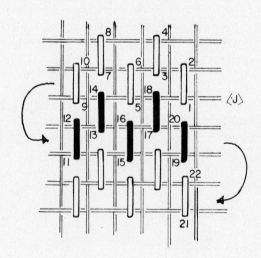

This stitch may be worked over four or six mesh with an even step (see page 185).

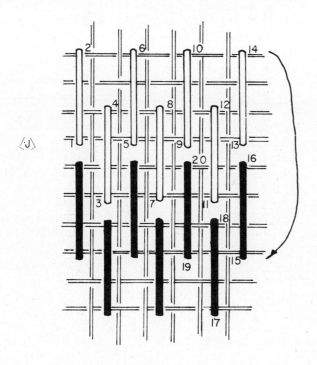

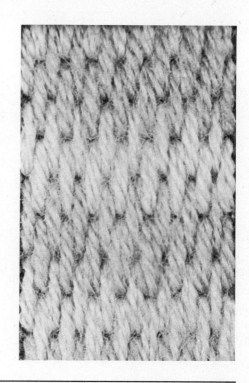

Double brick

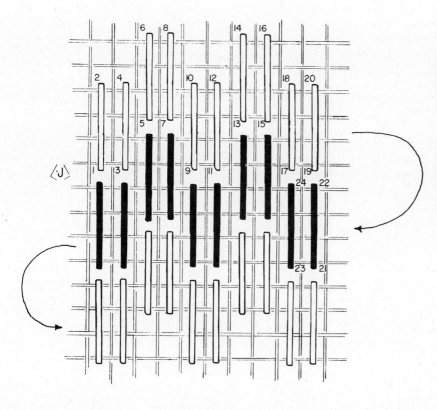

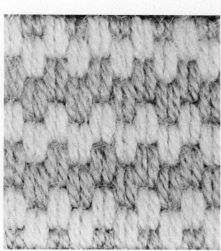

Horizontal brick

This stitch can be worked over two or four mesh.

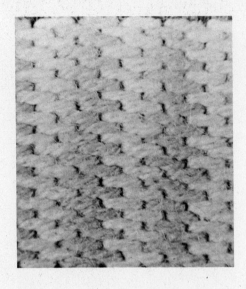

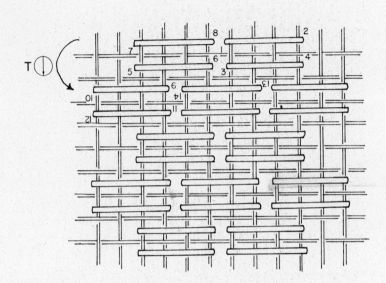

Parisian

Parisian is a combination of long and short stitches (over two and four mesh). The tall stitches are over the short stitches.

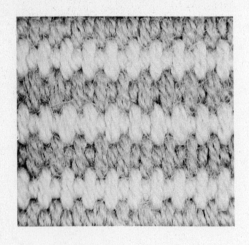

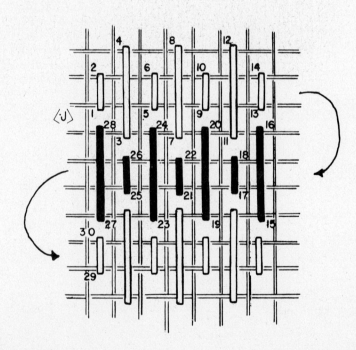

Plate 1.
Flower Purse.
Designed and stitched by the author.
(Moats)

Plate 2.
Wallet and Credit Card Case.
Designed and stitched by the author.
(Hagerty)

Plate 3. Cosmetic Case. Designed by Cindy Pendleton; stitched by the author. *(Moats)*

Plate 4. Pussy Willows. Designed by Cindy Pendleton; stitched by Carole Key. *(Moats)*

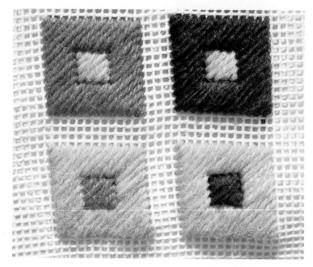

Plate 7

Plate 8

Plate 5 *(above).* Notice how colors change when surrounded by different colors. The blue-green center seems more blue with the purple around it, and more green with the green around it. Color relates to its environment. *(Moats)*

Plate 6. The lone square on the left seems orange when viewed alone; so does the one on the right. Yet, when compared with true orange in the center, they seem yellower and redder, respectively. *(Moats)*

Plate 7. The same colors when used in different amounts (but still with the same colors) appear different. The yellow seems more vivid and intense in small amounts and against darker colors. *(Moats)*

Plate 8. Three color values of green—light, medium, dark. *(Moats)*

Plate 9. Color Wheel. *(Long)*

Plate 10. Rainbow Plaid Pillow.
Designed by Chottie Alderson;
stitched by Betty Christensen. *(Moats)*

Plate 11. Plaid Floor Pillow.
Designed by the author; stitched by John J. Christensen. *(Moats)*

Plate 12. Sampler Pillow.
Designed and stitched by the author. *(Moats)*

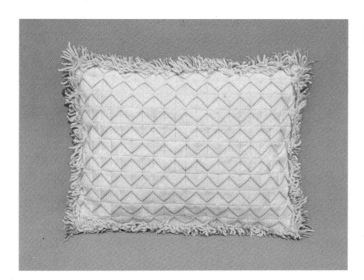

Plate 13. Reversed Giant Cashmere Pillow. Designed and stitched by Kathy Smith. *(Moats)*

Plate 14. Striped Sampler Pillow. Designed and stitched by Carole Key. *(Moats)*

Plate 16 *(below)*. Four-Way Bargello Pillow. Designed by the author; stitched by Carole Key. *(Moats)*

Plate 15. Mushroom Pillow. Designed by Cindy Pendleton; stitched by the author. *(Moats)*

Plate 17.
Farm.
Designed by Cindy Pendleton;
stitched by the author.
(Moats)

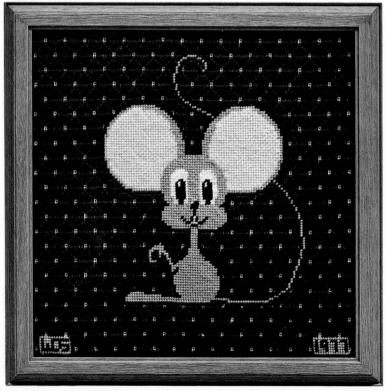

Plate 18.
Mouse.
Designed and stitched
by Wayne Stephens.
(Moats)

Plate 19.
Painting by Luciano Ippolito.
(Moats)

Plate 20.
Needlepoint from painting by Luciano Ippolito;
stitched by the author.
(Moats)

Plate 21

Plate 22

Plate 23

Plate 21. J-O-Y Banner. Designed and stitched by Needleworks, Ltd. *(Hagerty)*

Plate 22. Panda Christmas Ornaments. Designed and stitched by Needleworks, Ltd. *(Hagerty)*

Plate 23. Soldier and Drum Christmas Ornament. Designed and stitched by Needleworks, Ltd. *(Hagerty)*

Plate 24. Christmas Ornaments. Designed and stitched by Needleworks, Ltd. *(Hagerty)*

Plate 25 *(below).* Christmas Stocking. Designed and stitched by the author. *(Hagerty)*

Plate 24

Plate 26

Plate 27

Plate 28

Plate 26.
Tote Bag (Jo's Junk).
Designed and stitched by the author.
(Moats)

Plate 27.
Tote Bag (other side).
Designed by Cindy Pendleton;
stitched by the author.
(Moats)

Plate 28.
Man's Box Top.
Designed by Ed Sibbett, Jr.;
stitched by Linda Wilson.
(Moats)

ORBIS TERRÆ COMPENDIOSA DESCRIPTIO

Plate 29 *(above)*.
World Map.
Designed and stitched by Kay Kendall.
(Moats)

Plate 30 *(left)*.
Eyeglass Case with Initials.
Initials by Doris Drake;
designed and stitched by the author.
(Hagerty)

Plate 31 *(right)*.
Tie.
Designed by the author;
stitched by John J. Christensen.
(Moats)

Plate 32.
Mississippi River Boat Gambler Vest.
Designed by Luciano Ippolito;
stitched by the author.
(Moats)

Plate 33.
U.S. Postage Stamp.
Stitched by the author.
(Moats)

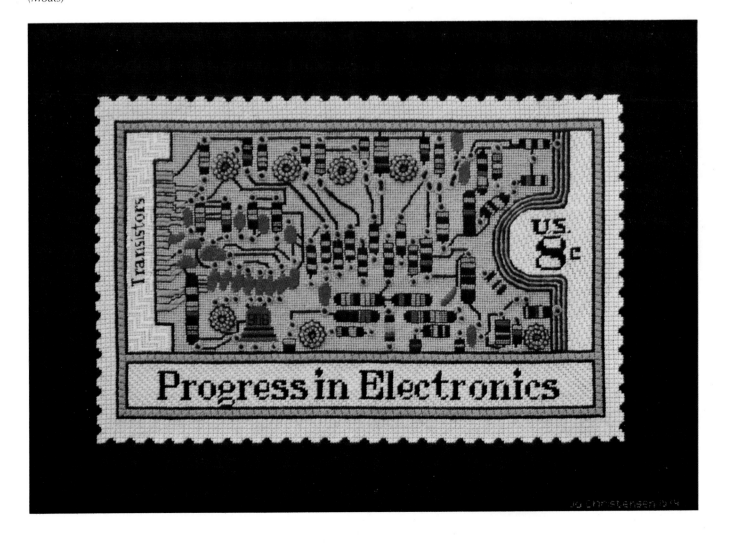

Plate 34.
Ukranian Wedding Picture.
Designed by Orest S. Poliszczuk;
stitched by the author.
(Hagerty)

Plate 35.
Egyptian Scarab and Sun.
Designed and stitched by Pat Biesiot.
(Moats)

Plate 36.
Mushrooms.
Designed and stitched
by Ruth Ippolito. *(Moats)*

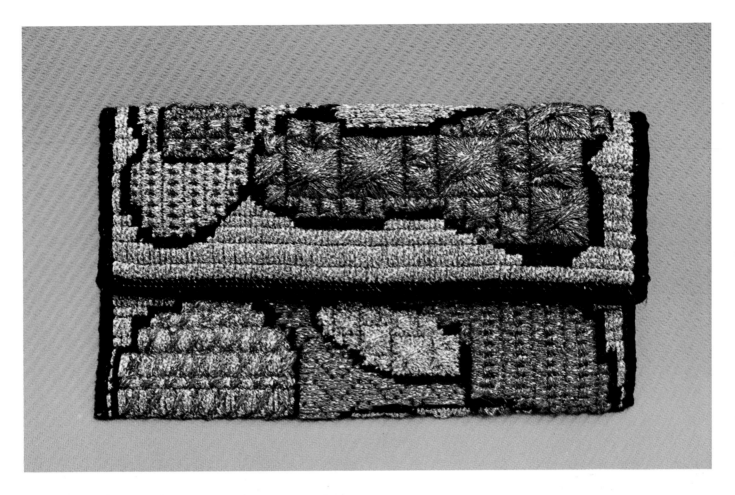

Plate 37 (above).
Non-Objective Metallic Evening Purse.
Designed by Carole Key and the author;
stitched by Carole Key. (Moats)

Plate 38 (left).
Footstool. Designed by Cindy Pendleton;
stitched by Mickey McKitrick. (Moats)

Plate 39 (below).
Plastic Key Chain.
Designed and stitched by Jackie Beaty.
(Hagerty)

Plate 40 (right).
Wooden Purse.
Designed and stitched by the author.
(Hagerty)

Plate 41 (below).
Place Mat and Coaster.
Designed and stitched by Wayne Stephens.
(Moats)

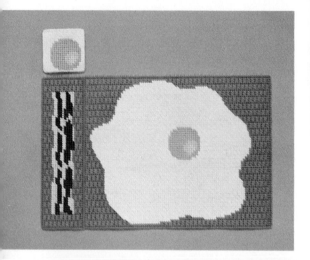

Plate 42 (below).
Tiger. Designed by Cindy Pendleton;
stitched by Carole Key.
(Hagerty)

Plate 43. Belt.
Designed and stitched by the author.
(Hagerty)

Plate 44. Checkbook Cover.
Adapted from designs by Doris Drake;
stitched by the author. *(Moats)*

Plate 45. Rose Brooch.
Designed and stitched by Nyla Christensen.
(Moats)

Plate 46. Bird Brooch.
Designed and stitched by Nyla Christensen.
(Moats)

Plate 47. Bargello Credit Card Case.
Designed and stitched by the author.
(Moats)

Plate 43

Plate 44

Plate 45

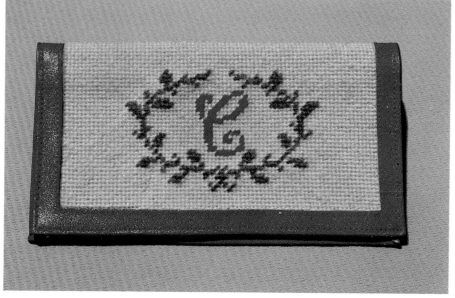

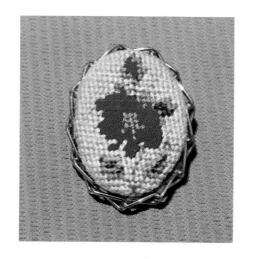

Plate 46

Plate 47

Plate 48. Value scales.

The first vertical scale on the left contains the familiar gradation of grays ranging from white to black in nine steps. The second column contains seven different *values* of one red hue. These red squares are placed alongside their matching values in the gray scale. The scales of the yellow and blue hues are arranged in exactly the same manner. Squint your eyes and move them horizontally across any level in this group of scales. You will see that the four squares of gray, red, yellow, and blue are *exactly the same in value*. The changes you see within each vertical scale are due to differences in *value*. The same hue simply becomes darker or lighter—it does not become a different hue, and it does not change its position on the color wheel. If this diagram were photographed in black and white, the red, yellow, and blue scales would all look exactly like the black-and-white scale, because the *value changes* in the *colored* scales are exactly similar to those in the black-and-white scale. *(Courtesy of Famous Artists School, Westport, Connecticut)*

This may be worked small (2:2:4:4:2:2:4:4, etc.) as in the photograph or large (4:4:6:6:4:4:6:6, etc.).

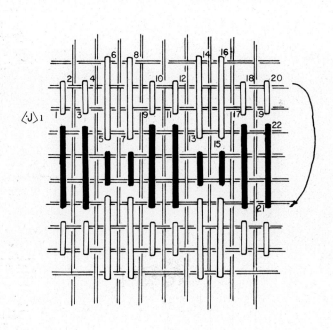

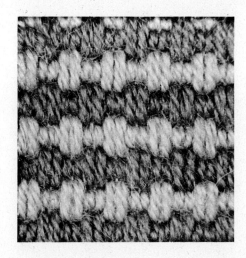

The diamonds share the short stitch.

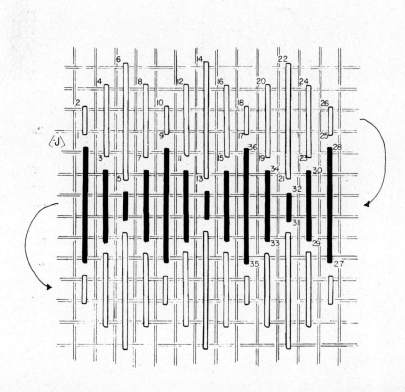

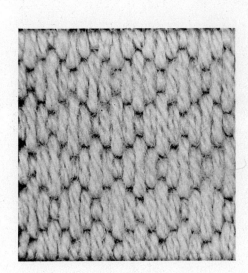

Hungarian

This vertical stitch establishes a diamond pattern. It is good in two colors, although it is stunning in one color. It is a set of three stitches—2:4:2. Skip a space. Repeat 2:4:2. Skip a space under the long stitch. Continue the pattern—2:4:2, then skip, then 2:4:2, and so on.

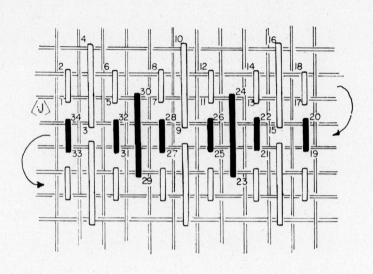

Hungarian ground

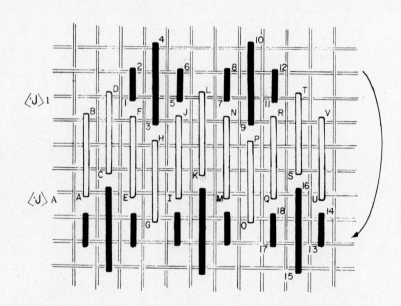

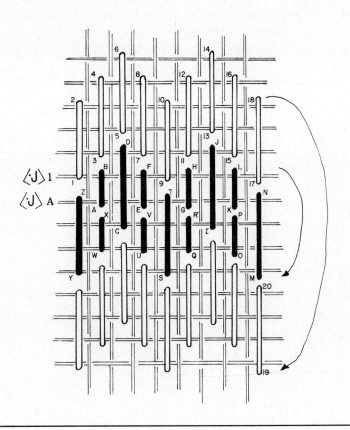

This stitch is a larger version of the Hungarian Stitch.

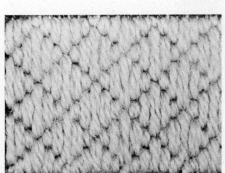

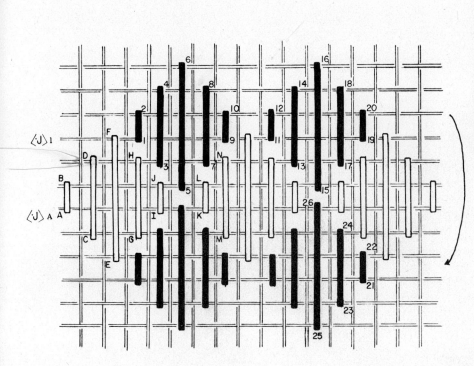

Tied pavillion

The long stitches need to be pulled slightly tighter than the short ones. The tie is over two mesh. Back-stitch in between the diamonds to cover the canvas if necessary.

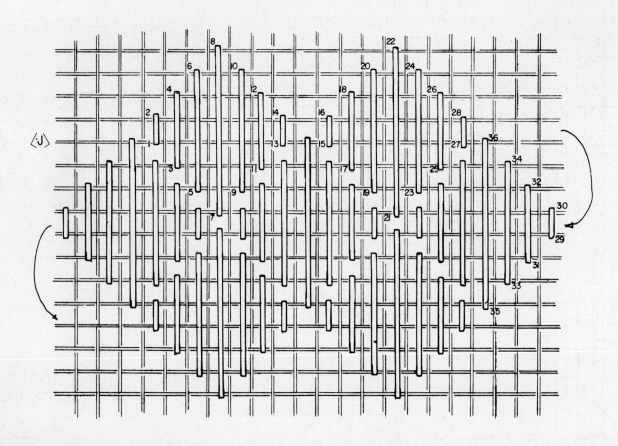

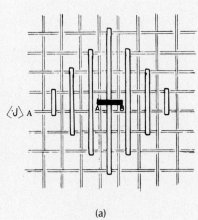

(a)

(b)

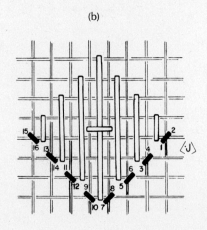

Short:long:short. The short stitch goes over the long. The smallest version is 2:6:2; the largest is 3:9:3.

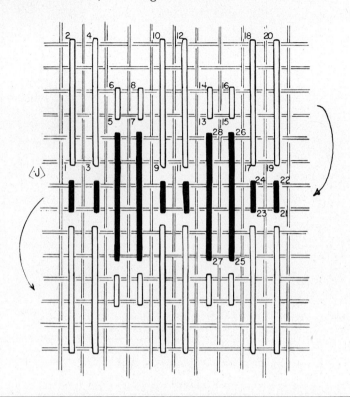

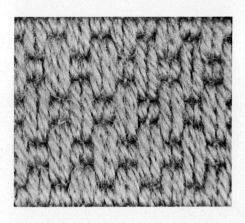

Horizontal old Florentine

When all the short stitches are worked in a second color, the stitch resembles a woven basket.

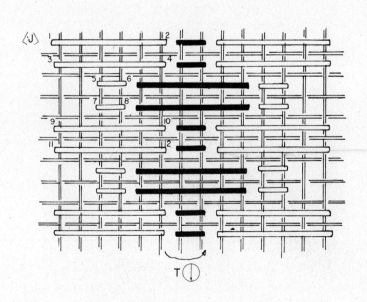

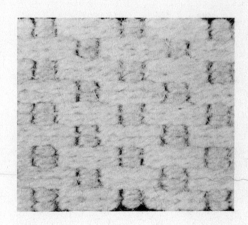

Beaty

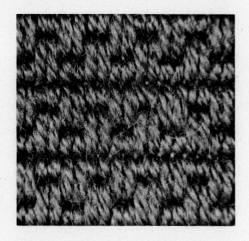

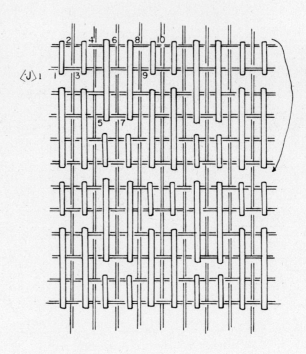

Wicker

As the name suggests, this two-color stitch resembles wicker. It will look different if you use three colors. Make other color variations by stitching in diagonal stripes and horizontal stripes of color.

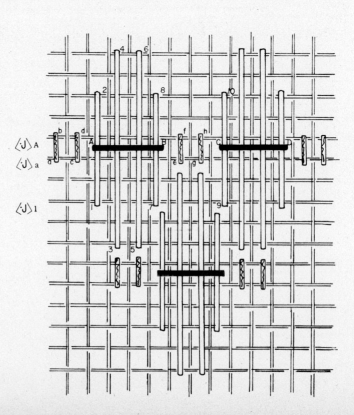

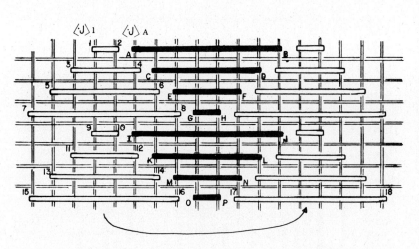

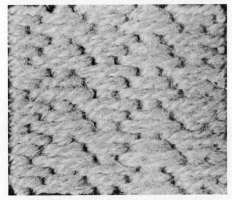

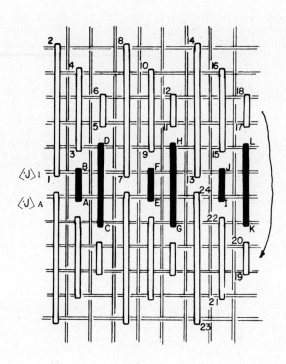

181

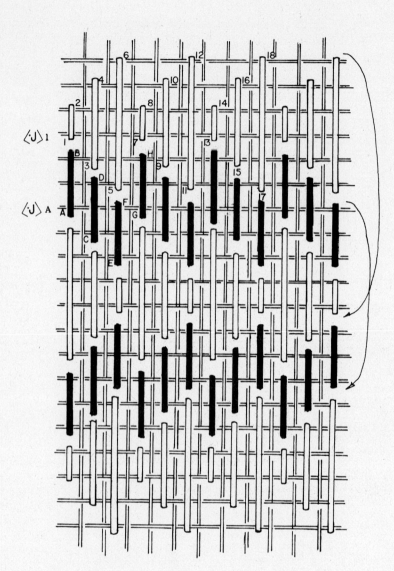

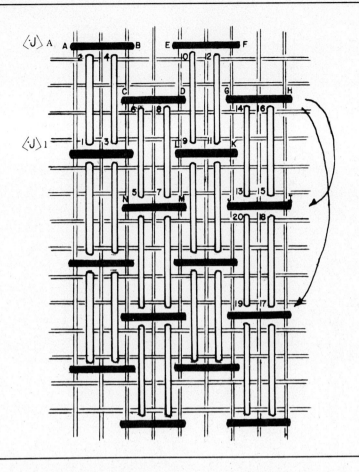

Pavillion boxes

Thin yarn for the diagonal stripes.

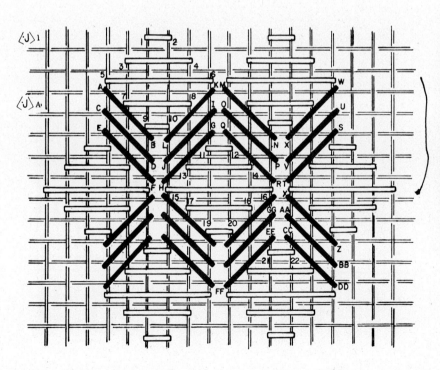

Triangle

It does not matter whether you cross the right arm of a Cross-Stitch over the left, or the left over the right—as long as you are consistent. Keep this in mind when putting in the crosses.

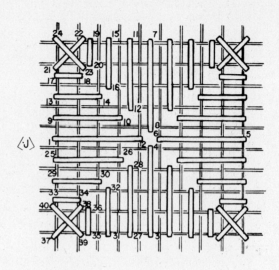

F-106

Various color combinations make this stitch look different.

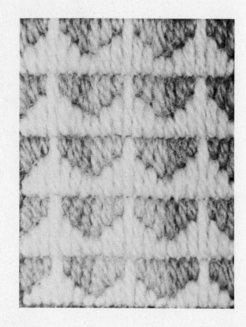

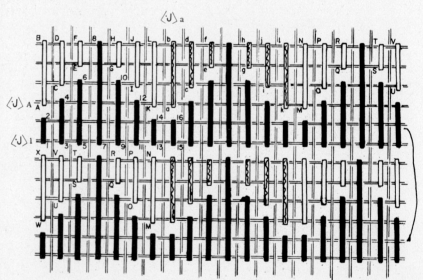

Bargello is straight stitches worked in a geometric pattern. These stitches can vary in size from two mesh tall to six mesh tall. When stitches are placed next to each other in a zig-zag line, the distance between the top of one stitch and the top of the next one is called a step. It is referred to by number—for example, "4:2." The "4" indicates how many mesh tall the stitch is; the "2" tells us how many mesh are in the step. A "4:2" stitch is the most common in Bargello. The smaller the step number is, the more gradual the incline (Figure a). The larger the step number is, the steeper the incline (Figure c).

A line pattern is a zig-zag line of stitches. Both the stitch size and the step number may vary within one line.

To produce arcs or curves, place more than one stitch on the same step (4:0). The more stitches there are on one step, the broader the curve (Figure d). These arcs or curves may be combined with a zig-zag line for a more interesting pattern.

A framework pattern can be made by turning a line pattern upside down (see page 187). Fill the center in with a secondary pattern of your choice.

Bargello has limitless variations, both in stitch and in color. There is much more to learn about Bargello and many other kinds of patterns.

NOTE: In working a whole piece in Bargello, start the pattern in the middle of the canvas to achieve balance.

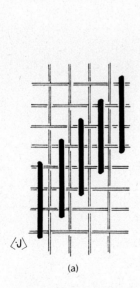

(a)

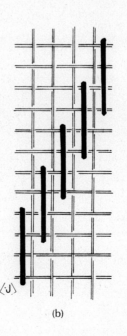

(b)

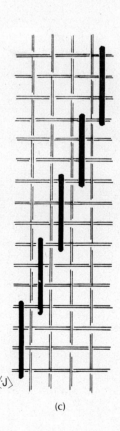

(c)

Bargello line pattern

This is an example only. Both stitch size and step number may vary within one line.

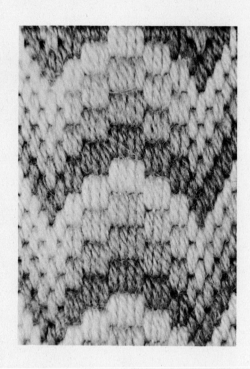

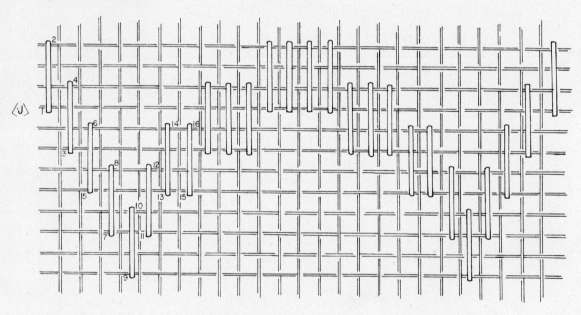

Try working the framework in the darkest color and shading the center. This is an example only.

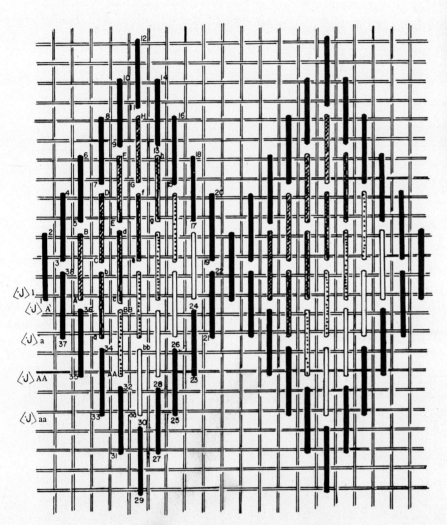

Four-way bargello

Draw lines from the center to each of the four corners. It is on these lines that you change from vertical to horizontal stitches. See page 96 for alternate stitching directions.

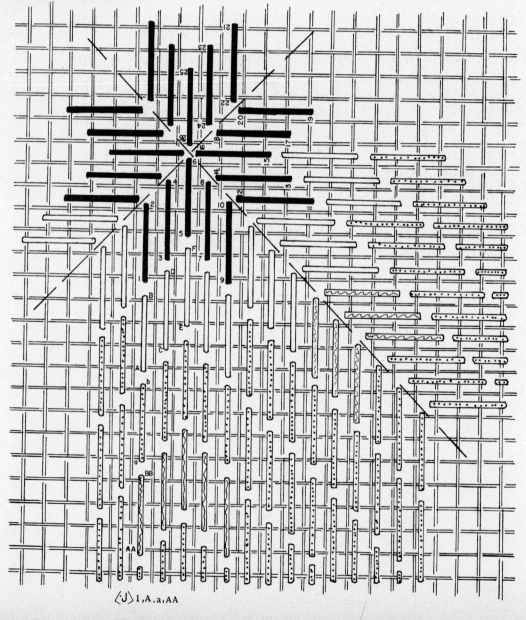

There are times when leaving the canvas blank adds to the design. This is one of them. If you do want to cover the canvas completely, stitch an Upright Cross in the bare spot.

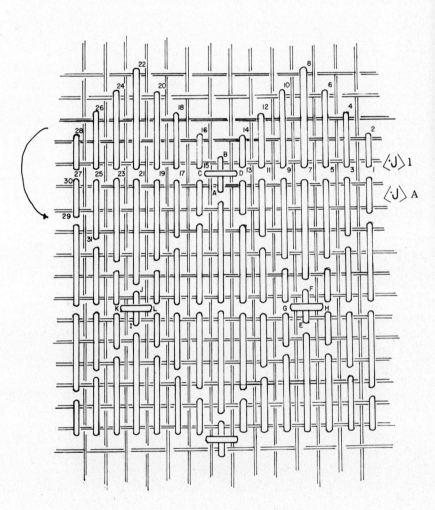

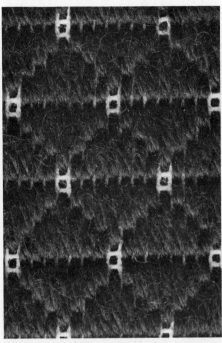

11 Diagonal stitches

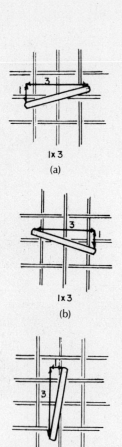

1x3
(a)

1x3
(b)

3x1
(c)

Diagonal Stitches cover the canvas by crossing junctions of mesh, rather than going between them. In referring to these slanted stitches, I have designated the angle or slant they take by two numbers. The first number refers to the number of mesh that you go up or down. The second number refers to the number of mesh that you go over. For example, a 1 × 1 stitch is a Tent Stitch; a 1 × 3 stitch is shown in Figures a and b. 3 × 1 and 3 × 3 stitches are also shown in Figures c, d, and e. For those stitches where both numbers are the same, you may count, diagonally, the junctions of mesh, instead of counting up three and over three. Whether you go up or down (for the first number) is shown in the sketch that accompanies each stitch.

Mono or Penelope 10 canvas usually accepts one strand of tapestry or Persian yarn for Diagonal Stitches.

Tent Stitches are Basketweave, Continental, and Half Cross.

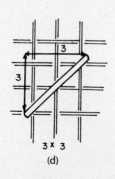

3 × 3
(d)

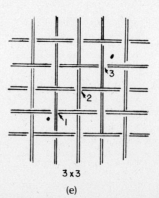

3 x 3
(e)

DIAGONAL STITCHES	Border	Good Backing	Poor Backing	Background	Design	Accent	Fast	Slow	Geometric Pattern	Shading	Yarn Hog	Snags	Snag-Proof	Little Texture	Medium Texture	High Relief	Flower Stitch	Weak Pattern	Medium Pattern	Strong Pattern	Distorts Canvas
Basketweave		•		•	•								•	•				•			
Continental		•			•					•			•	•				•			•
Chottie's Plaid	•	•		•	•				•				•	•						•	
Rainbow Plaid	•	•		•	•								•	•						•	
Half-Cross			•										•	•				•			•
Irregular Continental		•		•	•					•		•		•					•		
Petit Point		•		•	•	•		•		•			•	•				•			•
Rep		•		•	•	•		•		•			•	•				•			•
Slanted Gobelin		•		•	•		•		•					•						•	
2 × 2 Slanted Gobelin	•	•		•	•		•		•					•						•	
5 × 2 Slanted Gobelin				•	•		•		•					•						•	
Interlocking Gobelin		•		•	•			•		•	•			•				•			
Oblique Slav			•	•	•		•			•		•		•						•	
Encroaching Oblique				•	•					•		•		•						•	
Kalem		•		•	•						•			•						•	
Lazy Kalem		•		•	•							•	•	•				•			
Stem	•	•		•	•									•					•		
Diagonal Stem	•	•		•	•									•					•		
Byzantine #1		•		•	•		•			•		•		•						•	•
Byzantine #2		•		•	•		•			•		•		•						•	•
Irregular Byzantine		•		•	•		•					•		•						•	•
Jacquard		•		•	•									•						•	•
Irregular Jacquard		•		•	•		•					•		•						•	•
Diagonal Hungarian Ground		•		•	•		•							•						•	•
Staircase		•		•	•									•						•	•
Milanese		•		•	•	•						•			•					•	•
Oriental		•		•	•	•						•		•						•	•

191

Basketweave

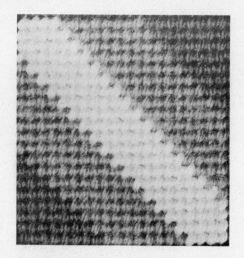

Basketweave is one of the most used and misused stitches in needlepoint. It is an excellent stitch to know and use. A durable backing, resembling a woven pattern, is created. This makes it a "must" for chairs, footstools, and other items that will receive lots of wear.

The finished piece is not distorted, but still needs blocking (see page 294). Basketweave allows a worked canvas to give a lot, yet still be strong. It can be worked without turning the canvas. Because it lacks maneuverability, it is not a good stitch for designing. (Use Continental for designing in very small areas if you want a Tent Stitch.)

Study the figure. Note that, basically, the stitch fills the canvas in diagonal rows, starting at the upper right corner.

As you work you will notice that a pattern is developing. In making an up row, the needle always goes straight across under two mesh. In making a down row, the needle always goes straight down under two mesh. Notice that the first of these two mesh is covered by a stitch in the preceding row. It is a very common error to go across or under three mesh by not counting the covered one.

At the end of each row there is what many students refer to as a turn stitch. Actually it is the first stitch of a new row. If it helps you to consider it a turn stitch, then do so. At the end of the up row this is a horizontal Continental Stitch and at the end of the down row this is a vertical Continental Stitch. The common error here is to leave the turn stitch out. Often students get carried away and make two turn stitches. If you have made an error somewhere, check to see if this is it.

When your yarn runs out and you must start another one, be sure to start *exactly* where you left off. If you do not, a line will show on the right side. For example, if your yarn runs out at the end of an up row, do not start the new yarn at the bottom of that up row you just finished, thus starting another up row. Instead you should be at the top of that last up row, ready to begin a down row. Most people tend to put their work away for the day when they have finished working the yarn on the needle. It might help you not to do this when working Basketweave. Leave the needle threaded with half a yarn and stitck it into the canvas in position ready to take the next stitch. This way you will not lose your place.

When working Basketweave on Regular Mono canvas, note that at the intersections of mesh in a horizontal row, the vertical mesh alternate between being on top of and underneath the horizontal mesh. However, on the diagonal, the vertical mesh are always on top of or underneath the horizontal mesh.

If you will take care always to cover the vertical mesh inter-

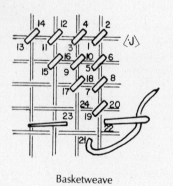

Basketweave

sections with a down row and to cover the horizontal mesh intersections with an up row, you will produce a stitch that is very even in appearance on the right side. This will also help you to keep track of up rows and down rows (see the preceding discussion).

When you come to the end of each strand of yarn, weave it under the yarns on the back side of the canvas for about an inch. Follow the weave that the stitch makes. Clip it closely to keep the back neat. If you work the beginning and ending tails under any other way, a ridge will form that will show on the right side.

Basketweave is not frightfully complicated. It may take some study on your part, but once you get the hang of the stitch you will enjoy working it. It has a certain rhythm that develops easily. You can achieve a perfection with this stitch that is unique. Use it no matter how small the area. (When the area is absolutely too small and when outlining, use the Continental Stitch.)

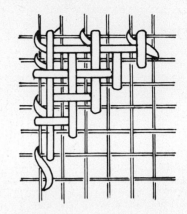

Basketweave: Wrong side—last row is *down* row (top); last row is *up* row (bottom)

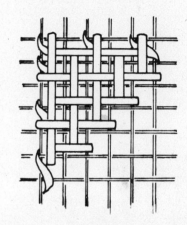

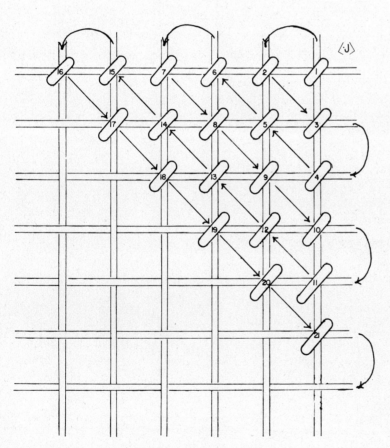

Basketweave: Sequence of stitches

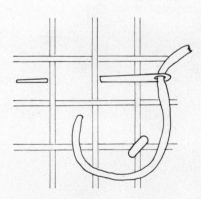

Basketweave: Right—up row covering a horizontal mesh intersection

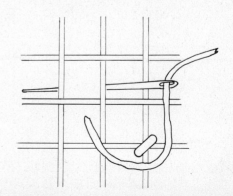

Basketweave: Wrong—up row covering a vertical mesh intersection

Continental

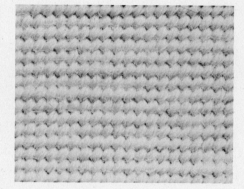

The Continental Stitch has the next-best backing after Basketweave, and it is the next most distinct stitch of the Tent Stitches. Its main drawback is that it pulls the canvas badly out of shape.

You really should use Basketweave wherever you can. But Continental will get the very small areas that Basketweave cannot.

If you insist on using Continental instead of Basketweave, you should try to make the stitches as even and uniform as possible. You may work Continental either horizontally or vertically. Choose the direction that best fills the area you have. Work the stitch in that direction for the whole space. Combinations of horizontally and vertically worked Continental will produce lines on the right side. Always work this stitch from right to left. If you are filling in a large space, do not run the canvas upside down for the second row; cut the yarn and begin the second row below the first on the right. The drawing does not show this because I do not recommend that you use this stitch in a large enough area to matter.

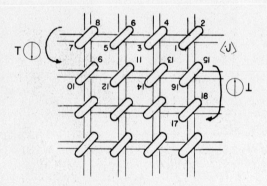

Continental: Horizontal—work left to right

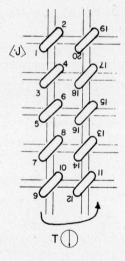

Continental: Vertical—work down

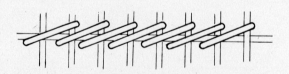

Continental: Reverse side

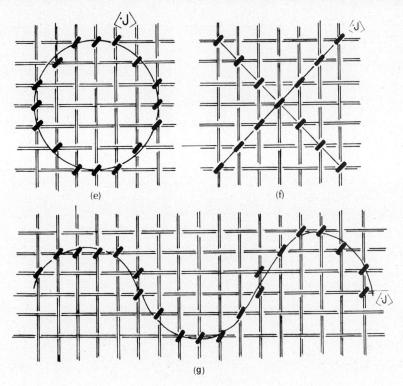

(e)

(f)

(g)

Continental: Outlining

Chottie's plaid stitch

A plaid is made up of a repeat count called a *sett*, so once you have determined your count and colors for a particular plaid, stick with it to make the plaid. If you don't repeat, you don't plaid.

IMPORTANT: Because the stitches are worked lying in the nontraditional slant, that is, lower right to upper left, the A-B corner directions are important to follow. When you have finished working the ''Chottie's Plaid,'' you turn the A-B corners to the top again and the stitches will lie in the traditional slant, that is, lower left to upper right.

If you are working the Chottie's Plaid stitch correctly, your piece will be reversible, that is, it will look the same on both sides—except where you tied on and off. If you really want it to be reversible (for instance, on a handbag flap or a coaster, etc.) tie on and off in the margins. If you don't care and are only interested in the plaid on the surface, tie on and off wherever you please on the back.

Following [Figures 4-33 a and b], work 10 rows of color A, then work 12 rows of color B, then 4 rows of color C, and 3 rows of color D staying in the same sequence of working every other stitch on alternate rows. Repeat this 10-12-4-3 count to cover the area you wish to be plaid. [Figure 4-33a] shows the method of working the stitch; [Figure 4-33b] shows 4 rows of Foundation worked.

To lay foundation

195

NOTE: Diagonal rows of worked stitches are formed, and diagonal rows of unworked stitches are also formed.

FOUNDATION

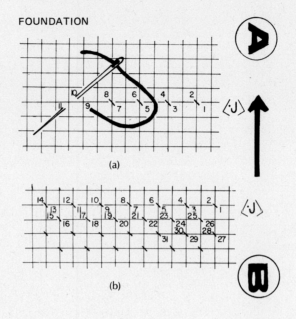

(a)

(b)

To cross hatch

NOTICE: "Cross Hatching" is filling in the unworked stitches that you skipped when laying the foundation.

Following the same "A and B corners" directions, work with [Figures 4-33 c and d]. Work 10 rows of color A, 12 rows of color B, 4 rows of color C, and 3 rows of color D. Continue in this count until you have finished the area. [Figure 4-33c] shows the method of working the stitch; [Figure 4-33d] shows 3 rows worked.

CROSS HATCH

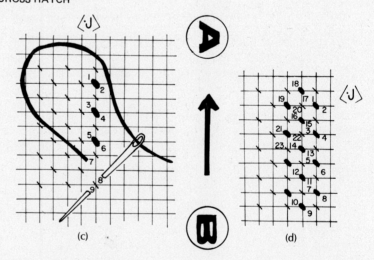

(c)

(d)

Be sure to check the back of your work occasionally as you work. It should look like the front except on the very edge or where you tied on or off. It's easy to slip into working a regular Continental (Tent) stitch but, if you do, you have lost the whole ball game.

196

Determine top left and right corners of your canvas. Mark top left corner of canvas with ''A'' and top right corner with ''B.'' Now note corners of this diagram page. Lay Figure 4–33 on your canvas, matching ''A'' to ''A'' and ''B'' to ''B.'' Turn canvas and diagram page (with ''A'' and ''B'' corners still matching) so that the arrow below is pointing up. Begin working.

In other words, on top of canvas, write A and B in the corners. Turn 90° to the right so A and B are on the right side. Stitch according to the diagram, and when you're through, turn canvas 90° to the left so A and B are again at the top. Then your stitches will slant in the correct direction for a Tent Stitch.

Rainbow plaid

This creates a beautiful pattern but you must follow the colors listed below—1 row of each color for foundation and the same for Cross Hatch. These colors must run in the sequence in which they are listed. (These are Paternayan Persian color numbers. You do not have to use Paternayan Persian. You can use any brand of yarn, but you must use the colors of another brand that are similar to the ones listed or it won't come out right.) This is a large pattern and requires a good-sized area to show it off.

Yellow-450	Violet-640
456	650
468	660
Yellow-Orange-Y40	Blue-Violet-611
Y42	621
Y44	631
Orange-960	Blue-731
965	741
975	743
Red-Orange-958	Blue-Green-718
968	738
978	748
Red-R10	Green-G54
R60	G64
R70	G74
Red-Violet-639	Yellow-Green-545
645	550
659	580

Repeat the entire sequence from Yellow through Yellow-Green as often as you wish.

Cross Hatch in the same count and color sequence.

Half-cross

The Half-Cross Stitch has the poorest backing of the Tent Stitches, and the stitch is not distinct. I do not allow my students to use this stitch, and I strongly suggest that you replace it with Basketweave and Continental.

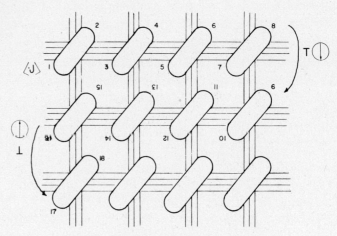

Half Cross: Horizontal

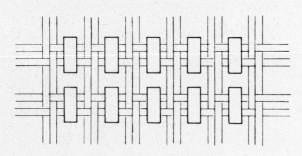

Half Cross: Reverse side

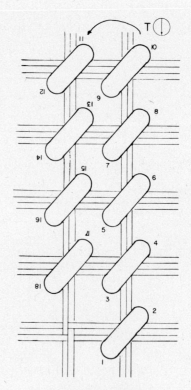

Half Cross: Vertical

This stitch is excellent for shading. In working it, be sure to keep it a 1 × 1, 2 × 2, 3 × 3, 4 × 4, or 5 × 5 stitch. Count the mesh junctions diagonally (page 190). The rows will be irregular. The drawing is an example only. Do your own. Take a Bargello tuck when you bury the tails (page 26).

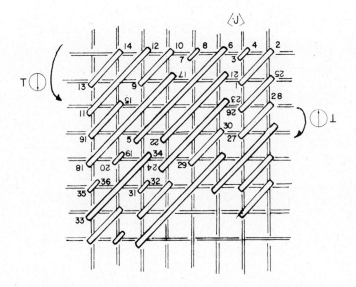

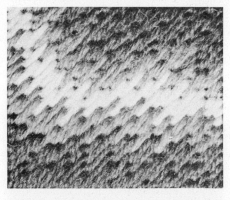

Petit point

Split the vertical mesh of Penelope canvas and work Continental or Basketweave. Thin your yarn. This is difficult to get smooth and even on Penelope canvas. Use it only if one or two small areas of your design demand Petit Point. For a whole Petit Point picture, use Petit Point canvas in 16 to 40 mesh per inch. Most of the stitches in this book can be worked in Petit Point, too.

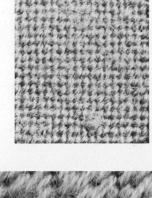

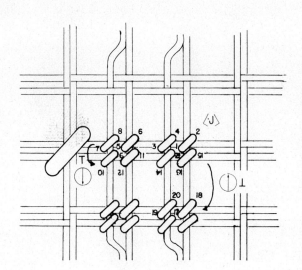

Rep

This makes a nice, small vertical stripe. In one color this is a good stitch. Work it vertically in two colors and make a pin-stripe fabric. Thin your yarn.

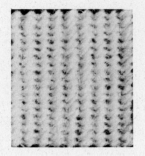

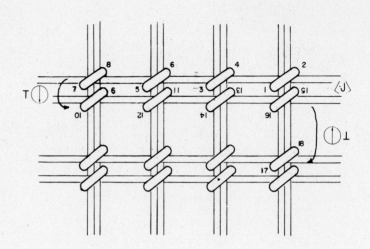

Slanted gobelin

This stitch is versatile, for it can be worked between two and six mesh tall and one or two mesh wide. When the stitch is taller than two mesh, you will probably need to thicken your yarn.

Slanted Gobelin makes a horizontal row. It is good for dresser drawers or anything else in rows.

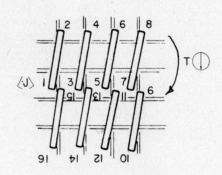

Slanted gobelin 2 × 2

This is the stitch that I used as a divider on my samplers.

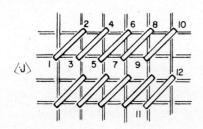

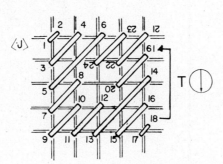

Slanted gobelin 5 × 2

Thicken your yarn.

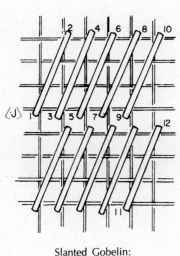

Slanted Gobelin:
4 × 2

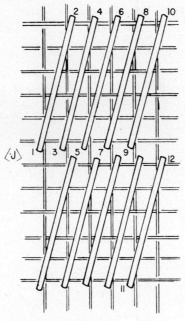

Slanted Gobelin:
5 × 2

Slanted Gobelin: (top to bottom)
2 × 2;
3 × 2;
4 × 2;
5 × 2

201

Interlocking gobelin

The second row's stitches rest beside the first row's stitches. It, too, can be worked two to five mesh tall and one to two wide.

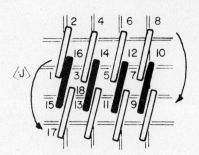

Oblique Slav

You will probably have to thicken your yarn for this stitch. There are two mesh between stitches.

Oblique Slav: Horizontal (upper right); Vertical (lower right and photograph)

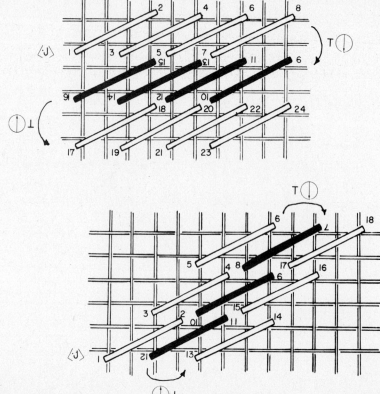

This stitch is Interlocking Gobelin turned on its side. Thicken your yarn.

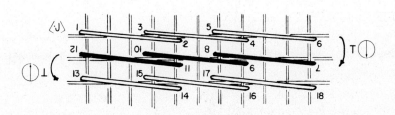

The Kalem Stitch looks like knitting. Be sure the tension is even.

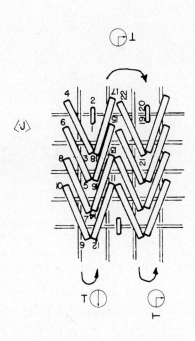

Lazy kalem

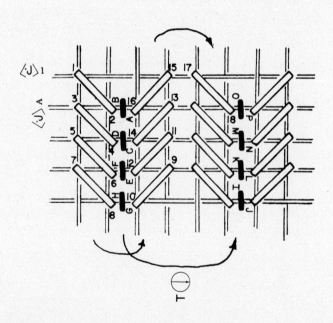

Stem

The Stem Stitch is usually best with two colors. Use a thinner yarn for the Back-Stitch. Complete one column of stitches at a time. Do a vertical Back-Stitch in a second color between the columns. This stitch makes good fences, columns, etc.

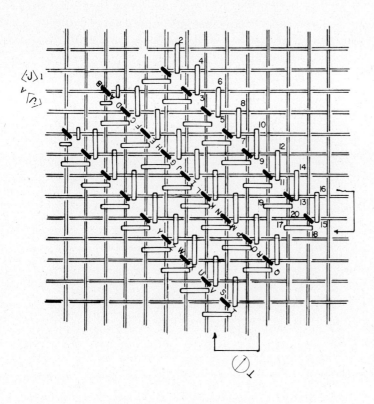

Byzantine #1

Byzantine makes good steps and fills in diagonally shaped areas well. Take a Bargello tuck as you bury the tails (page 26).

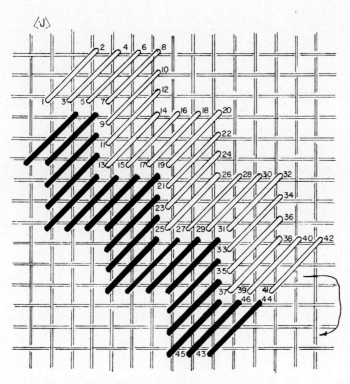

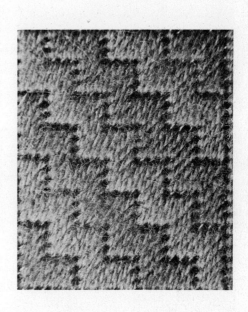

Byzantine #2

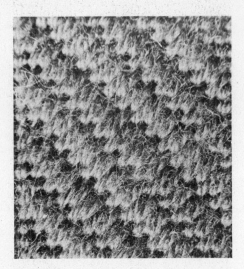

When filling in the canvas with a stitch in a diagonal row, work generally from upper right to lower left, as you do in Basketweave. This helps you to avoid snagging the yarn in the preceding row as you stitch.

Irregular Byzantine

Work rows of Byzantine 1 × 1, 2 × 2, 3 × 3, and 4 × 4 in order or mix them up. This stitch needs a very large area to establish the pattern. Take a Bargello tuck as you bury the tails (page 26).

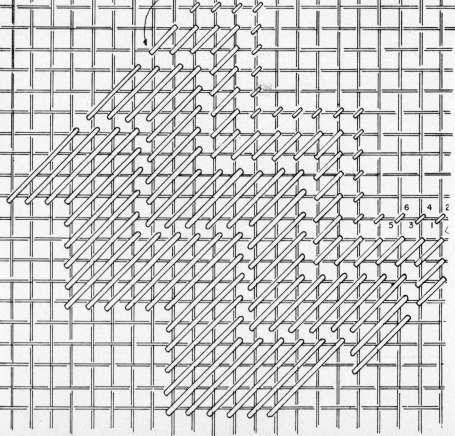

Jacquard is very much like the Byzantine Stitch with a Continental Stitch divider.

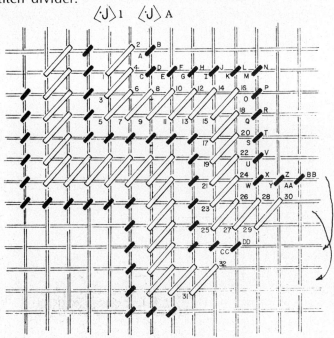

Do as many stitches as you want before turning the corner, but be consistent. Mix up the length of the stitches (2 × 2, 3 × 3, 4 × 4) or stitch them in order. A large area is necessary to establish the pattern. Take a Bargello tuck as you bury the tails (page 26).

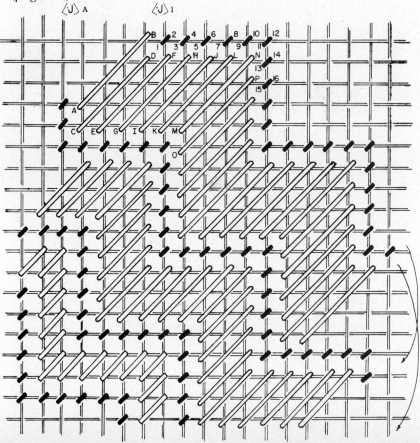

Diagonal Hungarian ground

Work this stitch in two colors, or work a very large, uninterrupted area in one color; otherwise, the pattern is lost.

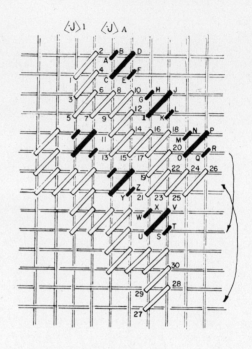

Staircase

This stitch, too, needs a large area to show off the pattern if it is worked in one color. It is also effective in two colors. This stitch is a variation of Diagonal Hungarian Ground.

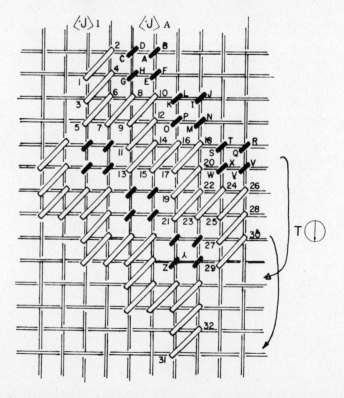

This is an especially pretty stitch, but it is difficult to work around lots of letters.

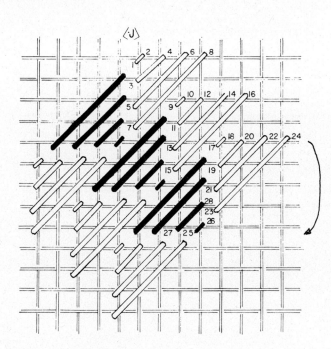

The Oriental Stitch is a good background in one color. It looks entirely different in two colors. Few stitches undergo such a change in appearance. Try it both ways.

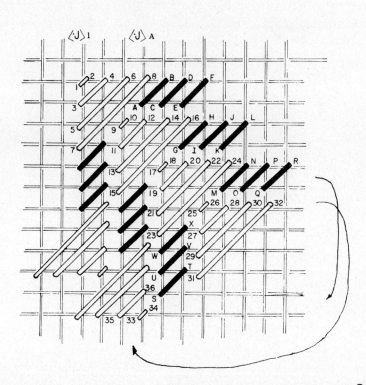

12
Box stitches

Box stitches are a series of diagonal stitches that form squares or boxes. The diagonal box stitches are simply boxes laid in a diagonal line, with the corners overlapping. (See the Diagonal Scotch Stitch.) Note how the short stitch is shared.

Most of these stitches make excellent borders. They lend themselves to beautiful geometric patterns in several colors. I have gone into only a few color variations, for there are whole books that discuss color variations of just a few stitches.

Box Stitches can be worked on Penelope 10 or Mono 10 with one strand of tapestry or Persian yarn.

Box Stitches almost always distort the canvas. However, reversing the boxes corrects this problem. Don't let a mistake slide—an error will stick out like a sore thumb because the pattern is more precise than in other stitches. Double-check your work every few rows.

All Box Stitches can be used in designing and many are good for background. Almost all produce a geometric pattern, and all have good backing, which means your finished piece will wear well.

BOX STITCHES	Border	Good Backing	Poor Backing	Background	Design	Accent	Fast	Slow	Geometric Pattern	Shading	Yarn Hog	Snags	Snag-Proof	Little Texture	Medium Texture	High Relief	Flower Stitch	Weak Pattern	Medium Pattern	Strong Pattern	Distorts Canvas
Mosaic	●	●		●	●		●		●				●	●				●			●
Mosaic Checker	●	●		●	●		●		●				●	●				●			●
Reversed Mosaic	●	●		●	●		●		●				●	●				●			
Diagonal Mosaic		●		●	●		●		●	●			●	●				●			●
Mosaic Stripe		●		●	●				●				●	●						●	●
Cashmere	●	●		●	●		●		●				●	●				●			
Tied Cashmere	●	●			●	●		●	●				●		●					●	
Staggered Cashmere	●	●		●	●		●		●				●	●				●			
Reversed Giant Cashmere	●	●		●	●		●		●				●	●				●			
Framed Cashmere	●	●		●	●				●				●	●						●	
Framed Giant Cashmere	●	●		●	●		●		●				●	●				●			
Elongated Cashmere	●	●		●	●		●		●				●	●				●			
Horizontal Cashmere	●	●		●	●		●		●			●		●				●			
Diagonal Cashmere		●		●	●		●		●	●			●	●						●	
Scotch	●	●		●	●		●		●					●				●			
Giant Scotch	●	●		●	●		●		●			●		●				●			●
Divided Scotch	●	●		●	●				●			●		●						●	●
Scotch Checker	●	●		●	●		●		●					●						●	●
Framed Scotch	●	●		●	●		●		●					●						●	
Reversed Scotch	●	●		●	●		●		●					●				●			
Framed Reversed Scotch	●	●			●			●	●				●		●					●	
Diagonal Scotch		●		●	●		●							●				●			●
Moorish Stitch		●		●	●		●		●					●						●	●
Wide Moorish		●		●	●		●		●					●						●	●

211

Mosaic

Mosaic is the smallest of the Box Stitches. It is just three diagonal stitches: short, long, short. It makes a box two by two mesh. Mosaic is an excellent background or design stitch. This stitch is a good background to work behind Continental letters. It can be worked horizontally, vertically, or diagonally.

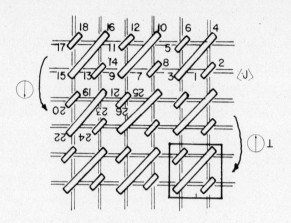

Mosaic: Horizontal

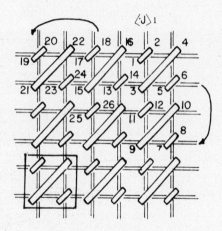

Mosaic: Diagonal

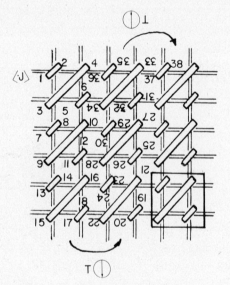

Mosaic: Vertical

Mosaic checker

Mosaic Checker must be worked in two colors. Do the Mosaic boxes in one color and fill in between them with Basketweave in another color. The Basketweave Stitches are lost in one color. This stitch wears well and creates a pretty pattern.

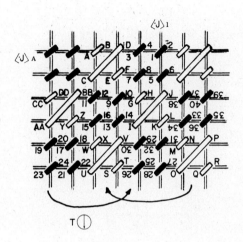

Reversed mosaic

This stitch is worked most easily by doing a diagonal row from upper left to lower right. Then turn the canvas 90° so that the upper right now becomes the upper left. Work the same type of diagonal row, filling in the blank spaces. I think this stitch looks best in one color.

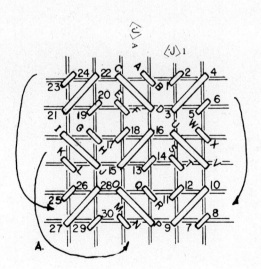

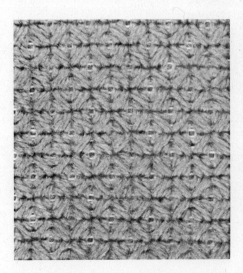

Diagonal mosaic

When Mosaic is worked diagonally, it becomes merely a line of short and long stitches. For this reason, you may use if for shading. Do this stitch in one or more colors.

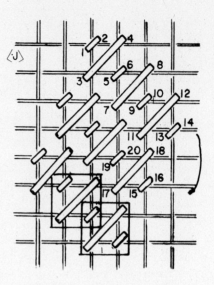

Mosaic stripe

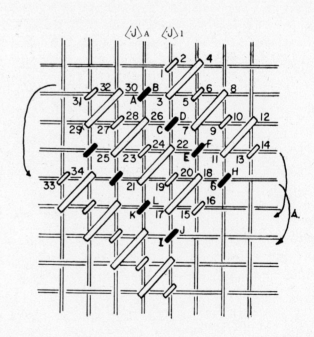

Cashmere is a rectangular Mosaic Stitch. It can be worked horizontally, vertically, or diagonally.

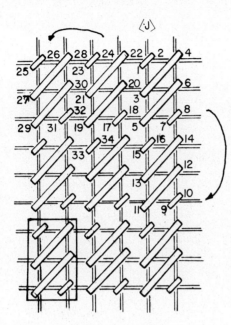

Cashmere: Diagonal

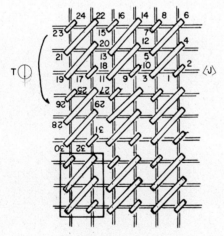

Cashmere: Horizontal

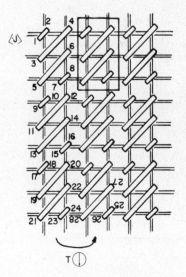

Cashmere: Vertical

215

Tied cashmere

Tie the two long stitches together. Use your thumbnail to move the yarns aside to see just where your needle must go. This tie creates a bump.

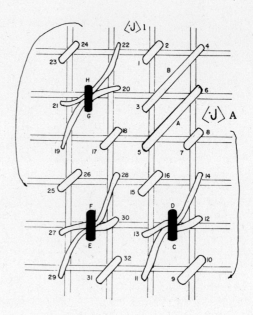

Staggered cashmere

This is just the same as Cashmere, except that the boxes are shifted one mesh on every other row.

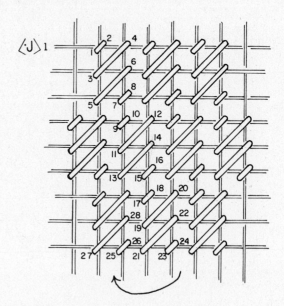

The Cashmere can be worked over any number of mesh, and as
long as you maintain a rectangle, you've got a Cashmere. Take
a Bargello tuck as you bury the tails (page 26).

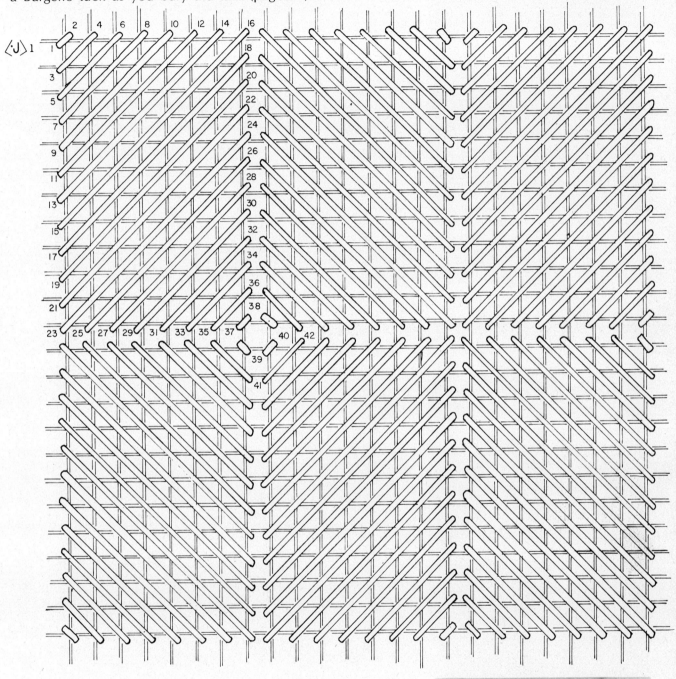

Framed cashmere

The Continental Stitch is used between the Cashmere boxes.

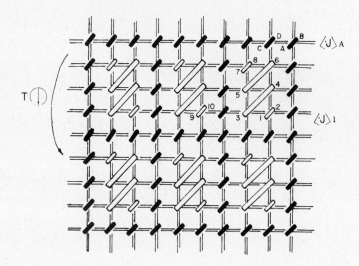

Framed giant cashmere

Take a Bargello tuck as you bury the tails (page 26).

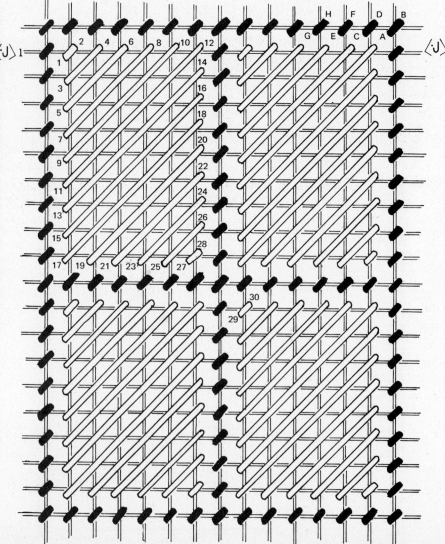

Elongated cashmere

Elongated Cashmere is just an extra-long Cashmere Box. In alternating rows, it reminds me of the outside of a barn. The number of long stitches may vary.

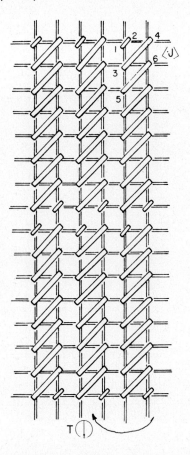

Horizontal cashmere

Turn Cashmere on its side and lengthen a little, but not as much as Elongated Cashmere. This makes nice bricks. Frame it with the Continental Stitch in white, and you have even more realistic bricks.

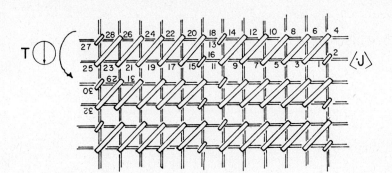

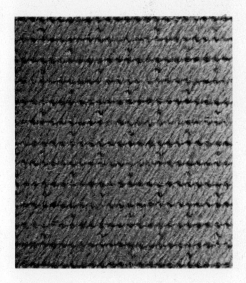

Diagonal cashmere

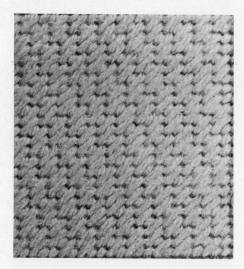

The second row of Diagonal Cashmere is a bit tricky to work. I try to remember that the first long stitch in the second row is diagonally below the last short stitch. After I have taken that stitch, I go back and pick up the first short stitch in the second row.

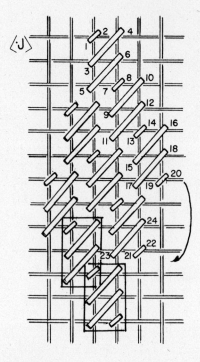

Scotch

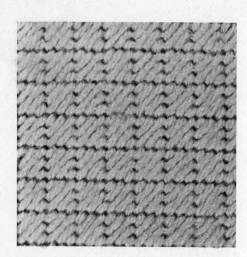

The Scotch Stitch is merely a large Mosaic Stitch. It has many lovely variations. This stitch can be worked three ways (see Mosaic and Cashmere Stitches).

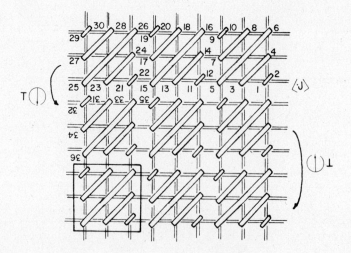

The Scotch Stitch can be worked in many sizes: five-stitch, seven-stitch, nine-stitch, and eleven-stitch. Keep in mind that the longer the stitches, the more likely they are to snag. Take a Bargello tuck as you bury the tails (page 26).

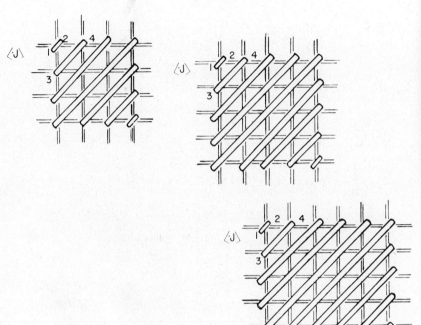

Divided scotch

I like this stitch in one color, although it may be worked with more.

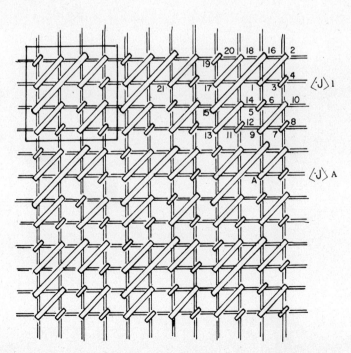

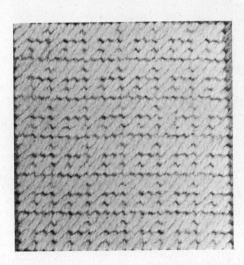

Scotch checker

This stitch is pretty in one or two colors. Fill in between each Scotch Box with Basketweave.

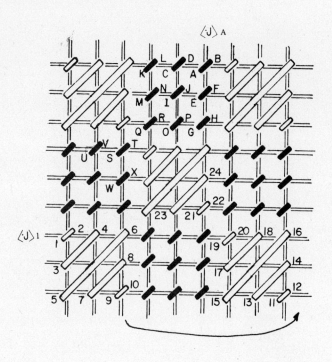

Framed scotch

Stitch the frame in the Continental Stitch. Work all the horizontal rows first. Work the vertical rows next, skipping the stitches that have been worked. Work a portion of vertical rows to ease turning the corner to the next row. Work missed areas as convenient.

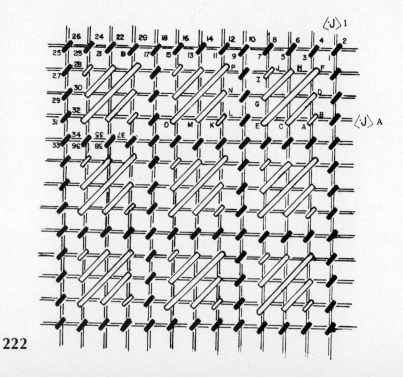

222

Try this stitch in one color. See Reversed Mosaic for hints on working Reversed Scotch.

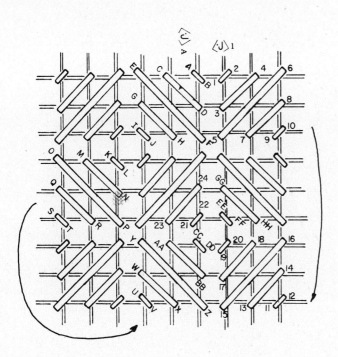

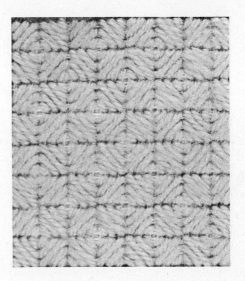

Work a ground of Reversed Scotch and then frame. This frame is made by making one straight stitch per side of each Scotch Box.

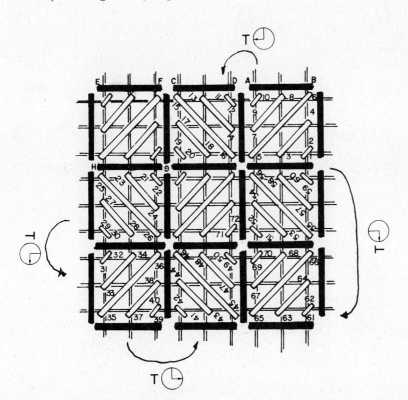

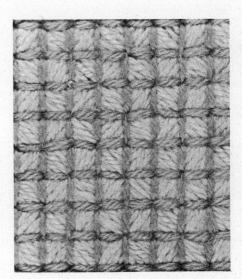

Diagonal scotch

Share the short stitch when making the next box.

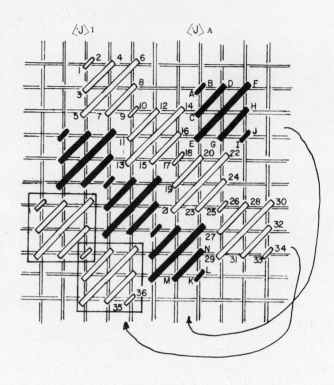

Moorish

This is simply a Diagonal Scotch with a separating row of Continental Stitch. It resembles stairs; it can be used for rooftops and geometric designs.

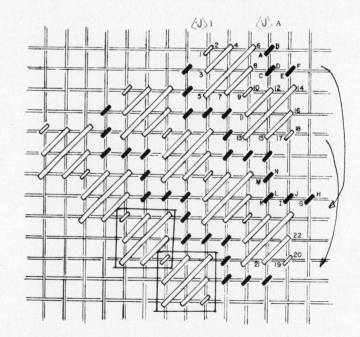

A 2 × 2 Slanted Gobelin separates the rows of Diagonal Scotch.

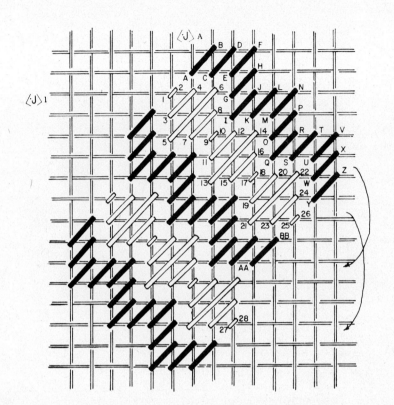

13
Cross
stitches

Cross Stitches make pretty filling, design, and border stitches. They often stand alone to represent flowers.

When worked on Regular Mono canvas, the Cross Stitch must be crossed as you go. Watch the numbering as you go through this section.

It does not matter whether you cross the right arm over the left or the left arm over the right—but you must be consistent. I find it easier to work the whole area in half of the cross first. Then I go back and cross those stitches. I manage to ruin it every time if I don't do this.

Penelope 7 or 8 is ideal for Cross Stitches. Many of the Cross Stitches do not need thickening; however, many do. When the Cross Stitch is worked on smaller canvas it is not distinct. Larger crosses can be worked successfully on smaller canvas.

Cross Stitches come in varying sizes, so as a group they are quite versatile—you can use them for accent, for design, and for background. They also create some variety of texture. Many produce a geometric pattern.

CROSS STITCHES	Border	Good Backing	Poor Backing	Background	Design	Accent	Fast	Slow	Geometric Pattern	Shading	Yarn Hog	Snags	Snag-Proof	Little Texture	Medium Texture	High Relief	Flower Stitch	Weak Pattern	Medium Pattern	Strong Pattern	Distorts Canvas
Cross Stitch				•	•			•	•	•			•	•			•	•			
Rice	•			•		•		•	•		•			•			•			•	
Giant Rice	•			•		•		•	•			•		•			•			•	
Double Cross	•			•	•				•					•				•			
Raised Cross					•			•	•			•			•					•	
Oblong Cross				•	•				•					•				•			
1 × 1 Spaced Cross Tramé				•	•				•					•				•			
1 × 3 Spaced Cross Tramé				•	•				•					•				•			
Alternating Oblong Cross				•	•				•	•				•				•			
Flying Cross				•	•				•			•			•				•		
Van Dyke	•		•	•	•		•		•			•		•					•		
Tied Oblong Cross				•	•				•						•				•		
Round Cross						•					•						•		•		
Hitched Cross	•			•	•	•			•					•		•			•		
Roman Cross				•	•				•			•		•				•			
Double Stitch				•	•				•						•		•		•		
Staggered Crosses				•	•				•					•					•		
Woven Square	•			•	•	•		•	•				•	•						•	
Bound Cross	•			•	•	•			•			•			•					•	
Upright Cross				•	•				•	•			•	•				•			
Long Upright Cross				•	•	•			•					•					•		
Combination Crosses				•	•				•				•	•				•			
Fern			•	•	•		•		•						•				•		
Binding Stitch	•							•				•				•				•	
Diagonal Fern			•	•	•		•				•				•				•		
Herringbone			•	•	•			•		•				•					•		
Herringbone Gone Wrong			•	•	•			•						•						•	
Two-Color Herringbone	•	•										•		•					•		
Six-Trip Herringbone	•	•						•		•				•	•				•		
Greek	•	•	•	•								•		•					•		
Diagonal Greek		•	•	•		•								•					•		
Waffle	•	•				•						•				•				•	
Trellis Cross				•	•	•		•	•				•	•			•		•		
Fancy Cross				•	•	•			•				•	•			•			•	
Double Straight Cross				•	•	•						•				•		•		•	
Double Leviathan	•				•	•			•		•					•	•		•		

227

CROSS STITCHES (cont.)	Border	Good Backing	Poor Backing	Background	Design	Accent	Fast	Slow	Geometric Pattern	Shading	Yarn Hog	Snags	Snag-Proof	Little Texture	Medium Texture	High Relief	Flower Stitch	Weak Pattern	Medium Pattern	Strong Pattern	Distorts Canvas
Triple Leviathan				●	●	●		●	●			●		●			●			●	
Medallion						●			●			●		●			●			●	
Chris Cross						●						●		●			●			●	
Rhodes	●	●				●					●	●				●	●			●	
Triple Cross						●			●			●				●	●			●	
Windmill						●			●			●				●	●		●		
Tied Windmill						●			●		●	●			●		●			●	
Butterfly	●			●	●	●		●	●			●			●				●		
Lone Tied Star						●									●		●		●		
Smyrna Cross	●			●	●	●			●			●				●	●			●	
Reversed Smyrna Cross	●			●	●	●			●							●	●			●	
Horizontal Elongated Smyrna	●			●	●	●			●			●				●	●			●	
Vertical Elongated Smyrna	●			●	●	●			●			●				●	●			●	
Alternating Smyrna				●	●	●			●		●					●	●			●	
Woven Cross	●			●	●	●			●			●			●		●			●	
Woven Band	●											●		●						●	

On Mono canvas, each Cross must be crossed right away. It is faster, however, to work Penelope Cross. Both look alike.

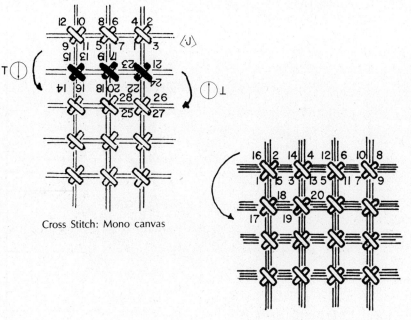

Cross Stitch: Mono canvas

Cross Stitch: Penelope canvas

Use this stitch for a border of varying widths.

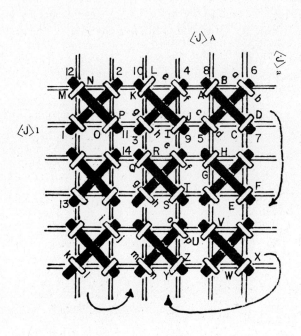

Giant rice

Take a Bargello tuck as you bury the tails (page 26).

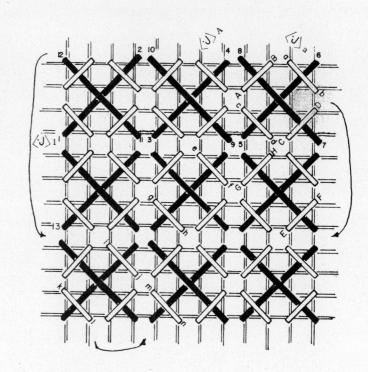

Double cross tramé

The tramé may be needed to cover the canvas.

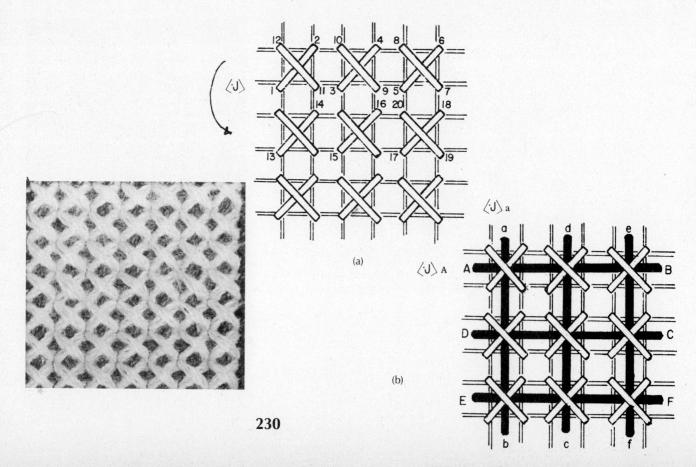

(a)

(b)

230

Thicken the yarn for the vertical stitches. Use three colors. Take a Bargello tuck as you bury the tails (page 26).

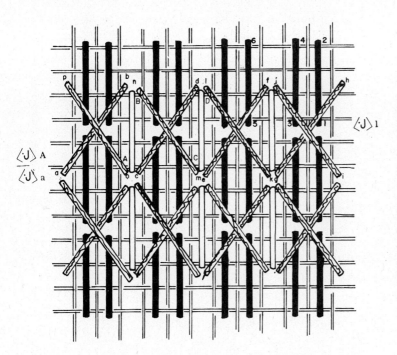

Oblong cross

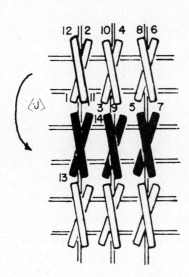

1 × 1 Spaced cross tramé

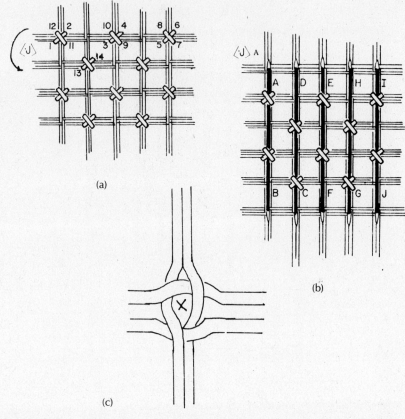

(a)

(b)

(c)

1 × 3 Spaced cross tramé

This stitch is worked most easily by stitching a checkerboard pattern of Oblong Cross Stitches first and then by running a Tramé under them.

When the Tramé is worked in a dark shade of green and the Oblong Cross in a lighter shade of green, this stitch resembles grass.

The Tramé and Cross-Stitches may run horizontally or vertically. Suit it to your needs.

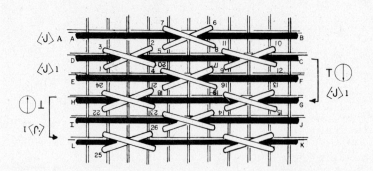

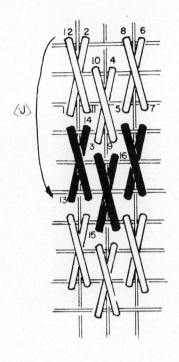

Thicken the yarn. Take a Bargello tuck as you bury the tails (page 26).

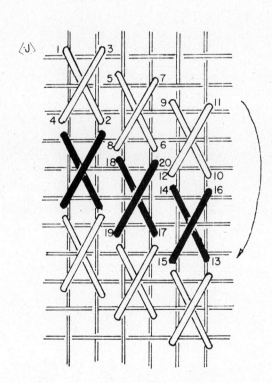

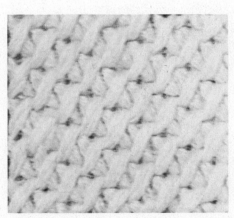

Van dyke

Always start the next row at the top. End and cut yarn each time. Good when used in single columns or as stripes.

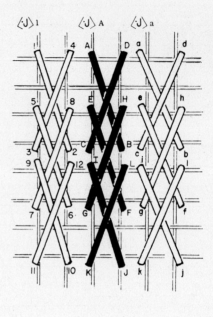

Tied oblong cross

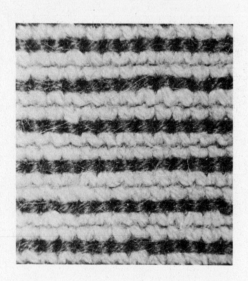

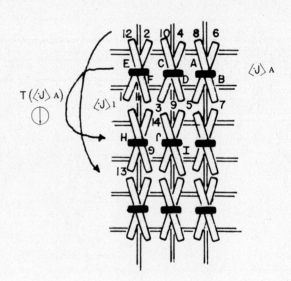

Round cross

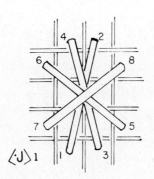

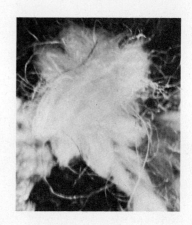

Hitched cross

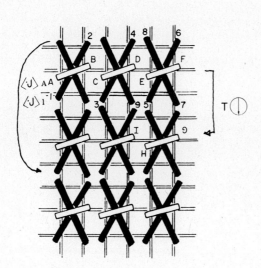

Roman cross

Take a Bargello tuck as you bury the tails (page 26).

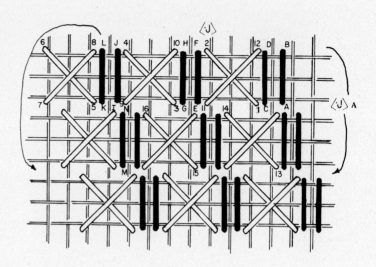

Double stitch

This is a good stitch for bumpy texture. When worked in one color it resembles tree bark. Good also for polka dots.

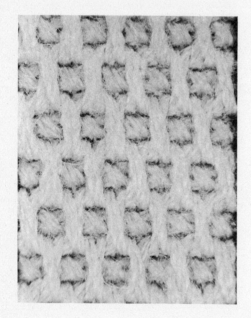

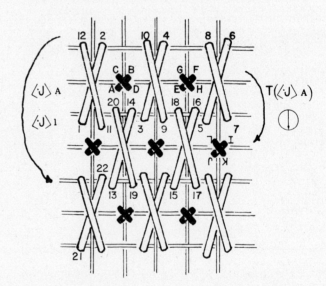

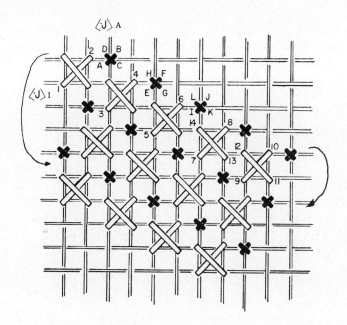

Woven square

Take a Bargello tuck as you bury the tails (page 26). Add a 2×2 cross between squares to cover the canvas.

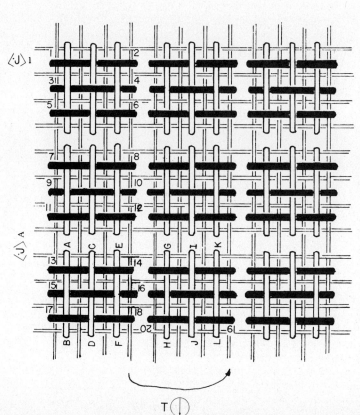

237

Bound cross

You can alternate the direction of crosses. Take a Bargello tuck as you bury the tails (page 26).

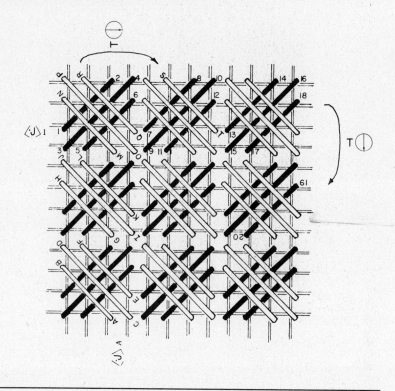

Upright cross

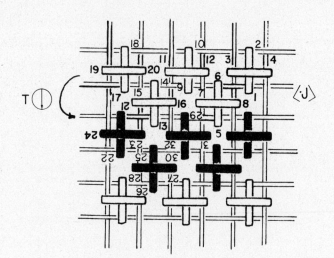

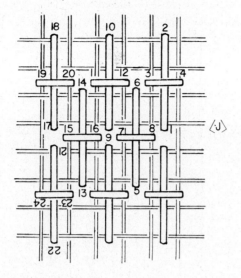

Combination crosses

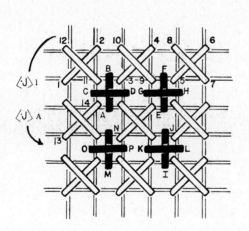

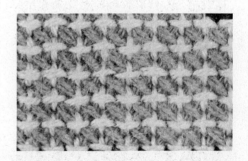

Fern

Work this stitch in vertical columns from top to bottom only. Do not turn the canvas upside down for the next row. It makes a fat, neat braid. Fill the space at the top of the column with a Cross Stitch.

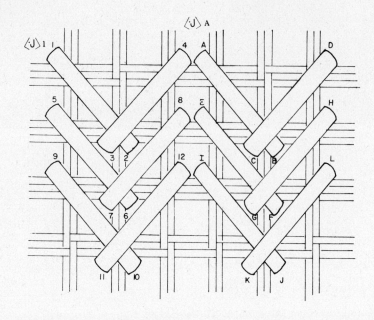

Binding stitch

The Binding Stitch is not only useful; it is attractive, too. It finishes edges and sews seams (page 78). It is worked only on the edge of canvas. You will need two threads of the canvas to secure it properly. On Penelope this is one mesh; on Mono, two mesh.

Take a Bargello tuck as you bury the tails (page 26).

It is worked much like the Fern Stitch and it, too, produces a braid.

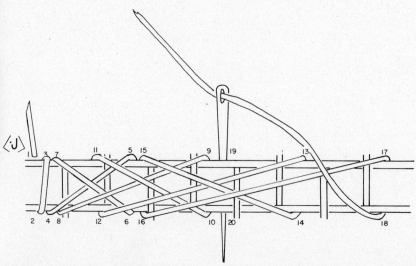

Right   Wrong

Bottom half is fabric
caught with Binding Stitch

Diagonal fern

Thicken your yarn to stitch Diagonal Fern. This is one of those
stitches that must be started with compensating stitches.

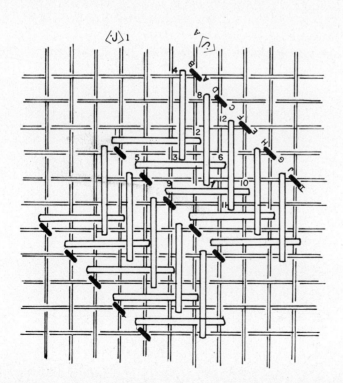

Herringbone

Work Herringbone from left to right only. Cut the yarn at the end of the first row and begin the second row directly beneath the first stitch of the first row, one mesh below.

You will have to move the yarn in the row above with your fingers in order to find the holes for the second row. This stitch is very tedious to work.

The common error is skipping a row. If you are having trouble, check to be sure every hole is filled along the edge of the stitch.

See page 26 for a hint on burying the tails.

Herringbone gone wrong

This stitch is worked like Herringbone except that you turn the canvas upside down to work the second row.

It is easier to learn if you end the first row with a stitch that slants upward.

You still have to move the yarns in the row below to find the holes for the second row.

It is a common error to skip every other row (see Herringbone).

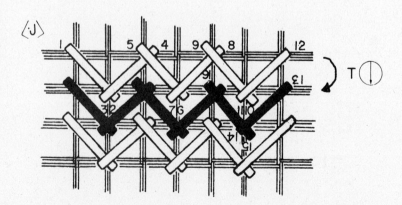

Two-color herringbone

Stitch the darker color first.

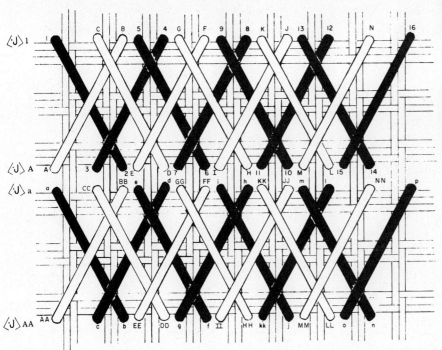

Six-trip herringbone

This is an excellent border stitch. Work it on Interlock Mono or Penelope canvas only; use all one color or many shades of one color. Put the darkest color down first. With only five colors, make the first and second trips in the darkest color.

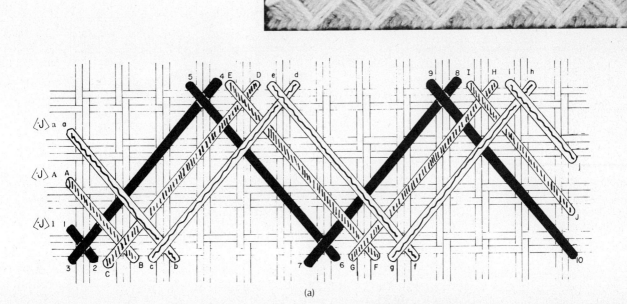

(a)

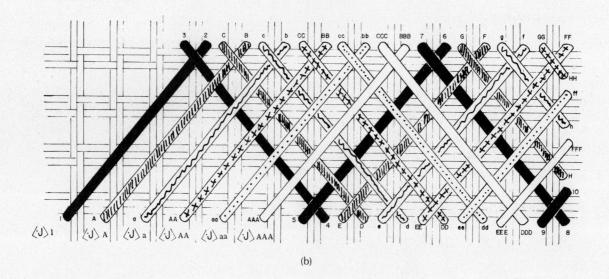

(b)

Greek

Work the Greek Stitch from left to right only. Break the yarn at the end of the row and begin again below the first stitch. It is actually a Cross Stitch with one short arm and one long arm. Each cross is intertwined with the next one.

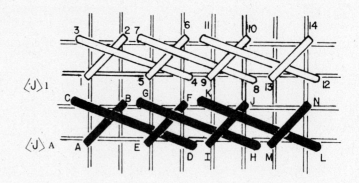

Work from left to right only.

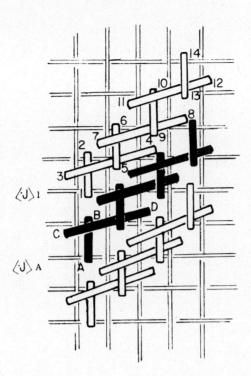

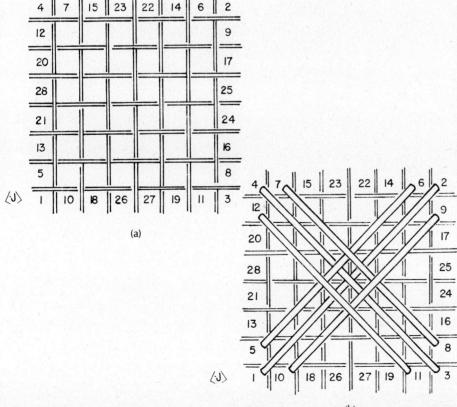

(a)

(b)

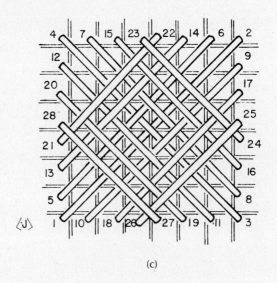

(c)

Trellis cross

This stitch resembles a basket.

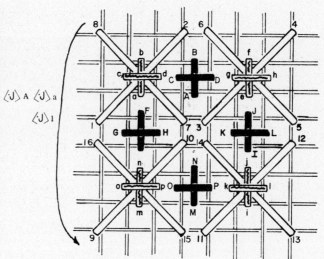

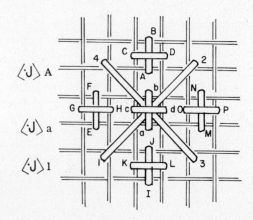

Stitch standing alone

246

You may need a Tramé to make this stitch cover the canvas.

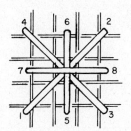

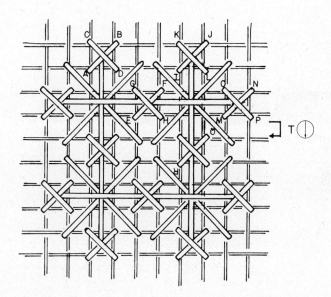

T ⊥⃘

Stitch standing alone

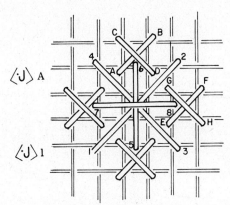

247

Double straight cross

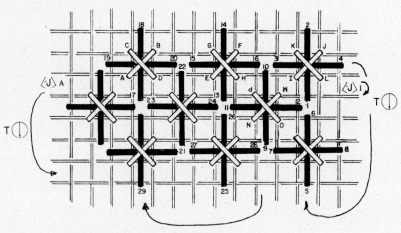

Double leviathan

Take a Bargello tuck as you bury the tails (page 26).

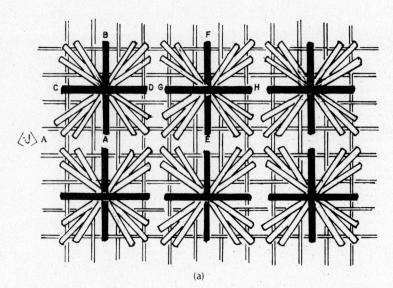

(a)

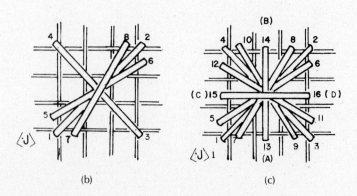

(b)   (c)

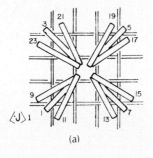

(a)

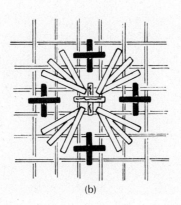

(b)

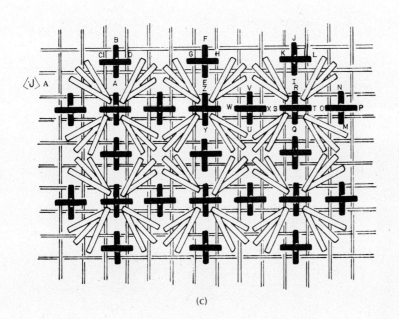

(c)

249

Medallion

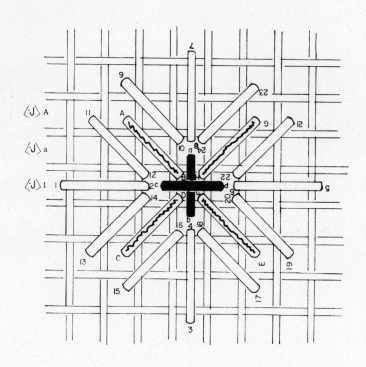

Chris cross

This stitch stands alone and serves well as an accent.

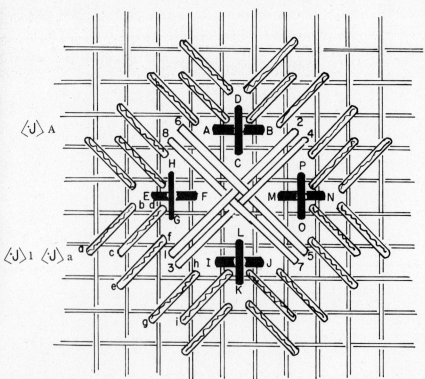

This stitch adds a fantastic texture to a needlepoint piece. Work it in varying sizes. Do not try compensating stitches; they won't work. Take a Bargello tuck as you bury the tails (page 26).

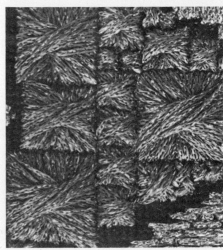

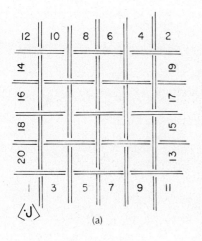

(a)

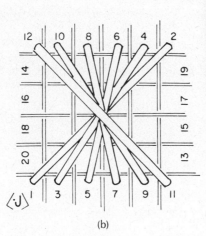

(b)

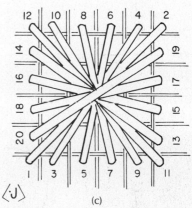

(c)

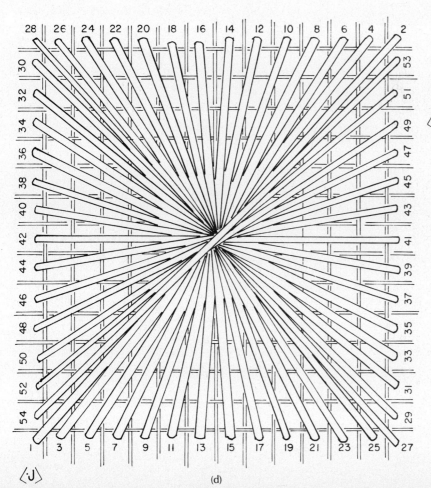

(d)

Triple cross

Triple Cross stands alone. It is similar to Triple Leviathan.

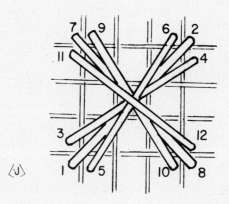

Windmill

This stitch stands alone. Fill the spaces with Cross Stitch.

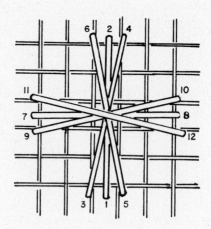

The Tied Windmill also stands alone. Put it on a ground of Cross Stitch, if you wish.

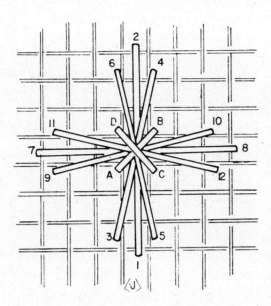

The Butterfly Stitch looks like a basket. When stitch E-F is worked in the same color as the numbered stitches and stitches A-B and C-D are on top, it resembles a butterfly.

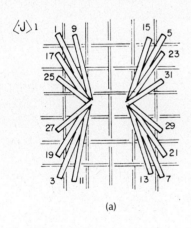

(a)

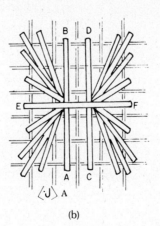

(b)

253

Lone tied star

This stitch stands alone. Fill with Continental, Upright Cross, or Cross Stitches. It resembles a bow or a bow tie.

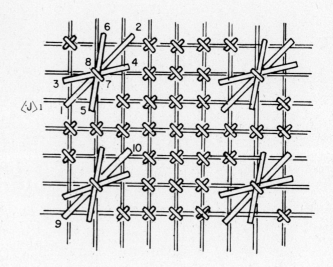

Smyrna cross

Make the × first, then the +. Smyrna Cross makes a good bump. When the + is worked in a light color, the stitch resembles hot cross buns. It is good for buttons, polka dots, etc.

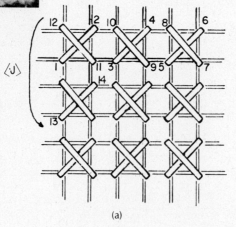

(a)

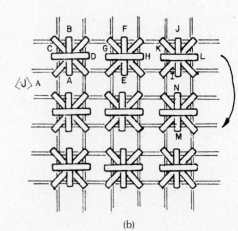

(b)

Reversed smyrna crosses

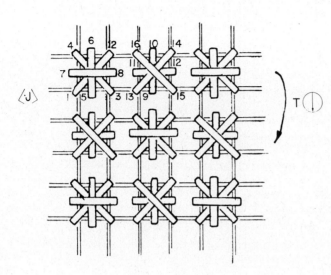

Horizontal elongated smyrna

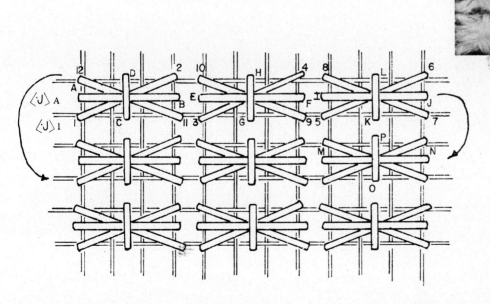

Vertical elongated smyrna

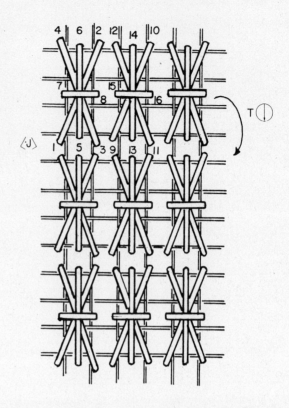

Alternating smyrna

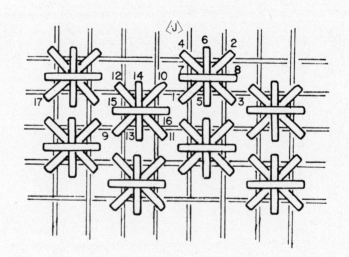

The yarn from #15 is worked under yarn #9-10 on its way to #16. Do not try to work compensating stitches; they cannot be readily done.

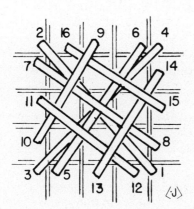

Woven band

This is an excellent border.

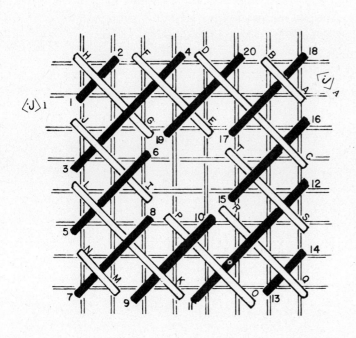

14
Tied
stitches

The Tied Stitches are pretty, and many are good stitches for shading. The Periwinkle Stitch was especially designed to be accented with beads.

These stitches are somewhat slow, but most give good backings with little snagging on the right side of the canvas.

It is most important that you tie each stitch or group of stitches as you go. Each of the drawings is numbered; follow them closely.

The Tied Stitches are best worked on Mono 12 or 14 with a full strand of tapestry or Persian yarn.

The Tied Stitches are good for design, and some can be used for background.

TIED STITCHES	Border	Good Backing	Poor Backing	Background	Design	Accent	Fast	Slow	Geometric Pattern	Shading	Yarn Hog	Snags	Snag-Proof	Little Texture	Medium Texture	High Relief	Flower Stitch	Weak Pattern	Medium Pattern	Strong Pattern	Distorts Canvas
Knotted Stitch		•		•	•			•		•			•	•					•		
Periwinkle				•	•			•								•				•	
Fly				•	•									•					•		
Couching			•		•	•	•					•		•				•			
Diagonal Roumanian				•	•					•			•	•					•		
Wheat	•	•		•	•	•		•					•		•				•		
Web					•	•		•		•			•	•				•			

Knotted stitch

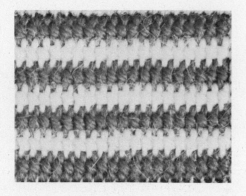

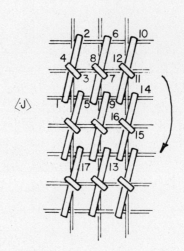

Periwinkle

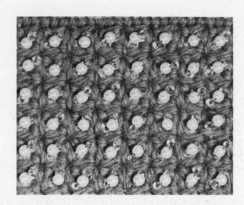

Because this stitch was designed to be used with beads, it does not cover the canvas unless beads are used. Use long, thin beads; one round one, large enough to cover, or three, as I have done. This stitch would make a particularly attractive background for an evening purse, especially if worked with metallic thread. Sew beads on afterwards with sewing thread.

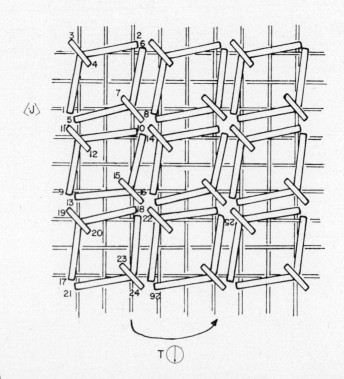

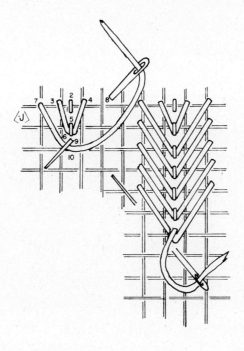

Couching

Couching is laying one yarn where you want it and tacking it down with another yarn. It curves well. Thread two needles. Try to tie at even intervals.

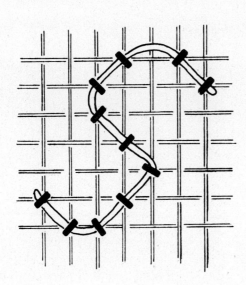

Diagonal Roumanian

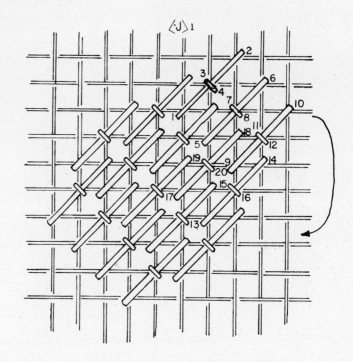

Wheat

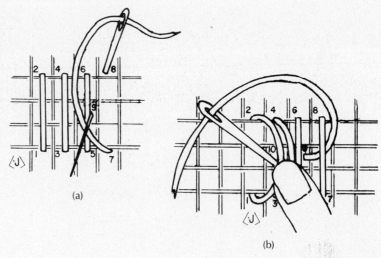

(a)

(b)

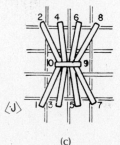

(c)

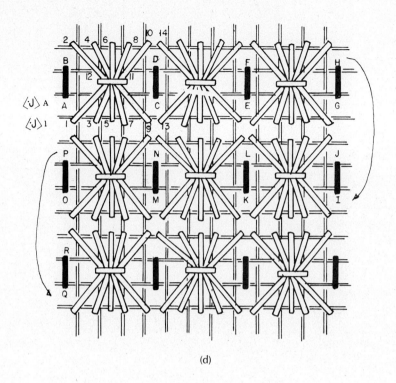

(d)

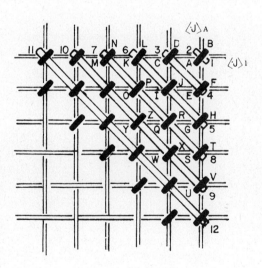

Web

15
Eye
stitches

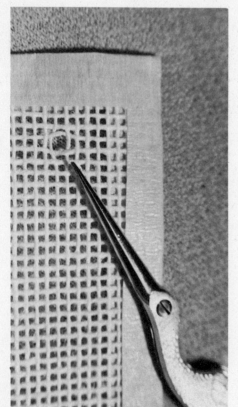

Eye Stitches are made by putting several stitches into one hole. This technique creates a hole, a dimple, or an eye.

Work Eye Stitches on Regular Mono 10. Use a full strand of tapestry or Persian yarn.

Eye Stitches are very pretty and interesting to do, but slow to work up. In stitching them, work from the outside to the center and always go down into the center. This will prevent splitting or snagging the yarn of the stitches you have already worked.

As you put what seems an impossible number of stitches into one small hole, take care that each of these stitches goes into the hole smoothly. If you are working on Regular Mono canvas, this task will be a little easier. It is a great help to enlarge the center hole by poking the point of a pair of embroidery scissors into it. Spread the mesh gently to enlarge the hole. This works only on Regular Mono (see photo at left). Use 2-ply Persian yarn on other kinds.

You may need to pull the yarn more tightly as each eye forms. This helps to make the stitch smooth, but be careful not to pull the canvas out of shape.

Note that Eye Stitches usually begin with an Upright Cross, going from the outside into the center. Next, one stitch is taken in each quadrant in a circular motion until all the remaining stitches have been taken. The even-numbered stitches are all in the center of the eye, and because the numbers do not fit easily, they have been omitted.

Eye Stitches lend themselves to broad borders, backgrounds, and pillows. Single motifs or clusters of two or three eyes make lovely flowers.

EYE STITCHES	Border	Good Backing	Poor Backing	Background	Design	Accent	Fast	Slow	Geometric Pattern	Shading	Yarn Hog	Snags	Snag-Proof	Little Texture	Medium Texture	High Relief	Flower Stitch	Weak Pattern	Medium Pattern	Strong Pattern	Distorts Canvas
Framed Star	•	•			•	•		•	•			•			•		•		•		
Square Eyelet	•	•			•	•		•	•		•	•			•			•			
Diamond Eyelet	•	•		•	•	•		•	•			•		•					•		
Triangular Ray	•	•			•	•		•	•			•			•				•		
Ringed Daisies	•	•		•	•	•		•	•						•		•			•	

Because the Eye Stitches have good backing, most of them will wear well. Those that will not are those that have long yarns on top, such as Triangular Ray and Square Eyelet. (Refer to Thickening and Thinning of yarn, pages 30-31.)

Framed star

Without the frame, this is simply the Star Stitch. The frame is necessary to cover the canvas, except on Mono 14.

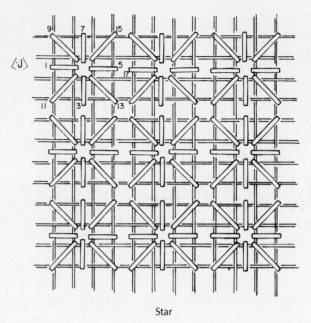

Star

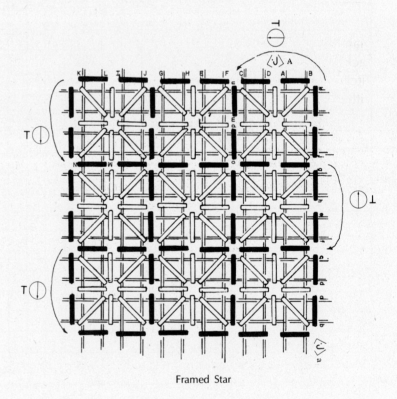

Framed Star

266

The Square Eyelet Stitch shown here covers an area 10-mesh square. It may cover 6 × 6 or 8 × 8. Take a Bargello tuck as you bury the tails (page 26).

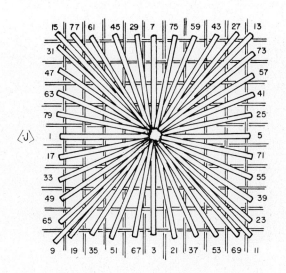

Diamond Eyelet lets you put a pearl or bead in the center. The Back-Stitch and Frame Stitch fill in between the diamonds. This stitch makes a good border, background, or geometric design with many color possibilities.

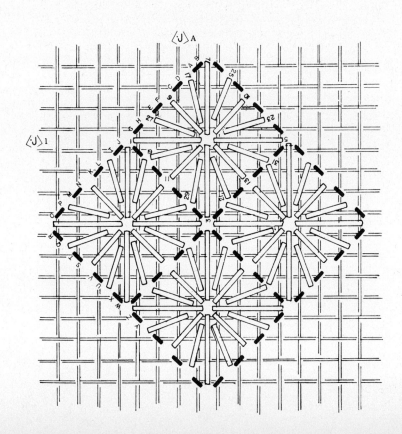

Triangular ray

This stitch makes a nice border. Arrangement of color can create rick-rack. Use a Back-Stitch, if it does not cover. Take a Bargello tuck as you bury the tails (page 26).

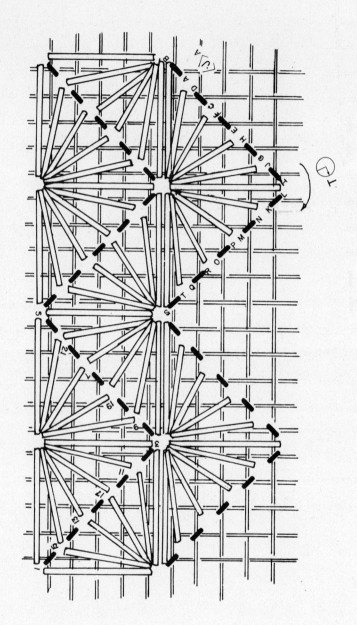

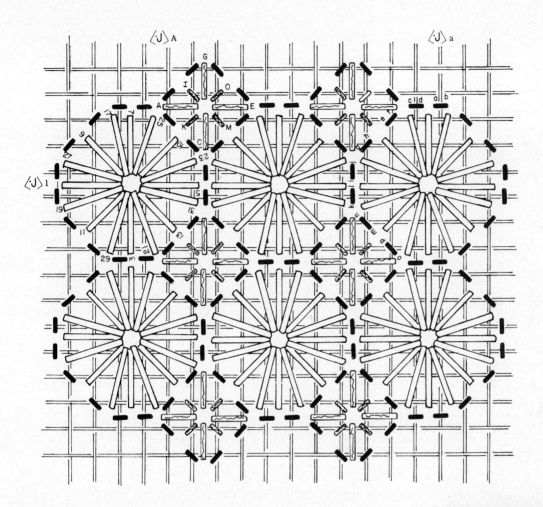

16
Leaf
stitches

Leaf Stitches have a charm all their own; they complement lovely flowers. Given on the following pages are a few of those you can use. Mix them up, use one or two favorites, or make up your own.

Use the Leaf Stitches as overall patterns, singly, or in pairs. Turn Leaf Stitches sideways or upside down to make feathers. They may be worked in three ways:

1. From the top, one stitch to the right, one stitch to the left, etc.
2. From the bottom, one stitch to the right, one stitch to the left, etc.
3. From the bottom, up one side, and down the other.

Work Leaf Stitches on Penelope or Mono 10. Usually a full strand of tapestry or Persian yarn covers.

Take a Bargello tuck as you bury the tails (page 26).

These stitches will also work up well in geometric patterns. Have fun with color. Most lend themselves well to shading.

LEAF STITCHES	Border	Good Backing	Poor Backing	Background	Design	Accent	Fast	Slow	Geometric Pattern	Shading	Yarn Hog	Snags	Snag-Proof	Little Texture	Medium Texture	High Relief	Flower Stitch	Weak Pattern	Medium Pattern	Strong Pattern	Distorts Canvas
Diamond Ray		•		•	•	•			•	•	•				•		•				
Ray Stitch	•	•				•		•	•							•	•		•		
Leaf #1	•	•		•	•	•			•	•		•		•					•		
Diagonal Leaf		•		•	•	•			•	•		•		•					•		
Roumanian Leaf	•	•				•	•					•			•				•		
Diagonal Roumanian Leaf		•				•	•					•			•				•		
Close Herringbone						•						•	•			•			•		
Raised Close Herringbone						•						•	•			•			•		

Diamond ray

The Diamond Ray Stitch makes a most interesting pattern and has a good backing. I generally like something faster to work up for a background, but you might want to use it that way. The longest stitch is not likely to snag.

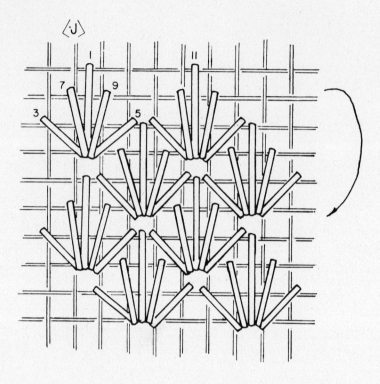

Ray

The Ray Stitch is also very slow to work up and is hard on the fingers. Try spreading the base hole with a pair of scissors as described on page 264. In spite of its drawbacks, this stitch is worthwhile, for it is lovely when finished. It makes a good, bumpy border, but it is not recommended for large areas.

These Ray stitches
are worked in one color

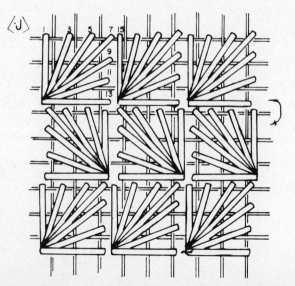

This is the basic and most familiar Leaf Stitch. It makes an interesting pattern. It is lovely when shaded within each leaf. This stitch has a good backing and makes a pretty border on vertical stripe.

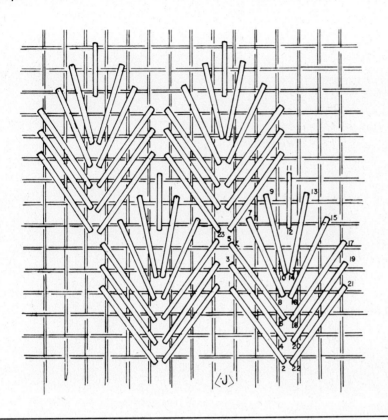

Diagonal leaf

Use this Leaf Stitch in groups or singly. The resulting pattern is pleasing to the eye.

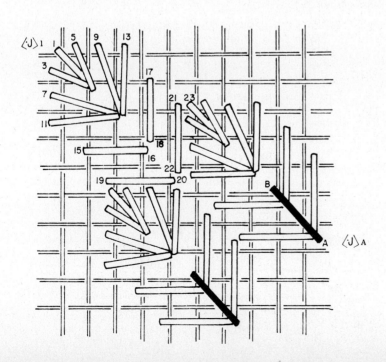

Roumanian leaf

The Roumanian-type stitches (Roumanian Leaf; Diagonal Roumanian Leaf, below; and Fly Stitch) are fast and fun to work. Refer to the Fly Stitch, page 261. Shading within the leaf can be done, but then the speed of the stitch is lost.

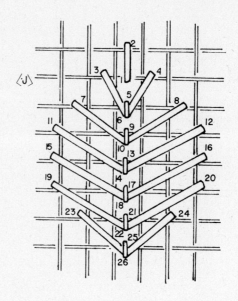

Diagonal Roumanian leaf

In order to give this more of a leaf shape, two stitches share one of the center stitches. Stitch #7 slips under #5-6 and goes down at #8. The pattern is then resumed.

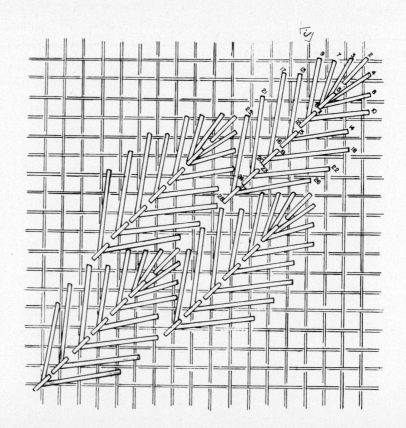

This makes a slightly raised leaf, made by crossing stitches over each other. There is some backing, but not a great deal. This stitch stands alone and makes a long, smooth leaf.

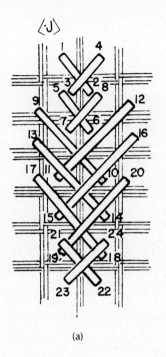

(b)

(a)

Raised close herringbone

This leaf is quite three-dimensional and is interesting to work. It is worked in steps that produce a fair backing. Again, this Leaf Stitch is used alone as an accent for a design. The needle penetrates the canvas only at the tip of the leaf and as it is worked to the rear. Only the first stitch at the base goes through the canvas. The rest of the stitches go under the first stitch on top of the canvas. The size and shape can be readily varied.

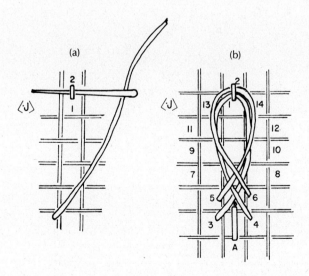

(a)

(b)

(c)

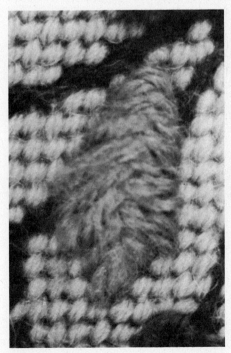

17 Decorative stitches

These Decorative Stitches have many uses, some quite specialized and some more broad. They are not related in construction technique.

Most Decorative Stitches have poor backing, and therefore are mostly used for accent. Many are poor choices for design and background, so when using one of the Decorative Stitches, choose carefully.

DECORATIVE STITCHES	Border	Good Backing	Poor Backing	Background	Design	Accent	Fast	Slow	Geometric Pattern	Shading	Yarn Hog	Snags	Snag-Proof	Little Texture	Medium Texture	High Relief	Flower Stitch	Weak Pattern	Medium Pattern	Strong Pattern	Distorts Canvas
Buttonhole	●		●	●	●	●		●				●		●				●			
Buttonhole in Half-Circle			●	●	●				●	●		●			●		●			●	
Chain	●		●		●	●								●						●	
Open Chain	●		●		●	●						●		●						●	
Diagonal Chain	●		●		●	●								●						●	
Woven Spider Web			●			●		●			●					●	●			●	
Smooth Spider Web			●			●		●			●				●	●				●	
Ridged Spider Web			●			●		●			●					●	●			●	
Wound Cross			●			●		●			●					●	●			●	
French Knot			●			●		●			●		●		●			●		●	
French Knots on Stalks			●			●		●				●			●		●		●		
Bullion Knot			●			●		●				●				●	●			●	
Twisted Chain			●			●		●				●				●		●			
Looped Turkey Work		●	●	●						●	●	●				●	●		●		
Cut Turkey Work		●	●	●						●	●	●				●	●	●			
Velvet			●	●	●	●						●				●	●			●	
Loop			●	●	●							●				●	●			●	
Lazy Daisy			●		●	●						●	●				●	●			
Needleweaving			●		●	●						●			●		●			●	
Raised Cup			●			●		●			●	●				●	●			●	
Running Stitch			●		●	●	●							●				●			

Buttonhole

The Buttonhole Stitch has many variations. Only two are given here.

This stitch creates a smooth area and a ridge. Arrange these areas to suit your purposes. Disregard the mesh. Treat the canvas as if it were fabric and stitch. When worked as shown here, horizontal stripes are created.

Work the rows from bottom to top and from left to right. To change from one strand of yarn to the next, you will need two needles, threaded with the same color yarn. If, for example, your yarn runs out at #8 on the drawing, insert the needle into the canvas at #8, leaving the yarn from #7 to #8 a little loose. Let this needle dangle on the wrong side of the canvas. Bury the tail, using a Bargello tuck (page 26), of the yarn on the second needle on the wrong side. Bring the needle up at #9. Let this second needle dangle. Adjust the tension on the first needle and bury the tail with a Bargello tuck. Continue with the second needle.

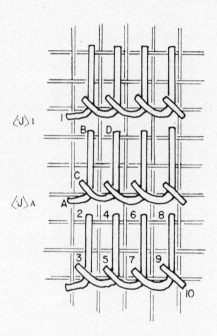

Buttonhole in half-circle

Take a Bargello tuck as you bury the tail (page 26).

This stitch makes a lovely filler for a field or faraway flower garden.

Make sure that the stitches that go into the middle are even. (See the chapter on Eye Stitches.)

278

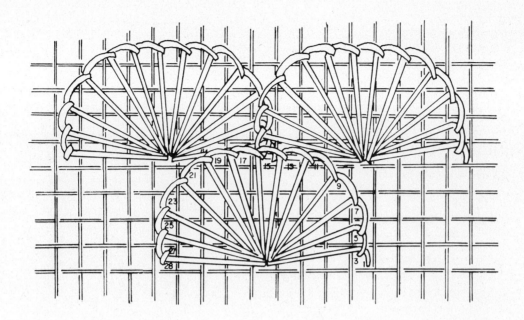

Chain

The Chain Stitch is quite a versatile stitch. It is one of a few stitches that curve. You may work it on top of the background or leave a space in the background to work the Chain Stitch.

This stitch is easier to work if you turn the canvas so that you are working horizontally and from right to left. Put one chain over 2 or 3 mesh.

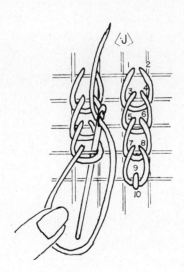

Open chain

This must be laid on top of an already stitched background.

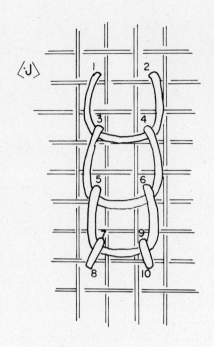

Diagonal chain

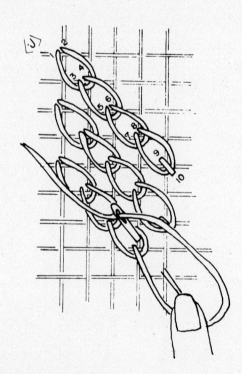

Some instructions for working Spider Webs are basic to all three versions.

Lay one of the foundations shown in the figure. Only the Woven Spider Web must have an odd number of spokes. If these spokes are not well secured, the whole thing will come undone. Take a Bargello tuck as you bury the tails (see page 26).

Bring the needle up as close to the center as you can without actually coming through the center. Work this yarn in the pattern of the stitch you are doing. Do not penetrate the canvas until you are through. Keep going around and around until the spokes are no longer visible. When you think you cannot possibly get one more round in, do two more—then you are through!

To make a high ball, pull the yarn tight, but not so tightly that the spokes become misshapen. As you take each stitch, pull the yarn toward the center. This helps to tighten the stitch.

You may change colors or techniques midstream. For example, you can make a wheel by working Woven Spider Web (for the hub), Ridged Spider Web (for the spokes), and Smooth Spider Web (for the rim).

Use Spider Webs for grapes, apples, other fruit, wheels, balls, buttons, flowers, ladybugs, spiders, and other insects—anything round.

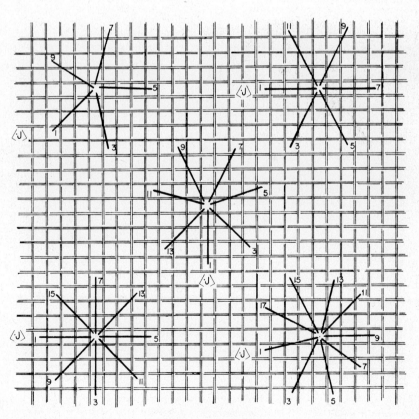

Spider Web Foundations

Woven spider web

Lay the spokes. You must have an odd number. Weave the yarn over and under the spokes. When you think you cannot possibly get one more row in, do two more. Then you are through.

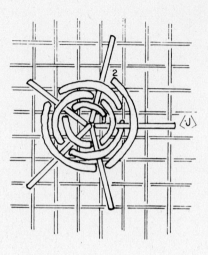

Smooth spider web

Go over two spokes and back under one; over two, under one, and so forth.

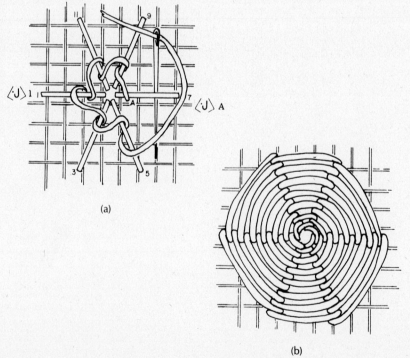

(a)

(b)

Ridged spider web

Reverse the process of the preceding stitch. Go under two spokes and back over one; under two, over one.

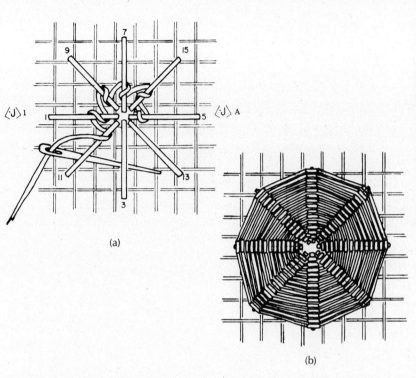

(a)

(b)

Wound cross

This is another good round stitch. Make it as fat as you like. Wind the yarn under all the spokes without penetrating the canvas.

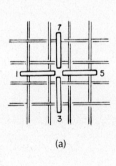

(a)

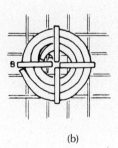

(b)

French knot

French Knots are handy. They fill bare canvas, make polka dots, flower centers, whole flowers, and so forth.

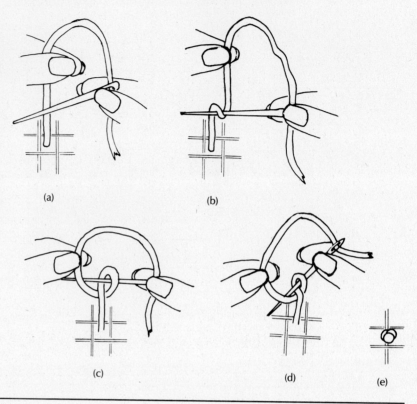

(a)

(b)

(c)

(d)

(e)

French knots on stalks

These are an expanded version of the French Knot. They make lovely flowers.

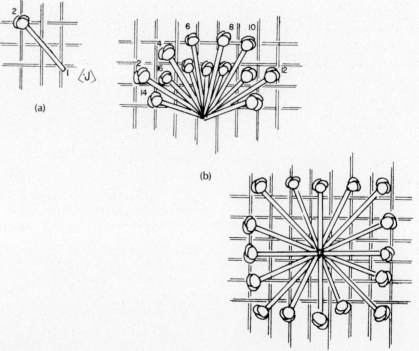

(a)

(b)

(c)

Bullion knot

The Bullion Knot is worked by laying a thread and wrapping a yarn around it, without penetrating the canvas. Be sure that the tail is well secured. Pull tight and it will curl. Worked loosely, this stitch resembles finger curls.

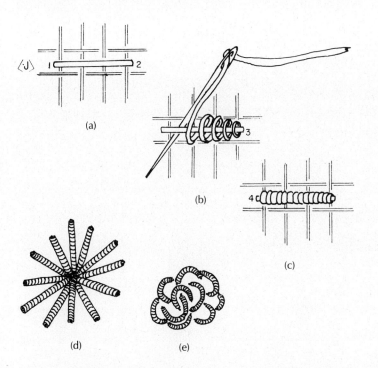

(a)

(b)

(c)

(d)

(e)

Twisted chain

This stitch can be worked in a single row and curved to meet your purpose. It may also be worked side by side to fill an area. It is imperative that your tension be even. Work from top to bottom only.

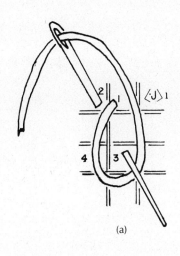

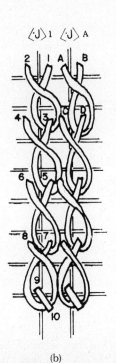

(a)

(b)

285

Looped turkey work

Stitch the bottom row first and work up. Work from left to right only. This means that you must cut your yarn at the end of every row. There is no tail to bury; it becomes part of the stitch. You may skip rows on a small canvas if it is too crowded.

Use a strip of paper to help you get the loops even (see following page, top). A drinking straw works well, too. In working Looped Turkey Work, try not to run out of yarn in the middle of a row unless you have to.

Turkey Work should be worked on an even number of mesh. However, when you get to the end of a row, there often is a mesh left over. Work the last three mesh by leaving the extra one in the center of the stitch. (You are actually skipping a mesh.)

Work your whole design first, then put this stitch in. If you do not, you will never be able to move this stitch aside to get the others in.

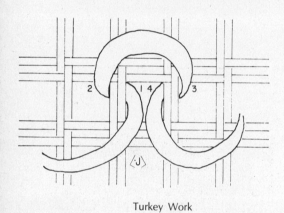

Turkey Work

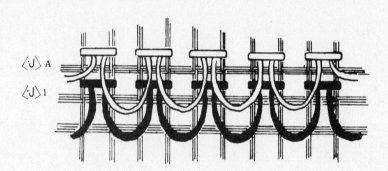

Looped Turkey Work

Cut turkey work

Work just as in Looped Turkey Work, but cut the loops as you go. After working Row 2, clip Row 1; after working Row 3, clip Row 2. If you cut each row immediately after it is worked, the pieces can be easily caught in the next row as you stitch it. However, if you wait until you have completely finished the area, it is quite hard to do a good cutting job. Cut as shown in Figure b.

Cutting the loops too short causes the rows to show. See top photo (right) and bottom photo (wrong).

It does not matter if you end a yarn in the middle of a row.

Persian yarn makes a fluffier Cut Turkey Work.

Work your whole design first; then put this stitch in. If you do not, you will never be able to move this stitch to get the others in.

To fluff your Turkey Work, pick at it with the point of the needle or brush it with a stiff-bristled nylon hair brush. Trim carefully.

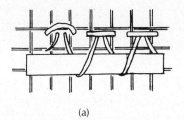

(a)

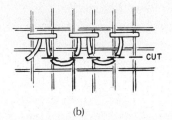

(b)

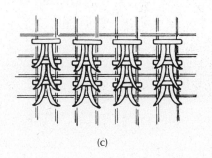

(c)

Velvet

This stitch is worked like Turkey Work—except that you must bury your yarn on the wrong side of the canvas—bottom up and left to right. Skip one mesh between rows. Do not lift your thumb off the loop until the ''X'' is completed; otherwise it will all come apart. Cut it or leave it looped.

The Velvet Stitch makes a nice thatched roof or a flapper's fringe. If the loops are cut it makes a good shag rug for a doll house.

Work your whole design first, then put this stitch in. If you do not, you won't be able to move this stitch aside to get the others in.

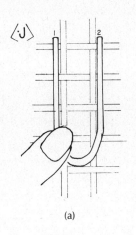

(a)

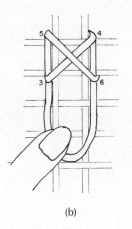

(b)

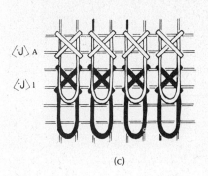

(c)

287

Loop

This stitch reminds me of Austrian drapes. Two rows of it, the second placed between the loops of the first, make a nice ruffle or lace trim (see elephant in Figure 3–46, page 138). You may want the loop longer in this case.

In going from #5 to #6, slip the needle under the horizontal bar created by stitch #3-4. The next stitch begins at #6. Let the loop hang down three or so mesh between #5 and #6. Place subsequent rows in the next holes up.

Work your whole design first; then put this stitch in. If you do not, it will be impossible to move this stitch aside to get the others in.

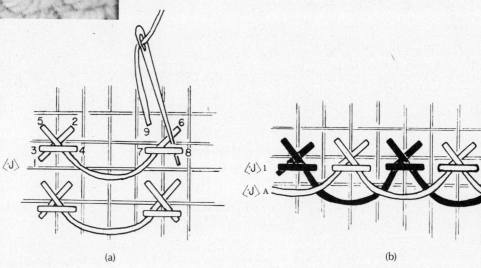

(a)

(b)

Lazy daisy

Work this stitch on top of a background stitch. It can serve as flower petals, leaves, and many other things.

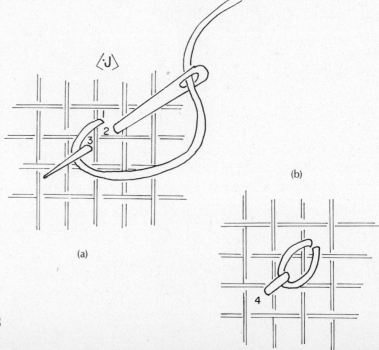

(a)

(b)

Needleweaving

This is a kind of surface embroidery. The yarn penetrates the canvas only at the outer edges of the area covered in Needleweaving. Any pattern you wish may be woven.

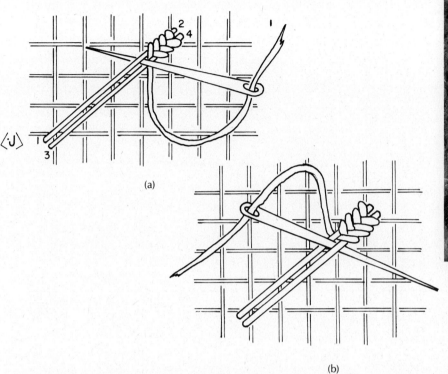

(a)

(b)

Raised cup stitch

Make a triangle of yarn as in Figure a. This is the last time your needle will go through the canvas. Slide the needle under one side of the triangle, without going through the canvas (Figure b). Put the needle under and then over the thread on the needle as in Figure c. Pull the needle through and tug gently, making a somewhat loose knot (Figure d).

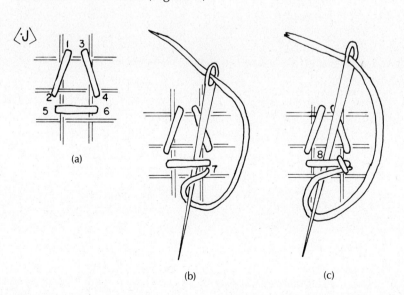

(a)

(b)

(c)

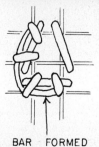

BAR FORMED

(d)

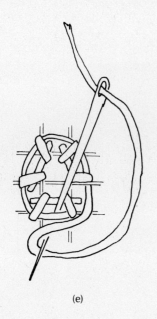

(e)

Do this again on the same side of the triangle. Keep going around the triangle making two knots on each side. Note that each of these knots is connected with a short piece of yarn. See the arrow in the photo. It is on this bar that you will secure the second row of knots. Make one knot on each bar as you go around the second time. Keep going around until the cup is as big as you would like it to be. Adding one knot on each bar merely makes the cup higher. You will have to place two or three on each bar as you go around if you wish to increase the diameter of the cup.

(f)

Running stitch

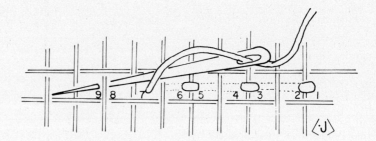

⟨J⟩

290

FINISHING

I am firmly convinced that finishing is the most important step in doing a needlepoint piece. Stitches of mediocre quality will be overlooked if the finishing is flawless. On the other hand, perfect stitching is never noticed when the finishing is poor. Of course, nothing can beat the winning combination of error-free stitching and exquisite finishing.

You can get a professional-looking finished product at home with good instructions, proper tools, and a little effort. The basic process for finishing your needlepoint project is blocking, which straightens the mesh of the canvas to the perpendicular shape it had and firms the stitches into that shape. Every piece of needlepoint must be blocked when you have completed the stitching.

The blocked needlepoint piece may be framed or incorporated into a useful or decorative item such as a pillow or purse flap. Chapter 19 gives suggestions for how to do this. Other needlepoint projects described in chapter 20 would make original gifts.

18
Blocking

Once the stitching is done, many people want someone else to do the finishing. Doing it yourself can save you money. Even doing just the blocking will save you enough to make it worth your while. It is not hard to learn to do, but it can be just plain hard work if your piece is out of shape. (That's why shops charge so much to block.) Pieces that are not out of shape take only a few minutes and very little effort to block.

Blocking board

The first step is to make a blocking board. Use insulation board or fiber board (without the tar). You can get it at a lumber yard. This product seems to have many names. It often helps to mention that it is the stuff bulletin boards are made of when they're not cork. Since the board breaks easily, there are often scraps lying around the lumber yard that they'll give you or sell you for a nominal charge. Most of the time they won't cut a 4' × 8' sheet for you, but if you'll ask the man who operates the saw, he might cut it for you. A square 2' × 2' is a handy size.

You need something that pins and staples will go into and pull out of easily. Also, it needs to be porous, so that the needlepoint can dry quickly. Therefore, I do not recommend plywood.

You've got to cover the board. The color on the board rubs off on you and your needlepoint, and the rough board may snag your needlepoint. Staple and then tape a piece of brown paper to both sides of your board. I've found a cheap paper bag does better than brown wrapping paper. Piece it with masking tape if you have to.

Next put the blocking board in the bathtub and pour water on the paper on both sides. Get it thoroughly wet. Then go to bed. The paper will look like such a gosh-awful mess that you'll be sure you've done something wrong! When you get up in the morning, you will have very smooth, taut paper on your blocking board!

Making the grid

Now draw a grid on your paper with a *waterproof* marker. The lines *must* be *perpendicular* and *parallel*. One-inch squares make the board easy to use, but I think lines that are the width of your yardstick are easier to get parallel, which is very important. After the ink dries, spray the paper with a spray plastic. This will make the paper last longer.

If you don't want to draw lines (or you want a prettier blocking board) you can cover the brown paper with gingham fabric. (You still have to have the paper because the insulation board will stain the fabric.) Use *woven* gingham; you can tell it from printed gingham because the fabric looks the same on both sides. Black and white or navy blue and white work best. One hundred percent cotton is best, but with all the permanent press around, it may be hard to find. One-inch squares on the gingham are the easiest to stretch over the board, but the ¼" or ½" squares make it easier to block. Do *not* pre-shrink the fabric.

The fabric must be stretched over the board so that it is *taut*. Secure with staples as you go. If it is not taut, you could catch a tuck in the fabric when blocking your needlepoint. It would throw the lines off and the needlepoint would be crooked.

Put the board in the bathtub again. Pour very hot water over the fabric. Let the excess run off. You want the fabric to shrink so the cover will be taut. 100% cotton will shrink. Some permanent press fabrics will not shrink enough, but most will.

Blocking

Before you start to stitch, measure the size of the area to be stitched. Write that measurement on the tape around the raw edges of your canvas with a waterproof marker. When you block the finished needlepoint, it should be this size.

Figure 5–1 shows how to block a needlepoint piece. Pieces that have all flat stitches should be blocked face down. This is because wool has a natural wicking action that brings the water to the surface. Any dye or paint that runs (heaven forbid) will, therefore, rise to the top with the water. This is, of course, the wrong side of the needlepoint.

However, pieces with textured stitches cannot be blocked face down. Your hard-worked texture will be squashed.

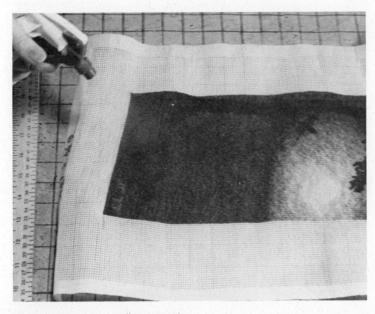

Fig. 5–1a. Wet your needlepoint with a spray of water.

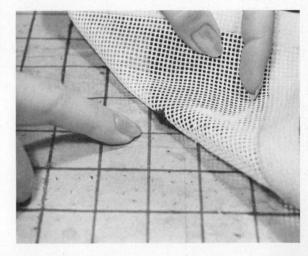

Fig. 5–1b. Put one corner of the needlepoint at the intersection of two lines on the blocking board.

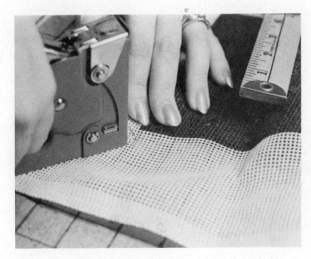

Fig. 5–1c. Staple this corner in place with 3 or 4 staples. They will be under lots of tension later.

Fig. 5–1d. Measure along one side as shown in Fig. 5–4b and staple the second corner.

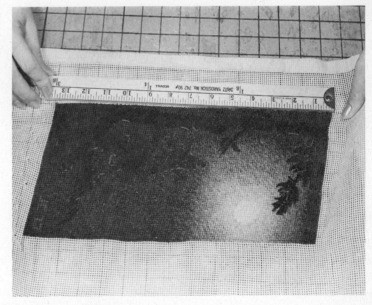

Fig. 5–1e. Measure between the second and third corners; staple the third corner. Then staple between the three corners.

Fig. 5–1f. Find the point for the fourth corner by measuring. Mark this point on the blocking board.

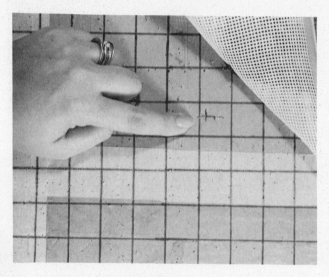

Fig. 5–1g. Your mark should look like this.

Fig. 5–1h. Pull the fourth corner to meet your mark. If your needlepoint is badly out of shape, you'll need one to three people to help you at this point. Staple the corner in place securely.

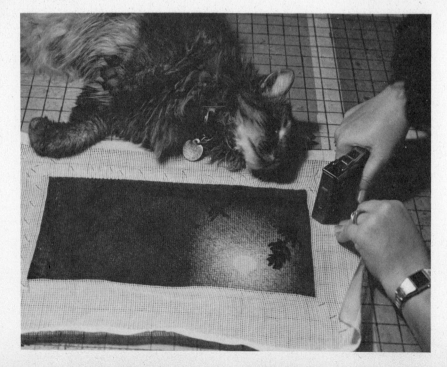

Fig. 5–1i. Usually you can use all the help you can get to block a badly misshapen piece. But with friends like this helping it takes a little longer!

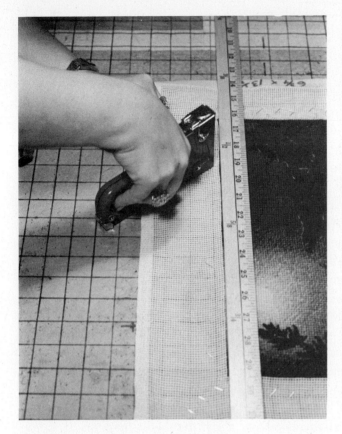

Fig. 5–1j. Lay a yardstick along the edge of the needlepoint to help you get the side straight.

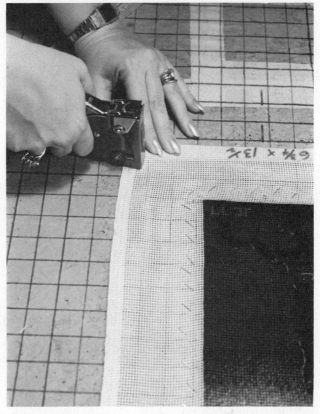

Fig. 5–1k. Staple the corners down so they'll dry flat.

Fig. 5–1l. Sometimes a badly distorted piece will need blocking again. It's easier to get it straight the second time around.

Fig. 5–1m. To block a piece with no margin of blank canvas, use T-pins. Follow the same basic blocking instructions given above.

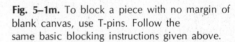

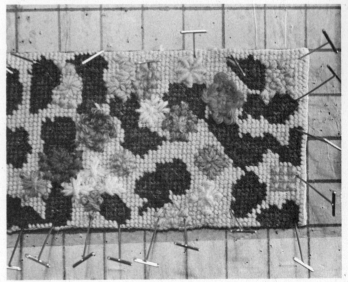

297

Fastening the canvas

When there is a blank margin of canvas around the stitched area of needlepoint, you can use a staple gun to block. Staple in this margin so that the staples are ¼" apart. If you put them at an angle to the mesh, the staples will hold the needlepoint better.

If you have used the Two-Step Edge Finishing method, there will not be a blank margin to staple through. Use the heavy-weight stainless steel T-pins. Place them carefully between stitches and 2 or 3 stitches in from the edge. They, like the staples, should be ¼" apart. Block *before* you do the Binding Stitch. It would be crushed in this process.

When the T-pins are taken out, holes will be left. Hold a steam iron over the needlepoint for a *short time*. Using a pin or a needle, push the yarns gently back in place. *Never touch the iron to the needlepoint.*

Don't take your needlepoint off the blocking board until it is *completely* dry. This usually takes 24 to 48 hours, but it can take as long as a week. If you take it off before it is absolutely dry, your needlepoint will, most likely, return to its former crooked shape.

Keep the blocking board flat until it dries. Under a bed is a good place unless you have a cat that will sleep on it! If you prop the board against a wall, a watermark will be on your needlepoint when it dries. *Nothing* removes a watermark. I've tried. You could get a watermark also if your needlepoint is not dampened evenly before blocking.

Stains

If your yarn, paint, or marker bleeds color during blocking, there are a couple of things you can do about it. First, cry a lot. But don't let your needlepoint dry. Soak it in cold water overnight. Maybe the color will keep running—right out of the needlepoint. This doesn't always work.

If it doesn't work, sponge the stain with a mixture of 1 tablespoon of ammonia and 1 cup of water. Then rinse thoroughly.

If the stain is still there, block the needlepoint and let it dry. The only thing left to do is rip (sorry) the stained stitches. Then you'll have to work them again, of course.

Hints

Textured stitches can be fluffed with a shot of steam. Be careful not to shrink or mat the wool.

A limp piece of needlepoint can be revived with spray sizing or spray starch on the wrong side.

Sometimes, no matter how carefully you've blocked, a needle-point piece pops out of shape again. This is particularly true of large canvases (3½, 4, 5, and 7).

Pieces that are only slightly out of shape can be held in place with an iron-on lining (page 310) or iron-on interfacing.

Badly distorted pieces will need rabbit skin glue. It can be bought in art supply stores. Rabbit skin glue comes in a powdered form which must be cooked. Several hours after it cools, it will gel. Follow the instructions that come with it.

You can put the glue on the wrong side of a needlepoint piece that has flat stitches while it is on the blocking board. Apply *thinly*.

Since textured stitches cannot be put on the blocking board face down, a frame is needed. Make it from strips of soft wood, 1″ × 2″. It must be larger than the finished area of needlepoint (Figure 5–2). Staple the blank margin of canvas to the frame. The needlepoint should be already blocked.

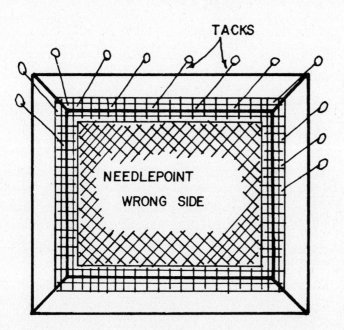

TACKS

NEEDLEPOINT

WRONG SIDE

Fig. 5–2. Frame for applying rabbit skin glue.

If there is no blank margin of canvas, you'll need to make a frame ¼″ smaller on each side than your needlepoint. If your piece is 11″ × 14″, the inside edges of the frame should measure 10½″ × 13½″. Cover the frame to protect your needlepoint; masking tape works well.

A frame of soft wood will enable you to use T-pins to attach the needlepoint to the frame. If you can't get them in, you'll have to use a hammer and rust-proof tacks. The thickness of the wood will lift your needlepoint off the table enough that the textured stitches will be protected. See Figure 2–31 a-d. Allow to dry overnight.

19
Framing, pillows, and linings

Framing

Needlepoint pictures can be the most costly item to finish. You can reduce the cost considerably by planning your project so that it will fit into a standard-sized frame.

Some of these frames come already put together, and some come in strips with easy instructions for you to put them together yourself. Go to the stores and check out the sizes these frames come in—*before* you cut the canvas. Choose a style and color (page 42-44) that will not overpower your needlepoint.

If necessary, I have a custom frame made and mount the needlepoint myself, still saving some money.

No matter which frame you get, it will have to be deep enough to cover a stretcher frame. The stretcher frame should not stick out beyond the back of the frame. If the stretcher frame is too deep, the framer will make you a thinner, custom stretcher frame. It will cost more than the stretcher strips you put together yourself. (You can buy them in an art supply store.)

Even then you may need a still thinner surface over which you can stretch your needlepoint. The needlepoint can be laced over a piece of Masonite (Figure 5–3). Do *not* use cardboard; it will bend under the tension put on it, and your needlepoint will not be taut.

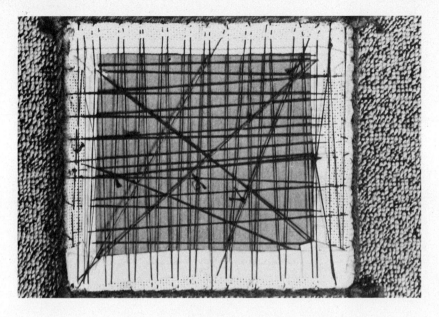

Fig. 5–3. To wrap a piece of needlepoint around a Masonite board, lace sides together with heavy thread. (This is a long job.)

Never put needlepoint under glass. It will hide your stitches as well as rob the wool yarn of the air it needs to breathe.

There is a trick to getting your needlepoint to fit a certain sized frame. You *must* measure carefully. You'll need a 3″ margin of canvas all the way around your needlepoint. So, if your finished needlepoint will be 11″ × 14″, you will need to cut a piece of canvas 17″ × 20″. This size was figured by adding 3″ + 11″ + 3″ = 17″ and 3″ + 14″ + 3″ = 20″. See Figure 5–4 for another example.

This might seem like a lot of wasted canvas, but it is *not*. When you're blocking a badly distorted piece, you need something to hang on to. The framing process also eats up much of this margin.

Fig. 5–4. (a) Margins for a needlepoint picture. (b) Measuring margins for a 3″ picture.

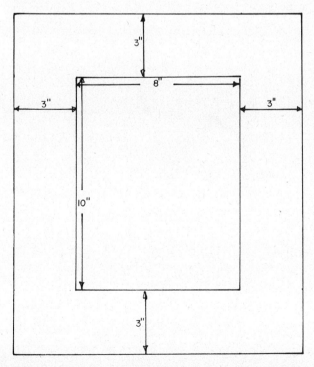

(a)

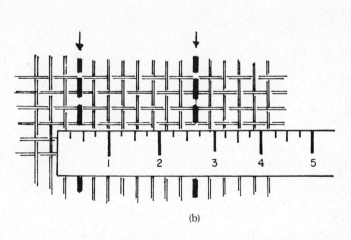

(b)

Next mark the margins with a *waterproof* marker. It should be marked two mesh (one on either side) short of 8″ and two mesh short of 10″ for an 8″ × 10″ picture (Figure 5–5). So actually, you have left a blank mesh all the way around the design area. This is your fudge factor.

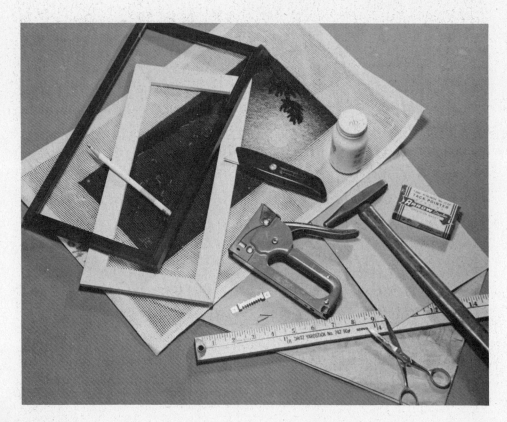

Fig. 5–5a. Equipment needed for framing needlepoint.

Fig. 5–5b.
(1) canvas
(2) stretcher frame
(3) frame
(4) pencil
(5) razor blade
(6) glue
(7) tacks
(8) cardboard
(9) hammer
(10) staple gun
(11) saw-tooth hanger
(12) tacks
(13) ruler
(14) paper bag
(15) scissors.

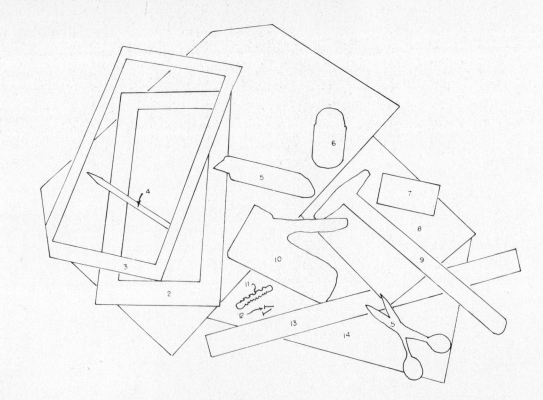

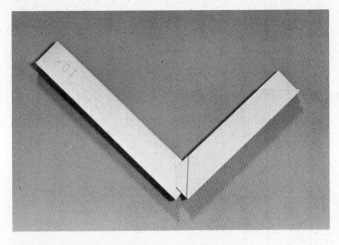

Fig. 5–5c. Stretcher frame pieces fit together at the corners like this; they may need a tap of the hammer to get them all the way together.

Fig. 5–5d. Use a square to be sure each corner is 90°.

Fig. 5–5e. A custom stretcher frame looks like this.
Try it in the frame.
Note that there is very little extra room.

Fig. 5–5f. Cut a piece of cardboard a little smaller than the stretcher frame and staple it in place on the stretcher frame. Wrap needlepoint around stretcher frame so that cardboard lies next to needlepoint.

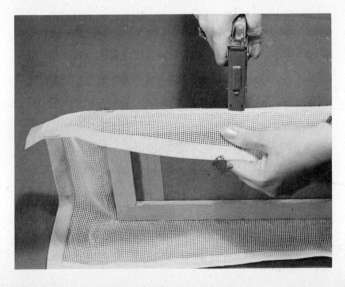

Fig. 5–5g. Staple corners first, then sides.

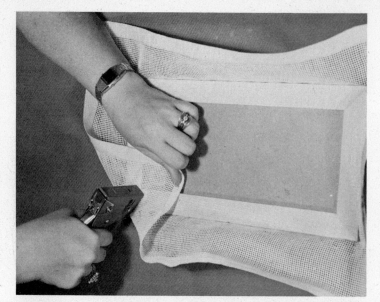

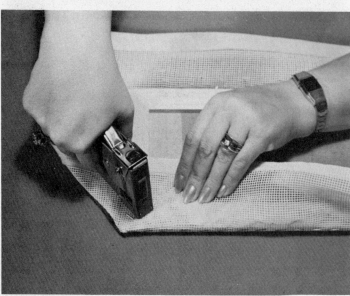

Fig. 5—5i. Next, staple sides of that same piece.

Fig. 5—5j (above). Fold one side of canvas to back to form one half of mitered corner, then fold other side back and staple. Do other three corners, then staple sides between mitered corners.

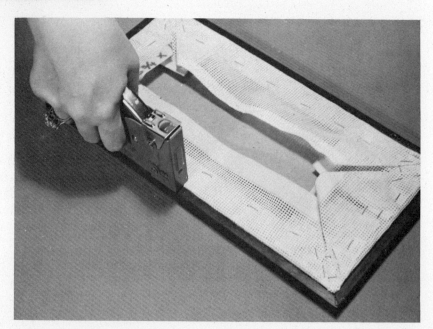

Fig. 5—5k (right). Put stretcher frame in frame; staple or nail stretcher in place.

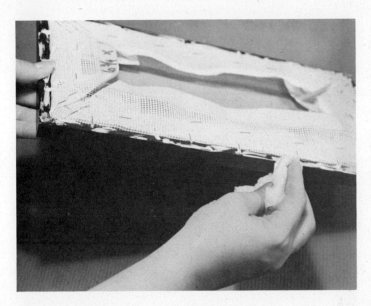

Fig. 5–5l. Apply Elmer's Glue to back of frame and wipe away excess glue with damp paper towel.

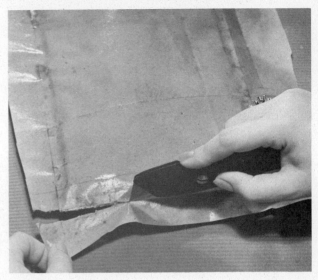

Fig. 5–5n. Place paper over back of picture frame and trim away excess paper with a single-edged razor blade; again, wipe away excess glue.

Fig. 5–5m. Wet a piece of brown paper for back.

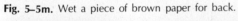

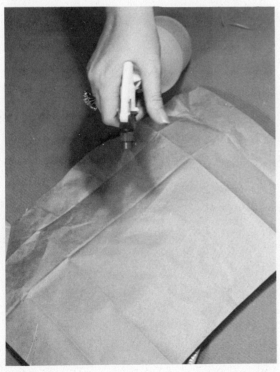

Fig. 5–5o. Find center of picture and attach saw-tooth hanger; the paper will dry out, and you will have a picture that looks better than a professional could do.

Fig. 5–5p. The finished product.

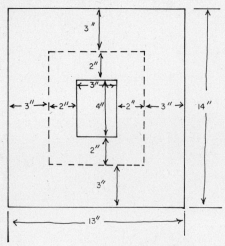

Fig. 5–6.
Cutting canvas for mat.

If you plan to stitch a border in needlepoint, remember that the lip of the frame covers about ¼" of your work. You will then need to stitch ¼" worth of sacrifice stitches (page 83).

Work the needlepoint and block.

See Figure 5–5 a-p. See the color plates for examples of good framing techniques.

If you wish to have a mat, it will be glued to an area of blank canvas. For example, if your needlepoint is 3" × 4", and you want a mat 2" wide, you will need to cut a piece of canvas 13" × 14". You will need 3" (margin) + 2" (area for mat) + 3" (needlepoint) + 2" (area for mat) + 3" (margin) = 13" for one side, and 3" (margin) + 2" (area for mat) + 4" (needlepoint) + 2" (area for mat) + 3" (margin) = 14" for the other side (see Figure 5-6.) The needlepoint is stretched over the stretcher frame as shown in Figure 5–5 h-l. The mat is then glued to the blank canvas. It should fit exactly to the edge of the stitching. If it overlaps, the mat will rise up over the stitches and look funny. If it falls short, the canvas will show. If you cannot make it fit exactly, overlap, rather than fall short. It is impossible to get circular needlepoint to fit inside a circular mat. It must overlap.

The mat board should be cut by a professional framer. His gadget cuts a very nice beveled edge. I'm sure a framer would charge only a nominal fee to cut it for you.

Pillows

Pillows are another popular item, yet they can be expensive to finish. If you sew, even a little, you *can* finish your own.

Don't forget the sacrifice stitches (page 83).

Choose a backing fabric that is: (1) washable (your needlepoint is), (2) durable (your needlepoint is), and (3) elegant (your needlepoint is).

Each of these points is not absolutely necessary to have, but it would be foolish to downgrade your needlepoint with cheap fabric.

I recommend *Ultra Suede*, for it meets all of these requirements. It is a synthetic suede that is washable and does not waterspot!

No-wale corduroy and cotton suede are both good choices, but nothing is quite so elegant as velvet! You may wish to give up durability and washability to have its marvelous feel.

Trimming

You must decide now what kind of trimming you want on your pillow.

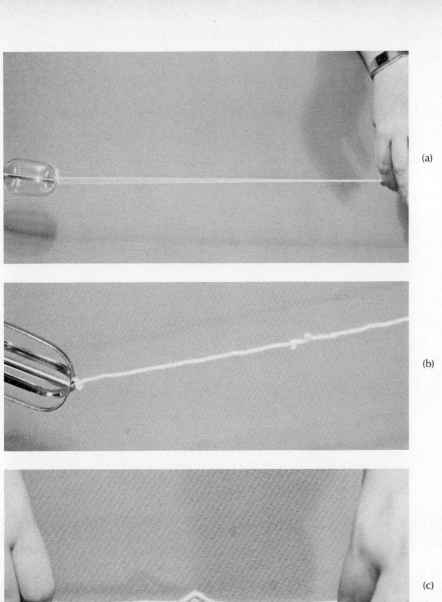

(a)

(b)

(c)

(d)

Fig. 5–7a, b, c, d.
Making a twisted cord.

If your heart is set on cording, I suggest you have the pillow professionally finished, unless you are expert at inserting cording.

A twisted cord resembles cording. It is much easier to make, and I think it's prettier.

Get a friend to help you. Measure the distance around your pillow (or whatever). Multiply this number by 3. This gives you the length of yarn you will need to make one twisted cord long enough to go around your pillow. If your pillow is 14" × 14", the circumference is 56"; so 56" × 3" = 168".

Cut 6 strands 168" long. (The number of strands you use determines the thickness of your cord.) Six makes a good thickness for a pillow cord. You obviously need an uncut skein of yarn for this.

Knot the strands at both ends. Knot all the strands together in the *middle*. Tie one end to one of the beaters of an electric mixer. Have your friend hold the other end. Hold the yarn taut. One of you will be on one side of the house and the other will be on the other side of the house! Turn the mixer on and run it until the yarn kinks. Keeping the yarn taut, hook the center knot over a hook (or a third person's finger). Give your end of the yarn to the friend who's holding the other end. Remove the yarn from the hook and slowly release the tension. The two sections of yarn will now twist together. If you go too fast it will get sloppy (see Figure 5–7). Tie the ends together with another piece of yarn so that it will not untwist. Hand sew it in place along the finished seam. Don't let your stitches show. Tuck the ends in to minimize the lump.

Pillow construction

Place the right side of the backing fabric and the right side of the needlepoint together, stitch together between the sacrifice stitches and the rest of the needlepoint (Figure 58). Round the corners slightly and stitch as shown in Figure 5–9.

Fig. 5–8. Stitch between the sacrifice stitches and the pillow on the machine.

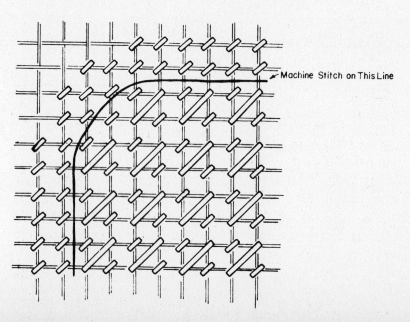

Machine Stitch on This Line

Trim the seam to ⅝″—even if you have to cut the needle-point at the corners. Zig-zag the raw edges together except at the opening; do those separately.

Turn and stuff with polyester batting. Don't skimp on the corners. The pillow should be plump, but a fat pillow will wrinkle on the sides between the corners.

Pin the opening together. Use the Blind Stitch (Figure 5–10). Run the needle inside the fold of the fabric. Bring it out to catch the canvas and insert it again into the fabric. Take stitches every ¼″ to ⅜″.

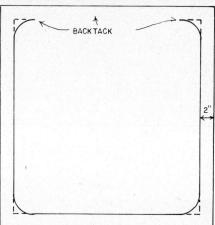

Fig. 5–9. Stitching pillow.

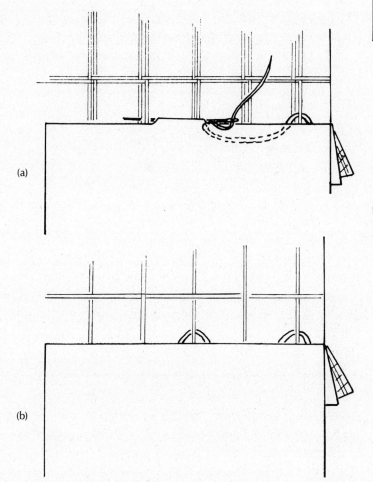

(a)

(b)

Fig. 5–10a & b.
Blind stitching fourth side of pillow.

Insert

Plate 15 shows needlepoint inserted into fabric, which was then made into a pillow.

This procedure must be done by hand, and the measurements must be precise. On the wrong side of the fabric, mark the desired finished line with tailor's chalk. Measure *in* ⅝″ from that line: This is your cutting line (Figure 5–11). Cut away the shaded portion. Slash the seam allowance *almost* to the dotted line. Use a thick craft glue to glue the seam allowance back. Be careful not to get any glue on the right side; it doesn't come off!

Turn the pillow top right side up. Place the needlepoint under the hole. *Carefully* glue it in place. When it is *completely* dry, Blind Stitch it in place.

Cover the seam with a twisted cord or a braid or leave it as it is. Finish the pillow.

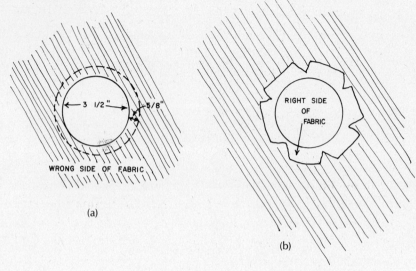

Fig. 5–11a & b.
Inserting needlepoint into fabric.

(a)

(b)

Linings

Linings can be attached in two ways: (1) iron-on and (2) sew-on. These two methods can be used to make two different kinds of linings: (1) drop-in lining and (2) separate lining of each piece.

Iron-on lining

Use double knit fabric, because it does not ravel. Bond it to the needlepoint with Stitch Witchery or Polyweb and an iron. Cut the Stitch Witchery so that it is *slightly* bigger than the stitched area. Cut the double knit fabric so that it is exactly the size you need. (There is no need to turn the raw edge under.) Place the needlepoint face down on the ironing board. Put the Stitch Witchery on next and then the fabric. Cover it all with a *wet* press cloth. The excess Stitch Witchery will come off on the cloth and not on your iron. Be sure the Stitch Witchery has melted completely; otherwise it will separate later.

You cannot use this method with textured stitches (they'll get crushed) or with plastic canvas (it'll melt!).

Sew-on lining

Use a lightweight lining fabric. Turn a ⅝" seam allowance under. Sew in place by hand with the Blind Stitch (page 309).

When you're lining an eyeglass case you can line each piece by sewing or ironing a lining on each piece of needlepoint. If you've made an object that is one piece of needlepoint that is folded to make a purse (Plate 37) or a credit card case (Plate 47), you should line it while it's flat. Then fold it and put it together with the Binding Stitch.

Drop-in lining

The tote bag in Plate 26 could have been lined piece-by-piece, but a drop-in lining is faster (less hand work) and it's easier to clean (just pull it out). It is made separately, dropped in, and sewn to the top of the bag only.

Cut the lightweight lining pieces the same size as shown on page 148, except add ⅝" for seam allowance. I think it's easier to handle if I add an extra inch to the top. Stitch the lining together on a sewing machine. Put the four sides together first, then sew on the bottom piece.

Drop the lining into the tote bag so that the wrong sides are together. Blind stitch the top of the lining to the top of the tote bag, turning under the raw edges as you go.

20
Other finishing techniques

Bell-pull

The sides of the Bell-Pull are already finished with the Two-Step Edge Finishing method. All that's left to do now is attach it to the hardware. Fold the blank canvas over and hand stitch it in place, leaving a space at the fold to slip the rod of the hardware through. (This must be done before rabbit skin glue, page 299.) Line (page 310).

JOY banner

Use a cotton suede fabric as the backing. Turn the raw edges under and sew or glue in place. Glue (or hand sew) a gold braid over the edges on the sides. Fold the top and bottom edges back, as above, leaving a space at the fold for the hardware to slip through. Line (page 310).

Glue the three squares of letters onto the fabric.

Christmas ornament in wooden ring

Trim the needlepoint canvas so that it does not show when a wooden ring is laid on top of it. Glue the needlepoint to the wooden ring. Cut a piece of felt just a little bigger than the canvas. Glue it over the canvas.

Screw an eye hook into the wood to hang it by. Trim it with a bow of ribbon and a ribbon hanger.

To make a tassel (Figure 5–12), wrap yarn (or embroidery floss) around a piece of cardboard that is as long as you want your tassel. Using one piece of yarn, about 6″ long, tie the yarn together at the top of the card. Slip the yarn off the card. Wrap another piece of yarn around all the strands of yarn. Tie. Let the ends hang down. Trim the bottom. Attach the tassel to your project with the strings at the top.

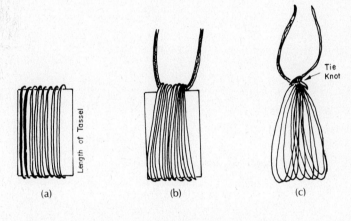

Fig. 5–12a, b, c, d, e. Making a tassel.

Brooch

Buy hardware for jewelry from hobby and lapidary shops. Also buy an egg-shaped piece of Styrofoam.

Cut the Styrofoam to fit the brooch form so that a slightly dome-shaped top is made. Glue the needlepoint to the top, stretching and molding it over the top so that there are no wrinkles. (Special glue must be used for Stryrofoam. Many glues dissolve it. You can get this glue in hobby shops, too.)

Glue the Styrofoam and needlepoint into the metal or wooden brooch form.

Footstool

The footstool in Plate 38 is a cheapie bought in a discount store. It came in pieces in a plastic bag. It was put together and stained at home. Yours need not be any fancier, but it could be as precious as an antique.

The needlepoint was attached as explained in Figure 5–13.

Fig. 5–13a. Equipment needed for finishing a needlepoint footstool.

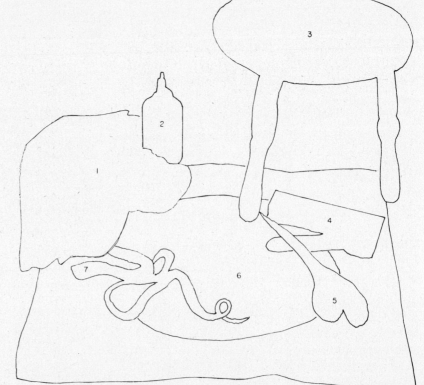

Fig. 5–13b.
(1) stuffing
(2) glue
(3) footstool
(4) staple gun
(5) scissors
(6) needlepointed canvas
(7) upholstery tape—for binding

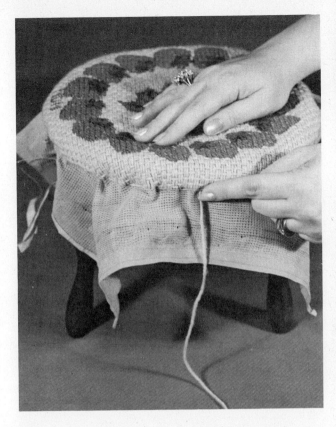

Fig. 5–13c. By hand, stitch a drawstring of yarn around the edge of the needlepoint. Put the needlepoint over the top of the stool. The needlepoint should be bigger than the top of the stool.

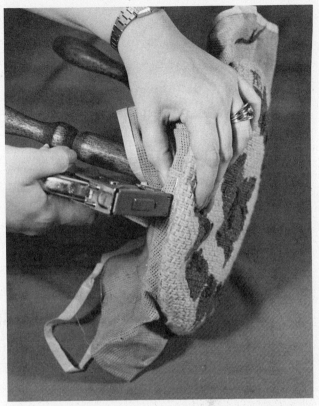

Fig. 5–13d. Staple the needlepoint to the edge of the stool. Staple at 12 o'clock, then at 6 o'clock, 3 o'clock, and at 9 o'clock. Then staple in between those first 4 staples, spacing the fullness as evenly as you can. Leave a hole big enough for your hand to go through.

Fig. 5–13f. Pull the drawstring tight and staple the hole closed.

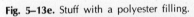

Fig. 5–13e. Stuff with a polyester filling.

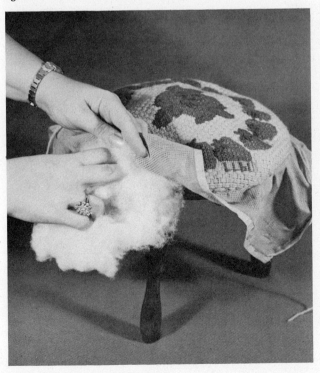

315

Fig. 5–13g. Trim off the excess canvas.

Fig. 5–13h. Some of the wood on the edge of the stool should show.

Fig. 5–13i. Apply the braid with thick craft glue or rubber cement (follow the directions on the bottle).

Fig. 5–13j. The finished product.

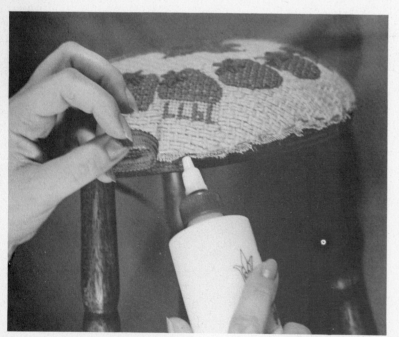

The backing fabric I chose is denim; the lining is red bandanna cloth. Insert a zipper as per the package instructions. Treat the needlepoint as if it were fabric. (Don't forget sacrifice stitches, page 83.) If you measured right when you started your needlepoint, the zipper will fit exactly.

With right sides together, stitch the side seams and bottom seams; be careful to put the sacrifice stitches inside the seam. Trim the seam allowance to ⅝". Zig-zag them together. Turn the right side out.

Make and attach a drop-in lining as on page 311.

Christmas tree ornaments

Although the Christmas ornaments in Plate 24 may be finished any number of ways, I'm giving you this method because it can be used with irregularly shaped pieces of needlepoint. For example, you could cut right around a Santa Claus ornament, and there would be no background.

Apply thick craft glue ¼" into the needlepoint area (Figure 5–14a) and ¼" into the blank canvas. When it is *completely* dry, trim right down to the stitches—*very carefully* (Figure 5–14 b and c).

Glue the cut needlepoint to a piece of felt. Trim the felt to within ⅛" of the needlepoint (Figure 5–14d).

Put a thin stream of glue on this ⅛" lip of felt. Place a decorative cord that you have bought or made (page 308) along this edge. Loop it at the top for a hanger. Stick the ends between the needlepoint and the felt.

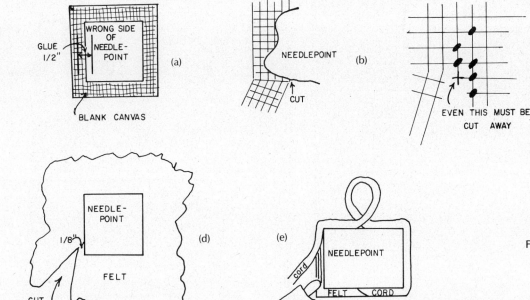

Fig. 5–14a, b, c, d, e. Finishing Christmas ornament.

Wooden purse

If your wooden purse has a hole already cut in it, it will also have mounting instructions for your needlepoint.

If you must, you can cut a hole in any wooden finish-it-yourself purse.

Glue your needlepoint to a piece of Masonite so that it will show through the hole correctly. Hold the Masonite in place with tiny nails inside the box.

Line with almost any kind of fabric. Cut separate pieces of cardboard that are slightly smaller than the sides, bottom, and top of the purse. Fuse the lining to the cardboard with Stitch Witchery, and miter the corners as shown in Figure 5–15. Glue the lining pieces into the purse.

Put an upholstery brad in each corner of the bottom, so that the nice wood will not be scratched.

(a)

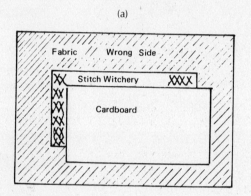

(b)

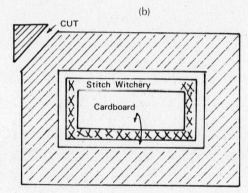

(c)

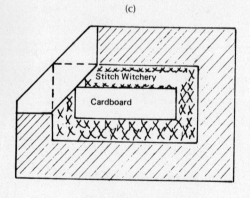

(d)

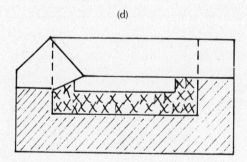

Fig. 5–15a, b, c, d, e, f.
Lining for purse and box.

(e)

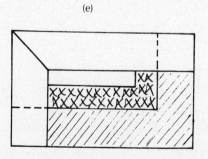

(f)

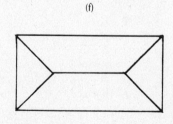

318

Finish the Box Top by wrapping the needlepoint around a piece of Masonite in a manner similar to that used for the footstool (page 313). Staple in place. Miter the corners as you did for a picture (page 300) (Figure 5–16b). Stuff the top with polyester batting through a hole that you have left. Be sure the batting is evenly distributed. Insert the top from the inside of the lid. The Masonite should be about ¼" smaller than this opening. For example, if the hole is 5" × 8" the Masonite is 4¾" × 7¾". Replace the back of the lid that should have come with your box.

Line as you did the purse (see also page 311). Glue felt to the bottom of the box to protect your furniture.

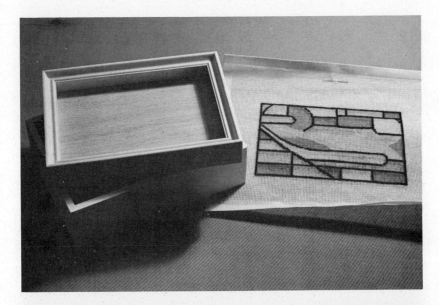

Fig. 5–16a. Type of box needed for a needlepoint box top.

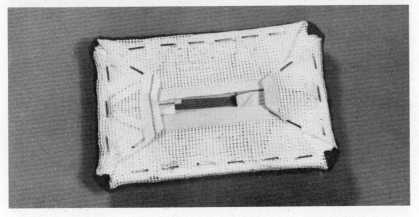

Fig. 5–16b. Place needlepoint on box lid as in Figs. 5–5h-j.

Tie

Sew the tie, with right sides together. Leave an opening at the top of the tie. The lightweight lining fabric should be just a little bit smaller than the tie. When you turn it right side out, the lining will not creep to the right side.

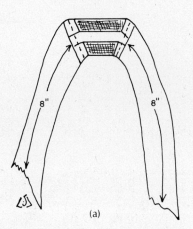

(a)

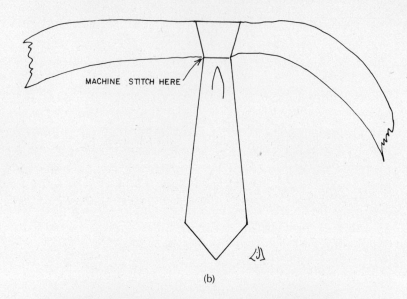

MACHINE STITCH HERE

(b)

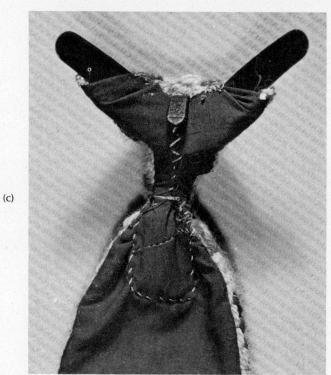

(c)

Fig. 5–17. (a & b) Putting tie together. (c) Final hand stitching of tie. It will look like a mess up to this point. Just start stitching by hand and pull it together. It should shape up.

There is no need to line the knot. Turn the blank canvas at the top and bottom under so that it doesn't show. Sew long (8″ or so) strips of lining fabric to both sides of the knot (Figure 5–17a).

Put the knot over the top of the tie, taking a tuck. Top stitch on the sewing machine. Try to place your machine stitches between the needlepoint stitches (Figure 5–17b).

Take an old pre-knotted tie apart, or buy a cheap one. Take the tie off *very carefully*. Notice how the tie was put on the gadget. Using the same gadget, put your tie on the gadget *exactly* as the other was. Hand stitch as shown in Figure 5–17c. I've used contrasting thread so that you can see it better.

320

SUPPLEMENTAL DESIGNS

G-R-O-W planter cover

Needlepoint in use

Desert (alternate design for hassock)

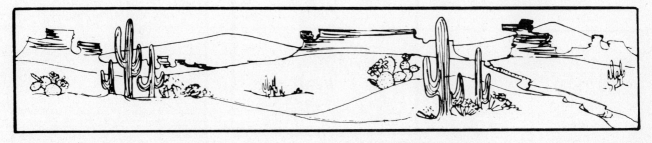

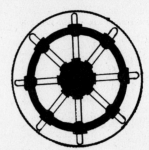

Underwater scene
(alternate design for hassock)

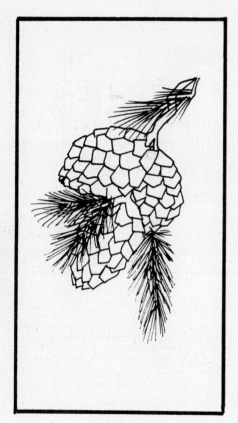

Pine cones

Sun Pillow

Bedroom door signs

Like Father, . . .

Desert scene

Checkbook cover
(Poor House/Fort Knox)

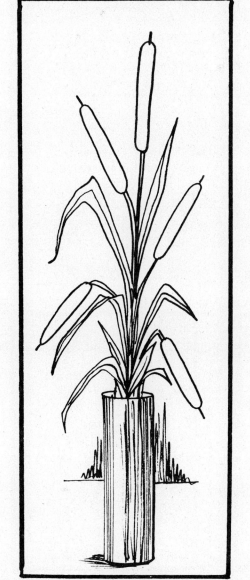

Cattails
(companion piece
for Pussy Willows)

Winter scene with Northern Lights

Canoe

Trailing vine *(Dover)*

Angel *(Dover)*

Book cover

Bear

Roses (Dover)

Child's Grow Chart

Wedding sampler

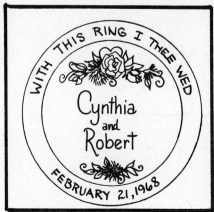

PRACTICE MAKES

PRACTICE MAKES

PERFECT

PERFECT

Practice Makes Perfect

Round pincushion designs

Owl eyeglass case

Apple tree *(Dover)*

St. Francis of Assisi

Butterfly *(Dover)*

Fish *(Dover)*

329

Purse or totebag design

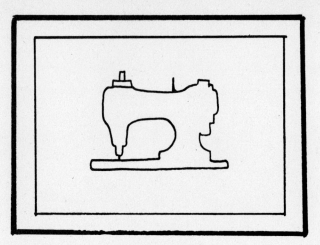

Needlebook cover

Four Seasons

(a)

(b)

(c)

(d)

Index

General index

Stitch index